EVALUATING HUMAN CAPITAL PROJECTS

How can we be sure t.... ....ose projects, programmes and activities that depend for their quality, efficiency and effectiveness on people's performance have met their objectives?

How can we improve the ways in which these projects, programmes and activities are planned so that realistic and useful measurement of their outcomes and value for money becomes possible?

How can we produce from these evaluations data of the quality and a standard required to drive future improvement?

Evaluating Human Capital Projects addresses these issues for professionals in the private, the public and the not-for-profit sectors. It shows them how to plan and track their investments with the professionalism and discipline widely applied to other capital investments. It is also written as a sourcebook for both professional and Master's-level students in business, health and a wide range of socio-economic disciplines.

It addresses effective planning, stakeholder engagement, result-tracking, and the identification and removal of barriers to good performance. It provides ideas, theoretical background, extensive references to practice and analysis from the authors' extensive experience or planning, collection of data, analysis of data and attribution, and reporting to drive future improvement.

It is intended to raise the bar on the professionalism with which human capital investments are planned and measured.

Jane Massy is the Founder Director and CEO of abdi Ltd.

Jeremy Harrison is a Director of abdi Ltd.

Accession no.
36137360

EVALUATING HUMAN CAPITAL PROJECTS

Improve, prove, predict

Jane Massy and Jeremy Harrison

LIS - LIBRARY	
Date	Fund
15·5·14	(w ſ
Order No.	
2501910	
University of Chester	

Routledge
Taylor & Francis Group

LONDON AND NEW YORK

First published 2014
by Routledge
2 Park Square, Milton Park, Abingdon, Oxon OX14 4RN

and by Routledge
711 Third Avenue, New York, NY 10017

Routledge is an imprint of the Taylor & Francis Group, an informa business

© 2014 Jane Massy and Jeremy Harrisons

The right of Jane Massy and Jeremy Harrison to be identified as authors
of this work has been asserted by them in accordance with sections 77
and 78 of the Copyright, Designs and Patents Act 1988.

All rights reserved. No part of this book may be reprinted or reproduced
or utilised in any form or by any electronic, mechanical, or other
means, now known or hereafter invented, including photocopying and
recording, or in any information storage or retrieval system, without
permission in writing from the publishers.

Every effort has been made to contact copyright holders for their
permission to reprint material in this book. The publishers would be
grateful to hear from any copyright holder who is not here acknowledged
and will undertake to rectify any errors or omissions in future editions of
this book.

Trademark notice: Product or corporate names may be trademarks or
registered trademarks, and are used only for identification and explanation
without intent to infringe.

British Library Cataloguing in Publication Data
A catalogue record for this book is available from the British Library

Library of Congress Cataloging in Publication Data
A catalog record for this book has been requested

ISBN: 978-0-415-66308-3 (hbk)
ISBN: 978-0-415-66309-0 (pbk)
ISBN: 978-0-203-07171-7 (ebk)

Typeset in Bembo
by Swales & Willis Ltd, Exeter, Devon, UK

MIX
Paper from
responsible sources
FSC
www.fsc.org   FSC® C013056

Printed and bound in Great Britain by
TJ International Ltd, Padstow, Cornwall

CONTENTS

FOREWORD

This book is for all those who are concerned to do a better job of planning projects, programmes and any activities which depend for their success on the buy-in, capability and good behaviour and practice of people. People may work independently, in pairs or in teams. They may be colleagues responsible for the main actions in an activity. Or they may be important stakeholders – colleagues or not – whose activities (or sometimes deliberate inactivity) are vital to good conduct and success.

So it is both for professional planners and managers, and for evaluators.

In fact, one of the strong messages from the book is that, at work, we all need to be better at ensuring that the things we do are linked to the most important objectives of our organisations; that they are driven by demand; that we have set realistic and measurable objectives; and that we take the time and the trouble to collect just enough data against these objectives to find out whether our activities have been of benefit, and if so (or if not), why that was so.

We both took our first steps in this active evaluation with Jack Phillips in the United States. We are always grateful to him and to Patti Phillips for introducing us to this powerful approach, and then for the support they gave us in our early years. In recent years we have added a great deal to that initial learning, and we are still adding.

We have consolidated what we know into a fully accredited (Pearson) ladder of professional learning and a 60-credit post-graduate certificate (University of Derby). Our approach is also accredited by the Singapore Institute of Adult Learning. It is mapped by Napier University against Scottish Vocational Qualifications.

This sourcebook for our approach has been developed from all of this experience, much of it drawn from teaching more than 1,600 business professionals from all over the world, and much of it drawn from our consultancy work – again worldwide. We thank all of these past and present colleagues for their support.

Closer to home, the book would not have been produced but for our colleagues in our business, abdi Ltd. We need to give special mention to some of them.

Deneise Dadd, whose PhD at the Open University we have been delighted to support, has drafted all of the case study extracts and has produced all of our references to research and practice, as well as the glossary and index.

Lianping Dong (Kay) and Hassan Mourtada have turned all of our sketches and ideas into graphics.

Diane Arnott, Arman Baroyan, Sandeep Joshi and our chair, Sally James, have provided encouragement and support when we've needed it.

Our colleagues at Routledge saw the point of it all, and were very patient.

1

THE QUEST FOR VALUE

There is growing agreement in organisations of all types and sizes that the cost and the value of human capital effort and achievement must be better tracked and reported. The demand to understand impact and value for money is intensifying. This can be met only by better planning and by rigorous and consistent evaluation. Human capital is reported as a cost rather than as an asset, in spite of claims that 'people are our greatest asset'. Too often, ambiguity about the benefit of investing in people leads to a black hole of accountability in which large sums of money get lost. This results in a cycle of ignorance about the outcomes of this expenditure, and a failure of accountability for the consequences. It is urgent to improve the way in which organisations align spend on human capital with their key priorities and objectives. But there are no magic bullets or quick fixes. The only way to measure the impact and value of human capital is through disciplined planning, rigorous tracking and objective reporting of robustly tested outcomes.

'Soft' activities, hard money

You are a manager and one of your team comes to you for approval for £20,000 worth of new equipment. Would the conversation go something like this (Figure 1.1)?

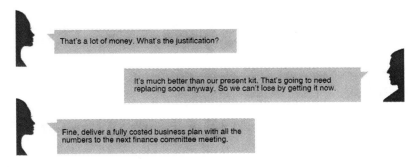

That's a lot of money. What's the justification?

It's much better than our present kit. That's going to need replacing soon anyway. So we can't lose by getting it now.

Fine, deliver a fully costed business plan with all the numbers to the next finance committee meeting.

FIGURE 1.1

It almost certainly would. But what if the request were for some training (Figure 1.2)?

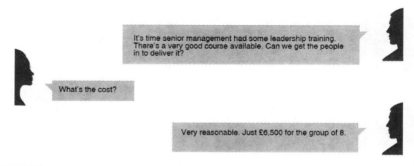

It's time senior management had some leadership training. There's a very good course available. Can we get the people in to deliver it?

What's the cost?

Very reasonable. Just £6,500 for the group of 8.

FIGURE 1.2

Stop here. Would this be your response (Figure 1.3)?

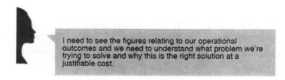

I need to see the figures relating to our operational outcomes and we need to understand what problem we're trying to solve and why this is the right solution at a justifiable cost.

FIGURE 1.3

Or this (Figure 1.4)?

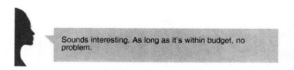

Sounds interesting. As long as it's within budget, no problem.

FIGURE 1.4

Why?

Experience suggests that many, perhaps most, managers will apply different standards to approving human capital initiatives than those they would apply to equipment. Most managers would also fail to spot that the real cost of the two is likely to be much the same. The human capital initiative may, in the end, be the more expensive. The indirect costs of human-intensive activities like training – the price of time committed by those being developed, and all the other 'hidden' but very real costs – are often at least *three times* the direct costs, and can even go as high as *ten times* the total of those costs.

So the real cost of both of these investments is likely to be virtually the same: £20,000 for the equipment, and at least £19,500 for the leadership development.

Why do so many experienced people bring a different set of attitudes to human effort than to what they consider common good practice when they consider physical things like plant and equipment?

Is it because it is commonly held to be much more difficult to measure the 'soft' outcomes of human effort than it is to measure the 'hard' impact of a piece of equipment? We think so. As a result, they avoid trying to do it.

But this is changing. There is growing agreement in the private, the public and the not-for-profit sectors that the cost and the value of human effort and achievement need to be better measured and reported. Demand from governments, donors, sponsors and shareholders to show value is intensifying.

Alongside the drive to show value comes the focus on aligning 'people' investments with business priorities (or key performance indicators, KPIs) using the same rigorous standards as organisations routinely apply to other important investments. In general, organisations find this very difficult.

In this book we examine the issues raised by these demands for more rigorous and credible evaluation. We show how it can be done. We also show how good evaluation stimulates a virtuous cycle of better planning, consistent performance improvement and better quality.

Three decades ago 'quality' was measured at the end of the production line. If a product came off a line faulty, it was rejected. Now the focus on quality has moved to the beginning of the line. We expect smarter planning and implementation. We look for quality indicators to prevent faults, and to provide the basis for continuous improvement. Lean management systems develop these concepts of quality further by placing business process under the microscope to identify ways to deliver quality and to achieve improvements in efficiency and effectiveness.

As we write this book, a further key shift is occurring: the growth of analytics (some driven by big data) applied to all human capital investments. All of this should be leading to a transformation in the culture and practice of human capital planning, monitoring and evaluation. Why are we not seeing the results we expect? Part of the answer has to be that too many organisations are ignoring the evidence that collecting, reviewing and carefully analysing data about performance, rather than simply exchanging descriptions and anecdotes about it, leads to better planning, better decisions and improved results.

Human capital: asset or cost?

Can we explain why so few organisations – governments, public sector bodies, large companies, not-for-profits, small firms and local organisations – have developed coherent ways of showing links between the resource they spend on their people and the impact outcomes they achieve?

Language is important. It is significant that whilst people and their endeavours are widely described as human *capital*, they never figure on any balance sheet. In fact, standard accountancy practice shows human endeavour, time and activities as a *cost*. This is particularly ironic, given that so many senior managers (including HR managers) regularly talk about people as their 'greatest asset'. Does it mean that they do not really see their expenditure on these people and their development as 'investment'?

This has two obvious consequences:

- They are left with no means of showing the impact that comes from 'people' investments – education and training, change and reform initiatives, policy, process and structural change, leadership and coaching and changes in incentives and rewards.
- They are unable to demonstrate the role their people have played in achieving (or failing to achieve) key organisational targets and priorities.

These issues hamper the entire process of change management and place limitations on its benefits. The success rates of change management projects are modest. John P. Kotter of Harvard Business School has put the failure rate at above 70 per cent. He cites eight common errors that cause change initiatives to fail:

1.   allowing too much complacency
2.   failing to create a sufficiently powerful guiding coalition
3.   underestimating the power of vision
4.   under-communicating the vision
5.   permitting obstacles to block the new vision
6.   failing to create short-term wins
7.   declaring victory too soon
8.   neglecting to anchor changes firmly in the corporate culture.

Kotter's influential thinking here closely mirrors and supports the thinking behind our approach to impact planning, monitoring and evaluation. Readers of this book will see a response to Kotter's eight errors in the principles and processes we use.

The enormous sums that fall into this black hole of accountability

The UK government spends in all around £2 billion a day. A very high proportion of that, leaving aside the amount spent servicing debt, is spending where human activity is the crucial determinant of success or failure.

Across the world, governments and private sector organisations spend billions of pounds, euros, dollars, rupees each day on projects and programmes that cannot run or succeed without trained, organised human effort. Men and women acquire knowledge and skills, find and analyse information and data, make plans, organise and re-organise and report on progress. Processes and structures, all aimed at achieving the objectives of teams and organisations, are planned, developed, implemented and become the subject of reports.

The Inquiry into Future Lifelong Learning (IFLL), conducted in the UK by the National Institute of Adult Continuing Education (NIACE), estimated that in 2010 some 3.9 per cent of GDP (£55 billion) was spent on post-compulsory education and training. This includes spending from private, public, voluntary and community sectors, as well as by individuals.

This is an estimate, but likely to be realistic. To put it into context, the learning and development budget for a single healthcare region alone (one of the larger of the former strategic health authorities in the United Kingdom) in 2010 was around £500 million, and for the NHS in England as a whole some £4.5 billion. This includes medical and dental education and training, as well as mandatory training and continuing professional development (CPD).

But even these massive figures do not include indirect costs, the greatest of which are the cost to organisations of the time that their people spend in initiatives such as change teams, training, away days, conferences, coaching etc. This omission results in true costs being typically understated by a factor of rarely less than three, and sometimes as much as ten.

These are huge sums of money. And how many of the courses, projects, programmes and initiatives on which they are spent are accounted for in a way that affords a credible account of the value for money that they provide?

The answer is very, very few: fewer than 1 per cent for sure.

A cycle of ignorance

This sustains a self-perpetuating cycle of ignorance in respect of which we need to highlight four key messages.

1. This consistent failure to measure and report the outcomes of human capital expenditure is a failure of accountability.
2. If individual investments are not justified by specific impact outcome targets, then collectively there is no clear way of confirming that they have been aligned with key organisational targets and priorities.
3. One of the key purposes of evaluation in operational settings is to apply immediately the lessons from robust outcome data so as to drive improved behaviour, task performance and changes in practices.
4. Sufficient performance data, systematically collected and analysed, provides a way of avoiding a cycle of operational ignorance characterised by vague objectives, unfocused activities and plans that are based more on guesswork and assertion than on attested experience.

A failure of accountability

One of the first things we do when people begin to learn our approach to planning, measuring and evaluating is to get them to list their key responsibilities, and also the things that they are held accountable for. Responses can vary a lot (Figure 1.5).

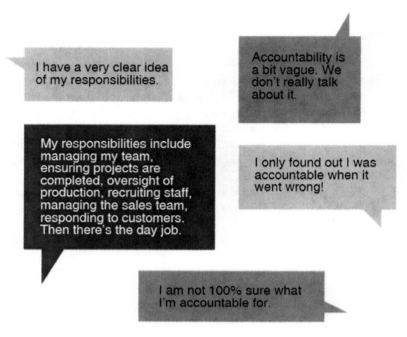

FIGURE 1.5

In part, this lack of clarity about responsibility (where the buck starts) and account-ability (where the buck stops) is a reflection of poor discipline in objective setting and project planning. In fact, most of our participants can list the main work activities for which they are responsible, although it is often the case that most refer to tasks rather than to management of the performance of their people. Approximately 90 per cent find it difficult, if not impossible, to state clearly what exactly they are accountable for.

This starts at the top, and its effects are felt everywhere. It may result in indif-ferent or average practice. Its consequences are likely to be a poor record of improvement, uncertainty about what is expected, disengagement and, at worst, a damaging culture of blame.

Accountability in organisations begins with the leaders. They must be the drivers of improvements in planning, measurement and reporting human capi-tal investments and their outcomes. Senior managers are not suddenly going to become experts in the measurement of human capital initiatives, but they do need to supply the impulsion and resources to ensure that rigorous measurement takes place. They will never do this until they make each major item of human capital spend stand up to three questions.

1. 'Does this plan link with our most important organisational priorities and objectives?'
2. 'Do we know what its full cost will be to the organisation – direct and indirect?'

3. 'How will we know whether it's been worth doing? What evidence will be given to show that planned changes have occurred and have contributed to a change in impact outcomes?'

None of these is in any way radical, but they carry messages loaded with signifi-cance. Merely asking them compels others to revise their assumptions and review their responsibilities and accountability.

It is worth pausing a moment to consider how broadly accountability may be shared. Take the apprenticeship programme described in the following box.

Apprenticeship programme accountability

A healthcare academy, part of a major teaching hospital's learning and devel-opment function, is accountable for training entry-level and support staff. Following a situation analysis, the need was identified to increase the num-ber of entry-level staff. Staff shortages, due to retirement, were anticipated. The academy decided to increase the number of apprenticeships. It had been training apprentices since 2004, but for the year 2009/10 the numbers were planned to increase from 44 to 100.

The academy also recognised its accountability for demonstrating the impact of this significant additional investment. An evaluation was set up to determine the impact of the apprenticeship scheme on the organisation's human resources requirements. Clear impact objectives were set for staff retention, career progression, patient satisfaction and overall value for money.

Accountability for the success of the scheme was seen to be shared between the stakeholders: apprentices, managers, clinical and nursing staff, existing support staff, trainers. Essential behaviours (in some cases involving change) were identified, and objectives set for them. These guided the learning content and the types of training provided. By outlining their desired outcomes they had a clearly defined road map for their journey.

This apprenticeship programme, focused on recruiting and retaining new entrants with the right competences to deliver rising standards of care, could attain its objectives only by ensuring that all the main stakeholders backed up the work and commitment of the apprentices by fulfilling their own roles and responsibilities to the required standards. Their behaviour, and the manner and timeliness of their actions, needed to be tracked. Their shared accountability was clear.

Accountability in public and private sectors can be a particularly vexed issue when outsourcing or contracting is involved. At a recent meeting between a public sector client and a services provider, at the point when contracts were ready for signing, the client stated that their legal department had advised them that project managers were now being held personally liable for achieving the objectives stated on the contract. They were surprised, then relieved to hear that only managers over a certain grade were therefore now expected to sign contracts, as they would be covered by professional indemnity.

Aligning key organisational priorities with operational and performance objectives

A large industry has grown up around the provision of learning and the development of learning materials. A parallel industry develops and sells business and project management tools, services and courses. Another major growth sector is in social and economic development services in emerging economies and conflict and poverty zones. You might suppose, since expenditures on training, education, coaching, apprenticeships, international aid and development and business consulting services of all kinds and at all levels are widely seen to be soft targets for cuts when times are hard, that these sectors would be visibly driven by demand.

In fact, almost the opposite is the case. Most of these human capital investments are strongly supply-sided. We can see this because when we ask why a piece, say, of training has been commissioned, we hear an answer like, 'Because we need people to go through it'.

Beware of magic bullets

The business world is richly supplied with commercial solutions. Some are solutions to specific technical or organisational problems. Some are more efficient ways of tackling issues that everyone faces at some time or another. Others claim to be 'magic bullets' (Figure 1.6). They are aimed at organisations' general health. They are solutions to non-specific problems. It is very hard indeed to know if they have worked or not because, usually, there was no specific justification for their use in the first place. Here are three fairly representative examples.

Case 1: Government has agreed to spend money on a major new 'innovative' project to improve healthcare or environmental outcomes. We hear the response: 'This is a great programme and we must try it because it comes recommended by a prestigious international agency and we must do (and be seen to be doing) something.'

Case 2: A major organisation has commissioned a change initiative from Business School X or Big Consulting firm Y. We are told: 'It must be the right thing to do because they are the market leaders.'

Case 3: The learning and development (L&D) lead went to a major exhibition and put in an order for the best-designed leadership training programme he'd ever seen. There was spare money in the budget and he was offered an introductory price. The suppliers will co-brand it with the L&D department.

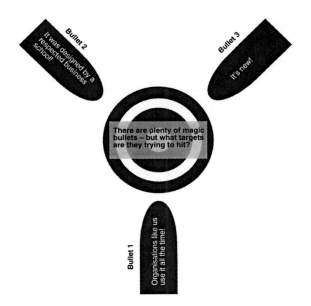

FIGURE 1.6

All three of these investments are essentially about *inputs*: money is being spent, so far as we can see, without a specific target or outcome in mind. If the spending were determined by *outcomes*, we would be reading about opportunities that needed to be pursued, or problems that needed to be addressed. As it is, all we can see is what amounts to testimonials for the interest or quality of the solutions themselves. They have the air of being cure-alls, including for corporate maladies that have not yet been defined.

This is not to deny that some organisations may want to test these 'magic bullets' to see what impact they cause. That is fine. What should not be regarded as fine is to use them just because they are thought to be 'a good thing', or a 'new thing'. That is just lazy and poor use of money.

The ADDIE approach

ADDIE is an acronym for a five-stage systematic instructional design model, where each stage feeds the next. It consists of:

1. *Analysis*: this includes identification of the learning problem, target audience needs, goals and objectives, existing knowledge, other relevant characteristics, as well as considering the learning environment, constraints, delivery options and project timeline.
2. *Design*: this includes the specification of the learning objectives by a systematic process.

(Continued)

(Continued)

3. *Development*: the creation of the content and learning materials, based on the design.
4. *Implementation*: this stage is where the plan is executed, where the content and learning materials are delivered.
5. *Evaluation*: this includes a formative and summative evaluation of the whole process.

There are many different variations of the ADDIE approach.

Source: http://www.learning-theories.com/addie-model.html.

The problem with ADDIE is that the evaluation (in this case, of 'learning') comes after the money has been spent. Too late! This is like the old quality model. We need to think of planning the evaluation or measurement at the start, as part of the analysis and design process, and then monitor all the way through until a final measurement analysis at the end.

The link between evaluation and good planning

We constantly point out that outcomes need to be planned before any final decisions are made about the scope and content of projects, programmes and activities. This means before the final amount of the investment to be made has been signed off. This is done most effectively by ensuring that evaluation – measurement of results – is part of that same planning process.

The key to this is establishing appropriate and genuinely SMART (Specific, Measurable, Attainable, Realistic and Timely) objectives that address the problems, or perhaps opportunities, that have prompted you to take action in the first place.

You will have explored the need for what you are doing, and framed your activities around it. Planning for your evaluation – ensuring that you have clear and useful data to collect, and that it can be collected – should be an integral part of planning the project or activity that you propose to evaluate. This means that not only will you have identified clear impact outcomes, but you will also have set measurable objectives for the key steps that will lead to them.

We will show in subsequent chapters how a 'chain of impact' can be built. This will demonstrate how data about the buy-in of individuals and teams, their capability and competence, and their operational effectiveness combine to drive results: impact.

2

DATA-LED PLANNING, MEASUREMENT AND EVALUATION

Many evaluations are a waste of money, telling stories without the data to back them up. A disciplined and logical approach to evaluation is demanding to apply. Many find it too difficult to sustain. The starting point for measurement is during the planning process, and the data collected needs to be applied to continuous improvement whilst a project or programme is in operation. Traditional evaluation approaches usually start after the activity is well underway, if not after it has ceased! Our active evaluation approach sets clear objectives, collects data throughout, reports and applies its lessons. The approach uses both formative and summative techniques and tools. It focuses strongly on the credibility of data and on the credibility of claims of impact. Those who claim it is not possible to measure human capital investments are wrong. But it is hard to do it well.

Robust outcome data

A chain of impact is only as robust as the data with which it is built.

> You need to look at your data, but you also need to remember what your data is supposed to represent and to assess whether it's actually doing that. Doing one without the other is only slightly better than doing neither.
>
> *(Eugene Eric Kim, from his blog, Eekim.com/blog)*

As many can testify from experience, and as others instinctively suspect, a large number of evaluations are a waste of money. Often this is because they are based on telling stories and cannot provide the data and rigorous analysis to support the conclusions they reach or the recommendations they offer. Moreover, carried out ex-post, and based on subjective perspectives and 'memories', they are often weak on evidence and high on justification.

The narrative approach to evaluation is seductive. It provides a convenient, if subjective, means of appearing to link what has been done with observed results. It is especially tempting when the subject of the evaluation is an investment in people. 'We can only really understand the results', the argument goes, 'if we hear from the people that we engaged or benefited.' 'Reducing people to data sets', it goes on, 'is crude, deterministic and too limiting.'

This book may be viewed as a refutation of this line. We don't deny that there is a place for narrative in evaluations. In evaluations of the activities of individuals and small groups, narrative tells the story. But it is most effective if it is backed with systematic, robust data, collected as objectively as possible. In large evaluations, narrative in the form of interviews or case studies humanises and provides context for the data. But the data should come first.

Many individual evaluators and organisations find themselves drawn to story-telling because of the challenges they experience in establishing measurable behaviour and performance objectives for individuals and which focus on *relevant* action.

A major European car manufacturer

The company's UK motor distribution network opened a National Learning Centre in 2005. It provides L&D services to the networks which sell and service the brands within its portfolio. The learning services provided to its networks are one component of a suite of services provided by the Group in order to ensure the highest standard of service to customers across all brands. Customer service and brand reputation are the global company's most important business metrics. Learning Services engages with the whole network population, including Heads of Business, Sales and Retail and Technical Service managers and staff and other employees. The Group needs to know that every person in the service chain has the highest standard of knowledge and skills that they need to do the job and meets the performance and business outcomes they are expected to help to drive. Learning Services collects and uses data to improve learning and performance outcomes across the networks and to measure the efficiency and effectiveness of the services to the networks. Its focus is to train all network managers and employees, including technicians and other staff, in the complex range of skills required to serve customers of the Group's brands. The Group's commitment to human capital investment is focused on providing its dealers with top-quality training, ensuring that their staff have the knowledge and skills needed to meet their customers' needs in the most effective and cost-efficient way.

The Group's board takes these human capital investments seriously and has made it clear that it wants to know what the company gets in return. This means that the Learning Centre carries out evaluations on all training programmes. For example, when the training programme for the launch of a new model was planned in 2009 a return on investment (ROI) evaluation was planned. The main

objective of the training programme in question was to improve sales performance by training sales specialists on all aspects of the new product. It involved
a mixture of face-to-face sessions and e-training. The trained sales specialists
were compared to a control group of salespeople who had not received this
additional training. The trained group demonstrated higher skill levels in all the
areas that were tested, and also sold more of the new model. The evaluation
reported a 116 per cent return on this human capital investment.

'It's all too difficult'

Our disciplined and logical approach can produce robust outcome data even for
the most complex activities. But it is demanding to apply, and that deters many.
They fear it may prove too difficult. This is partly because it brings evaluation into
the initial project planning stage (rather than starting it later, as an afterthought –
Figure 2.1). This demands a greater degree of planning discipline than many are
accustomed to applying to human capital projects (Figure 2.2). Some otherwise
well-intentioned evaluators just give up in the early stages.

But, significantly, analysis of the feedback that we collect from participants in
our evaluation competency-building workshops suggests that the most critical
problem that many of them face is that they were not included in the planning of
the projects they are expected to evaluate. When they are later asked to carry out
an evaluation, they find themselves playing catch-up, armed only with sketchy
baseline data, weak objectives, poor indicators and no clear consent from stakeholders, who are suspicious of someone they see as an 'inspector' rather than as the
'critical partner and friend' who could be of most value.

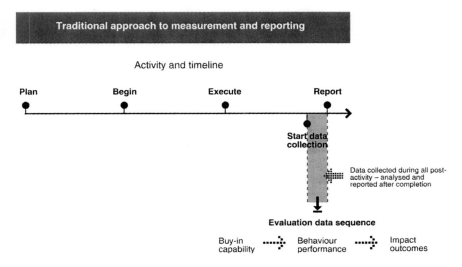

FIGURE 2.1

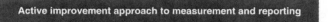

Active improvement approach to measurement and reporting

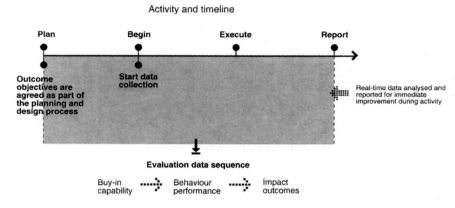

FIGURE 2.2

Of course, even when faced with such late-stage involvement, the competent evaluator does not give up. She or he grabs the opportunity to see what can be learned, but is likely to be forced to apologise for being unable to demonstrate why impact outcomes were, or were not, achieved. There will be no chance of a credible report of value for money.

Measuring social change initiatives

Arguably, some of the most difficult human capital initiatives to measure are social change initiatives. Yet, this is being done daily within development organisations across the globe, some more robust than others. The British Council carries out numerous evaluations, most evaluating social change initiatives in developing economies and countries where poverty and conflict are widespread. These evaluations are grounded in the logic model, where short-, medium- and long-term outcomes (or legacy) need to be identified as objectives and then later measured for change.

One such programme aimed to drive public sector reform in a large Asian country's civil service. This country has around 700,000 civil servants. Securing attitude changes essential to implementing structural change in everything from recruitment to reporting structures is a major challenge. A programme was designed to create a critical mass of reform-minded civil servants by targeting middle and senior civil servants to participate in leadership and policy development programmes. It was proposed that following their participation in the programme, civil servants would be able to develop and deliver government policies that better met the needs of the poor.

The results were in general positive although there were limitations due to weak indicator and data collection planning for monitoring changes in practices and behaviours as well as impact outcomes. The participants worked on Performance Improvement Projects (PIPs). These were projects where participants first explored and proposed and then implemented reformed human resource (HR) policies, systems and procedures including Client Focused Service and Service Improvement, People Development, People Management, Programme/Process/Resource Management, and Understanding Organisations. Participants were also expected to deploy some of the leadership concepts and theories they had learned and to demonstrate day-to-day changed behaviour, for example, through initiating regular staff meetings and including general staff in decision making.

Summative and formative

Clearly, it is essential to take human capital-intensive activities very seriously, and to accept the importance of undertaking much more measurement of their effectiveness than is currently done. That assertion is now very widely accepted. But its implications are not.

We need to apply both summative and formative evaluation approaches. We have to establish alignment between investment in projects and their impact and value that is both practical and credible. Some suggest it can't be done. There is a body of opinion that doubts if it is possible to measure the outcomes of human capital investment at all, or at least to do it with any degree of reliability.

One argument says that attempts to measure outcomes can never provide an accurate answer as to whether and how an investment delivered a specific outcome. This argument suggests that many influences or variables often contribute to impact outcomes, and claims that it will always be impossible to say what exactly influenced any improvement.

Another argument concedes that outcomes can be measured, but only through classic research methodologies such as randomised controlled trials (RCTs).

How randomised controlled trials work

RCTs are experimental trials comparing groups of people to determine whether an intervention works or if there are any benefits or adverse reactions to its implementation. Traditionally used in the medical field since 1948, RCTs have been a cause of much debate within the non-scientific fields, such as anthropology, social sciences, education and, more specifically, among evaluators.

(Continued)

(Continued)

Before the initiative starts, at least two groups of people are randomly selected from the same eligible population. Each group must share similar characteristics, the only difference being that one will participate in the initiative and the other(s) will not. The participating group is the experimental group and the other(s) is the control group(s). Ideally, participants should not know they are part of a trial. The groups should not communicate, and influencing factors should remain constant. In real life, however, these conditions are very difficult to achieve, especially in human capital interventions.

Sources: Haynes et al. (2012); Leeuw and Vaessen (2009); Melia (2011); Scriven (2008).

RCTs are used in healthcare drug trials, and they are increasingly used in the evaluation of public policy, but rarely in human capital projects because they need to be planned from the start, can be costly to apply and may pose ethical dilemmas. They must be applied correctly, and are dependent on rigorous conditions.

A misconception that leads some to favour RCTs over other approaches to measurement is that important stakeholders are invariably thought to be concerned only with summative evidence of impact. In our experience, this is not so.

Summative evidence of impact is of overwhelming interest to some stakeholders, mainly those concerned with organisational policy and financial and operational accounting. It is often the case that board members, funding agencies, policy commissioning teams, chief executive officers (CEOs), chief financial officers and investors want to hear about impact outcomes and value for money, and little else. However, everyone else – operational managers, team members, staff representatives, field teams, project designers and developers – is likely to be far more interested in why and how the impact results were (or were not) achieved. These stakeholders require evidence on which they can act to create and sustain the improvement that gets the best results. Moreover, on-going project concurrent monitoring can identify what is or is not working effectively and efficiently and use the data to address problems and, potentially, leverage the potential for impact and value during the project's lifetime.

RCTs can be highly effective in comparing results between different groups and in showing how variations in results may reveal differences in the groups that achieve them. But they do not help to reveal what people actually did and how the changes in practices and behaviours actually occurred. It is this, in all its complexity, that is so important in organisational or wider social and economic change settings.

To illustrate this important point, it is instructive to look at what RCTs try to do, alongside a view of what this approach to impact evaluation offers (Figure 2.3).

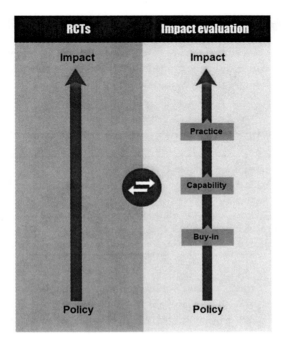

FIGURE 2.3

RCTs compare data sets of randomly selected individuals and groups that are directly targeted or involved in the project against a randomly selected comparable group that had no involvement. The rationale is that the only difference between the groups is the project intervention, and any improvements in planned outcomes can therefore be attributed to the project.

Our approach to impact evaluation described in this book, on the other hand, aims to fill in the gap between the same policy and its impact by tracking the activity of those who make or contribute to making the policy work. It examines data about the level of their buy-in and motivation and their capability. It then tracks their actions and behaviour changes and looks to establish the strength of the connections between each of the data sets and the impacts that have been achieved.

This is a qualitatively different journey, and the links it makes span microsteps, as opposed to the major leap from policy to impact. It is also a journey that provides data not just about cause and effect, but also about performance and explanations for success or failure. It is this that enables impact evaluations to be practice-improvement tools, as well as policy guides.

Our approach

This problem is overcome by the chain of impact, which is based on the Kirkpatrick Levels (Table 2.1). These in their turn have their origin in logic models.

This approach clarifies demand by working from the top (Level 4) down (to Level 1). The result or impact sought is associated with the performance and behaviour required to achieve it (Level 3), the knowledge and competence required to drive that performance and behaviour (Level 2) and the degree of engagement and buy-in needed to ensure strong motivation (Level 1).

TABLE 2.1

	Needs/priorities
Level 4	The problem or opportunity
Level 3	The individual or collective performance or behaviour changes required to achieve it
Level 2	The skill, knowledge or confidence investment required to drive the performance or behaviour change
Level 1	The circumstances under which engagement and buy-in can be assured

The strength of this approach lies in the iterative process by which we clarify why we are doing something and, in reverse sequence, from Level 1 to Level 4, the operational sequence by which we discover whether or not it has been done. This enables us to establish a robust chain of impact.

Finally, all of this comes down to developing sharply focused descriptions of need. When you set out to do it for your own project or activity, be careful to avoid the classic pitfall of focusing on inputs instead of outcomes, process instead of impact.

'We need a problem-solving organisation' might be an example. We may do, but the question is why? Presumably because we need to resolve our problems better and more rapidly. Perhaps we can be more specific about the kinds of problems that are most urgent for us to address effectively. We can then frame impact objectives accordingly.

The best process for solving those problems will be our focus at Level 3. Successfully equipping our colleagues to play their part in problem solving will be our Level 2. At Level 1 we will need to be assured that they regard problem solving as a major priority.

Formative evaluation

This again is to misunderstand the purpose of evaluating organisational development and project activity. For the vast majority of these evaluations of projects, programmes, events, innovations and other activities much of the value lies in the extent to which evaluation is rooted in the improvement of both current and future practice.

The early data provided from evaluations that are conducted formatively is some of the most valuable for identifying and prompting improvement: signalling what is dysfunctional and should be stopped; identifying what is effective and should be repeated or intensified.

In a working context this is nothing but practical good sense. Their objectivity is not assured by distance, but by a clear process rigorously applied, and by a system of rules that guarantee impartiality, fairness and, above all, conservatism. Nothing more thoroughly undermines the usefulness of an evaluation than the suspicion that it may be overstating, even slightly, the results that have been achieved. Nothing more helpfully encourages stakeholders to focus on lessons learned and future practice than the certainty that, if anything, claims of benefit and credit have been slightly understated. An evaluation method that ensures that claims of benefit are always on the conservative side is a method that can be trusted. If people trust its conclusions, the likelihood is that it will be widely used.

Isolating and attributing

Evaluations are worth nothing unless they can be regarded as credible. Life is complicated, work is complicated and there are multiple and contributory causes and influences for pretty much everything that happens. Organisations are complicated and there are often several claimants for credit for the good things that happen within them.

For all these reasons, one of the most difficult issues that anyone faces in carrying out evaluation is that of securing sufficient credibility for the judgements and claims made to ensure that the lessons drawn will be accepted and used.

So a key function of any evaluation approach is to address the giant issue of credibility, and to deal with both friendly and unfriendly challenges to it.

Attribution

When they are conducting evaluations, evaluators face key questions as they address the issue of attribution. What really caused the changes in the organisation or community that we are evaluating? Were they a result of the initiative being evaluated or were there other factors that influenced the changes? How much can we attribute to the initiative that was implemented? Using a variety of methods, evaluators try to attribute the initiative's influence on the outcomes.

These methods include experiments, e.g. randomised controlled trials (RCTs), that compare an intervention group receiving the initiative with a counterfactual group depicting what would have happened without the intervention. Following the intervention, the difference between the outcomes of both groups is identified; causality is then inferred, and thereby attributed to the initiative. These types of experiments are normally useful in circumstances where a large sample can be drawn.

(Continued)

(Continued)

For smaller sample sizes, other methods, such as the abdi recommended ROI approach, are used. The focus is on understanding the causal chain (chain of impact) that connects the observed outcomes with the intervention, in order to explain what happened and how it happened. The aim is to find out what really caused the change and thereby attribute the effects to the initiative and/or other factors. To achieve this, detailed evidence is gathered to establish how each link in the causal chain is organised and related.

Source: White and Phillips (2012)

Cause and effect

Few, if any, evaluations are likely to result in absolute *proof* that some impact or result was directly and wholly caused by any particular action or initiative. In the absence of proof we must look for techniques that provide assurance of credibility.

Inevitably this will be a combination of strong process, rigorously applied, and relevant insight into the project, programme or activity that is being evaluated, and its context.

We need to confess that we do the best we can. We need to admit this at the outset, pointing out that our purpose is to provide a view of impact and benefit that can be shared, and from which we will be able to plan securely and move on. We are not setting out to present final proof of cause and effect. We know that is never going to be possible. We are seeking to establish an agreement about the amount of change or improvement that all parties will accept as having been achieved. We are looking for the common ground from which all parties can safely draw conclusions and determine next steps.

A simple common-ground illustration

This is illustrated below in Figure 2.4, where, following an isolation/attribution process, four views of the amount of change or benefits attributable to an initiative are significantly different.

The graphic shows one view of benefit equalling 100, another equalling 90, a third equalling 60 and a fourth equalling 80.

In cases like this, even when the option of reporting the highest level of benefit or improvement has been rejected, as it must be, many observers will suggest reporting an average of the views.

As the graphic shows, this would report a benefit of 82.5, which has the full consent of only two of the four views (even though it is only marginally above the level of the fourth view).

The only report that has the full consent of all four views is the lowest: View 3. It establishes the common ground (Figure 2.5). There will be no argument about possible over-claiming. The stakeholders will be able to use this report to discuss and decide on conclusions and recommendations. They may acknowledge the other, different views, but should avoid any conclusions or recommendations that depend on any of the higher views of benefit.

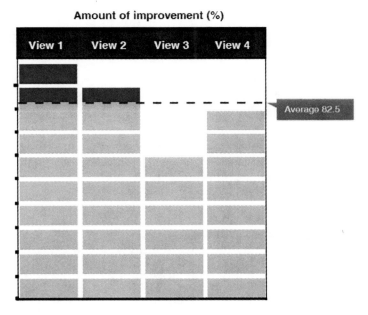

FIGURE 2.4

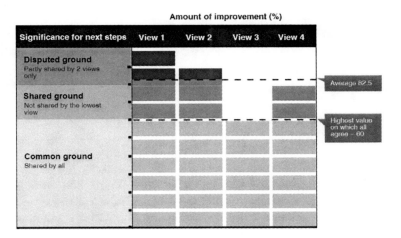

FIGURE 2.5

The effect of time

There is a second important principle governing the way that we approach attribution. It is the effect of time – and extended periods of time are our concern.

The proposition is straightforward. The further apart the investment we make and the impact that we want it to influence, the greater the potential quantity and intensity of other possible influences.

There is no formula to govern this effect, but common sense tells us that we must acknowledge that it is likely to be there. It suggests a pattern for a credibility life-cycle.

The credibility life-cycle

Figure 2.6 illustrates the fact that the further away an outcome is from the investment that was designed to encourage or produce it, the less credible becomes the link between the two. As time passes there are increasing numbers of other influences and circumstances that may have contributed to the impact. The pattern is merely a template because everything we plan and do is context driven.

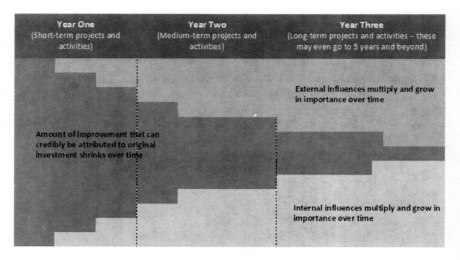

FIGURE 2.6

Some activities may be driven very little by external influences, even beyond the medium term. An example would be an organisation experiencing significant internal restructuring in order to maximise profits, but operating in a sector with very stable demand and little in the way of competition or regulatory change (Figure 2.7).

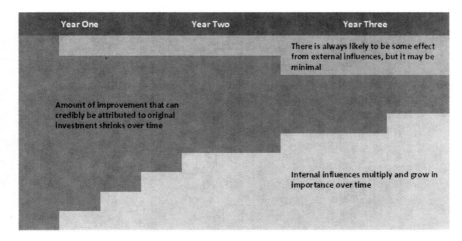

FIGURE 2.7

Or the pattern may be reversed. Say, in a very well-established organisation in a stable market, but which conducts most of its activities internationally or is subject to significant regulatory change (Figure 2.8).

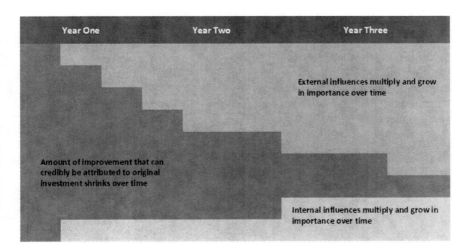

FIGURE 2.8

A credible view of impact

The evaluator's highest priority and greatest test is achieving credibility.

This is hard to do in itself, but is made even more testing by the fact that stakeholders and other readers of evaluations may have very different standards to bring to their judgement of whether a report is credible or not. This judgement may be influenced by any one or more of:

- their expert knowledge of some aspect of what is being evaluated
- their prior knowledge of the stakeholders in the evaluation
- their prior knowledge of the evaluators, or of the approach to evaluation that is being used
- the demands or opinions of funders or policy stakeholders
- their desire to see certain results reported.

We *can* measure the outcomes of human capital investments

Our conclusion after decades of experience is that we can measure, with reasonable accuracy, the outcomes of human capital investment. We can gather data to provide robust evidence of how these outcomes are achieved.

'Reasonable accuracy' is an important qualification. By this we mean a level of accuracy acceptable to all concerned, based on a clear evidence base, transparent in its assumptions and calculations.

On occasion this means that we must acknowledge the potential margin of error in the conclusions we reach. This becomes acceptable only when credibility is made the governing principle by insisting that every option is resolved by reporting only the most conservative of any alternative views of improvement or success.

This enables us to collect robust evidence, both quantitative and qualitative, that is of practical use during the project life-cycle and that can be used to help improve the final impact outcomes.

However, we have also learned to recognise that there are different outcome types and that these are crucial to our ability to make the link between investment and its outcomes.

As we will show throughout this book, there is no automatic causal link between spending money and achieving an outcome. Projects and programmes are driven by people, and the link with value can be forged only by tracking and understanding what they actually do.

3

PLANS

We must question why any and every investment in human capital is being undertaken: why it is important; what results it is expected to achieve or to influence. A high proportion of human capital investment is currently in effect supply-sided – commissioned because there is a good supplier, a good course or an available budget. It is important to shift to a demand-sided approach for this expenditure: to link these plans to impact outcomes that are important to organisations and funders. This means that planners of human-capital initiatives and projects must understand their organisation's business and working environment. We clarify organisational needs with the help of Theory of Change models or with Systems Analysis and Root Cause Analysis processes. Our planning is based on logic models.

The why question

Here's a very modest proposition: we should never accept a proposal to invest money or effort without asking 'Why?'

Agreed? Next proposition: the answer will be helpful only if it tells us the ultimate organisational reasons for the initiative. That may be a potential opportunity to be exploited. It may be a problem to be tackled. It may be a threat to be defused or risk-reduced.

We know if this question has been asked and the answer pursued with some rigour as soon as we read a set of plans for a new project or a fresh initiative. Figure 3.1 shows a selection of justifications for spending that come our way in one form or another with great regularity.

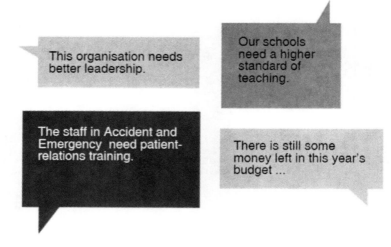

FIGURE 3.1

When we justify money and effort our minds seem to be drawn first and most strongly to the *inputs* that we feel are needed, not to the *outcomes* that should be achieved.

So, before proposing a solution, we must understand the problem or opportunity that we want to address. Then we can get our heads around the specific impact outcomes for which we will need to plan.

And before we can begin to formulate the outcomes, we need to look at the past and current position and assure ourselves of the scope and quality of the evidence base that has been used to establish it.

Analysing impact needs

When someone over sixty years old has a fall, this has a ripple effect on the individual and their family. Apart from the physical and emotional impact on the individual, it can often have a significant impact on children, partners, other family members and working relations.

In one large UK city the National Health Service (NHS) sees over 4,000 people at Accident and Emergency (A&E) departments each year as a consequence of falls. Over 60 per cent are later admitted to hospital. The impact goes further – ambulance service, pharmacies, physiotherapists and, of course, general practitioners.

A 'community falls pathway' has been developed. This aims to identify persons at risk and then to seek to mitigate or reduce their risks. The intention was that following the correct pathway should contribute to minimising falls. However, careful analysis showed that the pathway was not being used. A group of healthcare staff set about rectifying this by revamping the pathway, improving its accessibility and usability. In addition, a new training programme was developed to provide front-line community staff with the necessary skills in 'screening and assessment', 'appropriate patient management' and 'sharing information and assessments'.

During the planning stage, the team working to try to reduce avoidable falls identified the past/current status of over-60s patients coming to A&E as a result of falls and where and when the falls occurred; and examined what and who needed to change their everyday work practices and behaviour, as well as how to provide the skills needed and engage front-line staff. Not only will a reduction in numbers of falls reduce costs to the NHS, but also the city's elderly will enjoy a better quality of life. The team decided to carry out a pilot before full roll-out to check its assumptions about how the pathway works and how improving the knowledge and skills of staff might influence behaviour and, ultimately, numbers of falls.

The example above shows an organisation asking the *why* question. Instead of deciding that training was needed and 'selling' training as the solution to reducing falls, the team researched the exact numbers of falls, where they took place and when, and the real costs incurred. It reviewed how those at risk of falling were being identified. It looked at whether or not a care pathway was being followed to minimise the risks to the over-60s. Only then did it venture to say that it was clear as to where the problems lay, and what opportunities might be available to improve the situation.

Unfortunately, this logical and reasoned train of thought is by no means always followed. We live in a world of solutions in pursuit of problems to solve – and it's the wrong way round!

There are a number of tools and disciplines available.

The exhaustive why

The first is a discipline we all need. It is what might be called 'the exhaustive why'. It is one of the first things anyone measuring outcomes has to learn.

Our experience is that when we first discuss an evaluation with a client we are more often than not involved in a conversation along the lines illustrated in Figure 3.2.

FIGURE 3.2

This kind of progressive interrogation can become a matter of instinct and habit. It needs to be carried out systematically because until real motives for spending money and effort have been brought out there is no great chance of identifying relevant outcome objectives on which to focus the effort. Without clear objectives it is impossible to conduct good evaluation.

Evaluators find that the process of getting to this point is often difficult, and can be fractious. Partners and clients are often unaware of the extent to which they have fallen short of analysing the problems or the opportunities they need to address.

They may have spent a good deal of time thinking through their projects or programmes, but fail to identify the real demand for them. Without intending to, or appreciating what they have done, they generally end up supply-siding their investment. Their final objective becomes the implementation of the solution, not the solution to the problem, or the achievement of the opportunity.

Supply-side culture

This supply-side culture seems to be at its most dangerous in large organisations with bureaucratic tendencies. Here one of the strongest pressures on managers can be to spend their budgets. Budgets unspent, it is suspected, or perhaps threatened, may shrink proportionately in subsequent years. Where power can be gauged by budget size, this is a dire threat.

Much supply-sided commissioning is undertaken by people who believe they are protecting their jobs and those of their colleagues. If this is true in the short term, it may be tragically mistaken in the medium and long term as it becomes apparent that little can be shown in the way of impact. The supply-side culture is also continuously fed and watered by 'solution providers', organisations deploying smart marketing and sales techniques to convince buyers that their solution is the answer. That can be compelling even if the buyer has not yet completely framed the question.

References from previously satisfied customers are powerful reinforcers of supply-side culture. With great respect to General Electric (GE), it is extraordinary how many organisations we have met that say they are investing in leadership development programmes because they think that will make them like GE!

We need to go over to the demand side

The tendency to track and report inputs rather than outcomes is all too easy to follow, especially if one is close to a piece of action, and strongly involved in it.

'We spent £20,000 on the conference, and it was oversubscribed', might be an example. What this does is track the effort and money that went into the event (the inputs). The only other thing we know about it is that it was popular *before* it took place. We know nothing of what may have changed as a result of it, nor if the people who were so keen to attend believed that they had spent their time well.

We have no idea if anyone ever asked the question 'What do we need to see happen *as a result of this conference?*'

Understanding demand

How do we get to the demand side? There are no short-cuts, but we have found that there are three indispensable characteristics of those who do this well.

1. They really know their own organisations, and not just that, but the environment and the wider sectors and contexts in which they operate.
2. They use the business tools available (we use Theory of Change, Root Cause Analysis, Porter's Five Forces Analysis, Boston Matrix, SWOT analysis, Ansoff Matrix and PESTLE (Political, Economic, Social, Technological, Legal or Environmental Analysis).

3. They can list the most important indicators that report the performance of the organisation, not just the financial and operational indicators, but indicators such as customer loyalty, brand awareness and staff engagement (the key signs of a healthy organisation with a future).

Knowing the organisation, its business and its environment

Regardless of role, this should form a common basis of understanding in organisations. Anyone in a management role who is not familiar with the organisation's key performance indicators is likely to become peripheral to the activities associated with them, and will have great difficulty aligning their own work with that of others and with the organisation's most important goals.

There are two principal approaches to investigating impact needs. Both can be deployed for organisational performance indicators either where they are failing to achieve their expected levels or where there is an opportunity to achieve new goals that were previously unconsidered. The first is well described in management literature and combines Systems Analysis with Root Cause Analysis. The second, Theory of Change, is more common for public sector initiatives and is increasingly used in international development and aid programmes.

The first, Root Cause Analysis, is a systematised inquiry process.

Root Cause Analysis

Root Cause Analysis (RCA) is a process for solving issues or concerns involving problems, incidents and non-conformity. As the name suggests, the aim is to examine the root cause(s) or underlying reason(s) for the occurrence of a particular situation, so that corrective procedures can be implemented that will stop it from happening again.

Although there isn't one specific method for carrying out an RCA, there are a number of methods and tools used across industries. Two popular methods are the '5 Whys' and 'Fishbone Diagrams'.

*   The 5 Whys. This is a question-asking method where the simple question 'Why?' is asked at each stage of the investigation until the real cause(s) of the situation has been identified. The question is asked at least five times and further questions are added, as appropriate.
*   Fishbone Diagrams. These are also called the Herringbone Diagram or the Ishikawa Diagram (after its creator, Kaoru Ishikawa). This method is very useful in complex situations where examination of smaller components of the situation is required. Some of the questions used to identify the primary and secondary cause(s) include 'What actually happened?' 'When?' 'Where?' 'Why?' 'How?' and 'So what?'

Source: BRC Global Standards (2012, 20).

Systems Analysis is a problem–solving process for investigating the best way to resolve a complex problem.

Systems Analysis

The process includes stakeholders from multidisciplinary professions and involves both quantitative and qualitative analysis. The International Institute for Systems Analysis (IISA) uses a nine-step framework in its process, employing computer modelling where appropriate.

1. Assemble all the information and scientific knowledge available on the problem in question, gathering new evidence and developing new knowledge, if necessary.
2. Determine what the goals of the stakeholders are, both people and institutions.
3. Explore different alternative ways of achieving those goals, and design or invent new options, where appropriate.
4. Reconsider the problem in the light of the knowledge accumulated.
5. Estimate the impacts of the various possible courses of action, taking into account the uncertain future and the organisational structures that are required to implement the proposals.
6. Compare the alternatives by making a detailed assessment of possible impacts and consequences.
7. Present the results of the study in a framework that facilitates choice by the stakeholders.
8. Provide follow-up assistance.
9. Evaluate the results.

Source: Hordijk, L. (2007).

A simple example of a sales activity

Peter is the sales director of a firm manufacturing and selling packaging to food producers. For five years sales rose on average 3 per cent per annum, mainly through new customer growth. The small sales team was having little difficulty meeting targets and it seemed that the firm was on a steady growth pathway. Then, in 2011 sales fell by 5 per cent on the previous year, and they fell again in 2012. Peter's team worked harder than ever to identify potential leads. However, it was clear midway through 2013 that sales were likely to fall for a third year in a row. Data suggested that there was still growth in the market, and competitors did not appear to be suffering. A wider Systems Analysis, combined with an environmental scanning exercise, provided no evidence that anything untoward was happening in the wider market. The problem had to be internal.

With the rest of the senior management team, Peter decided to undertake a more serious investigation. They used RCA. Working with his sales team Peter examined a small selection of successful and failed 'leads', first looking at how each lead was identified, then moving through the entire sales process. They identified a point in time when the firm had introduced a new way of describing the packaging processes and the preparation of the product prior to shipping it to clients. The analysis suggested that it was this changed 'message' which was the root cause of the problem. Its use coincided with the point from which new customer acquisitions began to decline. The analysis showed that the information about this process and the new shipping arrangements for the packaging were suggesting to 'leads' that it would increase the effort they would have to make to fill each package with their food products. So a number of them looked for other suppliers. Strong, established relationships with existing customers had either prevented this confusion arising among them, or had it enabled any anxieties to be dealt with swiftly.

The second approach, Theory of Change, is developed from the logic model which, at its simplest, organises information about projects into inputs, activities, outputs and outcomes. It combines many of the techniques found in PESTLE and other environmental scanning activities.

Theory of Change

As defined by www.theoryofchange.org:

> All building blocks required to bring about a given long-term goal. This set of connected building blocks – interchangeably referred to as outcomes, results, accomplishments, or preconditions is depicted on a map known as a pathway of change/change framework, which is a graphic representation of the change process.

Theory of Change is based on certain assumptions about the theories of cause and effect – to make this social change, these things need to happen. The Theory of Change approach takes this on board by documenting the outcomes desired and the assumed journey(s) to get there. The aim is not only to evaluate the contributions that the initiative makes to outcomes, but also to identify any learning that can be applied to future initiatives. A critical component is the contribution of key stakeholders. With stakeholders' input, data collection and analysis is undertaken to monitor and evaluate the progress of the initiative to identify the assumptions contributed to any changes.

Source: ActKnowledge Inc. (2012); RAND Corporation (2009).

At its most basic, it sets out to show how early results and outcomes can lead to longer-term results. In more elaborate versions it looks more deeply into the process of change in question and provides help with tracking the links between the early and later outcomes.

Creating a Theory of Change model for a specific project or activity is likely to involve:

1. identifying the ultimate goal
2. looking backwards to clarify the preconditions essential to its achievement
3. setting out how the project or activity will create those preconditions
4. producing indicators for each one, so that performance can be assessed
5. backing the theory up with a narrative to explain how it works and achieves its results.

Using Theory of Change models

Within a good Theory of Change model there needs to be information on who will achieve the results, exactly what those results are expected to be, when they need to be achieved, how this will happen, what the context will be and why the approach has been chosen.

We find the most value in Theory of Change as a means of developing the demand-led objectives that can generate good data. Others see it as a complete evaluation model, valuing it for the discursive and descriptive approach that it encourages. The disadvantage of using it in this way is that, because the focus is more discursive, it will not provide evidence of the strong chain of impact that both shows why results have been achieved and, thus, provides a clear basis on which future improvements or innovations can be framed.

But the model certainly supports a full definition of needs and, if applied well, avoids the development of supply-sided projects.

Theory of Change models are increasingly widely used to plan activities and projects, as well as to understand and evaluate them later. They are designed to show a clear relationship between the investment and effort put into activities and the outcomes achieved.

Models can be framed differently to include more information, and they are quite often presented in more complex graphics. But what matters is the structured thought about the influences and potential contributions of all the factors expected to contribute to change and to help deliver improved impact outcomes. The message they all send is that one can never assume a causal link between investing money and effort and a subsequent outcome or impact. All of life is more complex than that, not least because people are involved.

The value of Theory of Change models is that they force the human element into the planning and evaluation of change.

In developing economies, one of the most important areas for development and improvement is education. Their systems and attitudes to education will have evolved over many years and are likely to be influenced by many economic, social, geographical and cultural considerations. Whilst the ultimate objective of reform is likely to be raising educational achievement levels in the population at large, funding may come from donors specifically concerned with improving teacher training, school facilities and discrimination. These will generate their own barriers. Change may be resisted by loyal adherents of existing systems. As well as entrenched interests at the top, and privilege reinforced by wealth and influence, some groups in the community may mistrust 'education' for political or religious reasons. It is complex, and takes time. Theory of Change models are used in many parts of the world to help organise thinking about these systems, influences and stakeholders. Well used, they present a broad and detailed picture that helps to clarify the motives and needs behind initiatives, and should also enable realism to be injected into expectations and objectives of impact.

A simple model might contain five columns showing a progressive relationship between inputs, activities, outputs and outcomes/impacts (Table 3.1).

TABLE 3.1

Assumptions (the thinking behind the project)	Inputs (the investment and resources put into a project)	Activities (what people do to drive the project)	Outputs (interventions designed to bring about the benefits)	Outcomes/impacts (the changes or benefits that occur later)

But it can be shown differently. In the example in Table 3.2 of a hospital project to prevent patients from developing pressure ulcers (Figure 3.3), we can first see how this might be represented in the format described above.

TABLE 3.2

Assumption (the thinking behind the project)	Input (the investment and resources put into the project)	Activity (what people do to drive the project)	Output (interventions designed to bring about the benefits)	Outcome/impact (the change or benefit that occurs later)
Pressure ulcer infections are too costly and 95% of them are preventable	The investment in the training	A series of training courses to teach better care and management of pressure ulcer infections	Staff applying the techniques on wards	Standards of care are achieved. Pressure ulcer infections are reduced by 5% in 6 months. Average nursing time on pressure ulcer infections is reduced by 10% in 6 months.

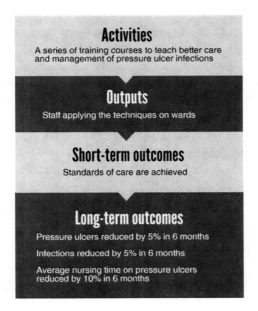

Activities
A series of training courses to teach better care
and management of pressure ulcer infections

Outputs
Staff applying the techniques on wards

Short-term outcomes
Standards of care are achieved

Long-term outcomes
Pressure ulcers reduced by 5% in 6 months

Infections reduced by 5% in 6 months

Average nursing time on pressure ulcers
reduced by 10% in 6 months

FIGURE 3.3

Theory of Change models and SMART objectives

Combining Theory of Change or Systems/Root Cause Analysis with an impact outcome framework built from the logic model provides the detail that we require to express the sequence of needs that will enable us to define SMART objectives from which we can build a chain of impact. The contribution of the levels in the logic model is to place the individuals or teams responsible for the key activities at the heart of the chain. A clear explanation of the knowledge, skill and competence we require from them, backed up with an understanding of the degree of buy-in we need to demand, provides the basis from which we can specify the performance and behaviour they will need to exhibit if they are to be responsible for the results and impacts we have in mind.

The challenge is then to set SMART objectives at each of these levels. We deal with this in detail in Chapter 4. But it is worth noting here that while most project managers and learning and development professionals understand what SMART signifies: objectives that are Specific, Measurable, Achievable, Realistic and Timely, understanding of what will actually work as a SMART objective in practice appears to vary widely. We see far too many unrealistic and unmeasurable objectives.

These poor objectives emerge for two reasons:

1. lack of what might be called specific rigour, which results in them being too vague to measure
2. insufficient relevance and lack of realism.

The issue of rigour is a key one dealt with in the next chapter.

The issue of relevance is a prior concern. It is generally caused by poor understanding of background and baseline data. It is extremely difficult to set achievable, realistic objectives for improving something unless you know its current state. You will have difficulty being objective about a realistic speed of improvement unless you know how that state has changed over a relevant past period.

Clarifying organisational needs

Whether demand needs to be clarified or investigated for the first time, it will have been driven by one or more of the seven motives shown in Table 3.3.

TABLE 3.3

Seven drivers of demand	Usefulness and caveats
Saving costs Saving time	These of course are closely related, and provide the shortest route to identifying a financial benefit from your project or programme. Beware though: neither of these is of any value unless it can be achieved without an unacceptable loss of quality – to be useful as clear statements of priority they both need to have the quality standard clearly articulated alongside them.
Increasing output	A measure of output is often the target that managers set. It is crucial to them, but it does have its limitations as an organisational measure taken on its own. Ultimately it is the profit or margin that results from that output which will tell whether we have a worthwhile result, and which will enable us to see if we have had value for money. Also, if increasing output is a metaphor for making greater effort, it does not necessarily signify commensurately improved results.
Improving quality	The challenge here is to articulate quality in a way that will subsequently be possible to measure – otherwise it will be hard to know what has been achieved. The most frequently used conventional measure of quality is the avoidance of the need to repeat or replace a product or service. In international development work, quality might be indicated by improved client loyalty or by strengthened reputation.
Improving internal climate	Most organisations have some means of surveying their staff. The problem often encountered, especially when regular surveys are used, is associating any improvement with a specific initiative.

Improving external climate	Customer or client satisfaction data is widely collected by questionnaire. Organisational compliance is noted with increasing frequency (and is the subject of more critical discussion on pages 88–9). Organisational awards and quality ratings are widely used in the service sector. In international development work, reputation – again gauged by questionnaire or survey – might be the measure.
Innovation	This might mean evidence of an innovative workforce (suggestions for new products, services or processes) or of an innovative organisation (new products or services successfully launched or patents filed). Of course, the innovating staff may lead directly to the organisational success.

Embarking on change

Being clear about what you want to change is a vital first step, and one that is often not taken with any precision. But this alone is no guarantee of robustness.

Think about your own past projects. How many of these, are you able to claim, were delivered exactly to plan, on time, to budget and with the required quality of outcomes? One suspects not many. Even the successful ones may not have happened completely as expected.

Research by the American change management guru John P. Kotter reports that relatively few change management initiatives succeed completely. A roughly equal, but small number, fail completely, and the majority fall somewhere in between, with most of these at the failure end of the spectrum.

Source: Kotter (1995).

Kotter suggests, as we noted in Chapter 1, that change initiatives often fail because they fall down in one or more of seven important tasks: establishing a sense of urgency; forming a powerful guiding coalition; creating a vision; communicating a vision; empowering others to act on the vision; planning for and creating short-term wins; consolidating improvements and producing still more change; institutionalising new approaches.

Kotter tells that by 'establishing a sense of urgency' he means 'Examining market and competitive realities and identifying and discussing crises, potential crises, or major opportunities'. In other words, looking at demand in precisely the way we have just proposed.

Organising objectives into logic models

Once priorities have been established, validated and strengthened by reference to relevant baselines, they will provide the basis for the creation of strong impact objectives, which themselves can be organised into logic models.

Conventional logic models place descriptions of activities and objectives in broadly sequential blocks of information and data, enabling the progress of projects and programmes to be tracked and analysed. The illustration in Figure 3.4 is fairly typical.

Resources ▸ Activities ▸ Outputs ▸ Short- and long-term outcomes ▸ Impact

FIGURE 3.4

The disadvantage of some logic models (e.g. the Logical Framework Approach) for planning and measuring activities that depend heavily on human endeavour is that they end up being presented as a linear process or sequence. This does not involve the active use of data collected at each stage to drive any necessary corrections or changes that might result in a better final result. The logframe implies evaluation that is biased towards the summative, not the formative approach.

Clear needs driving strong impact objectives

Using the project to prevent pressure ulcers that we used as an example of a Theory of Change model, we can see how a brief, clear expression of need can be used to build highly specific, genuinely SMART impact objectives.

Example: NHS – setting impact objectives in healthcare

Treating pressure ulcers costs the NHS billions of pounds each year, estimated to be up to 4 per cent of the total NHS expenditure. Yet, with the right care, around 95 per cent of pressure sores are preventable. This was clearly an area that required critical attention. One NHS region embarked on improving the education and knowledge of staff by developing a five-hour training course.

The training course focused on helping learners understand pressure ulcers. It was initially undertaken at five hospitals, with twenty learners from each hospital participating. The project aimed for an ROI of 30 per cent. The impact objectives were:

- to reduce the incidence and prevalence of pressure ulcers by 5 per cent after six months
- to reduce the rate of pressure ulcer infections by 5 per cent after six months
- to reduce the average nursing time spent caring for ulcers by 10 per cent in six months.

Achieving these objectives will extend to other areas not measured in the project, such as less patient time in hospital and fewer materials used for treatment, as well as fewer staff needed to care for pressure ulcers.

4

SETTING OBJECTIVES FOR IMPACT AND LEGACY

You will never know how far you've travelled when you arrive at your destination unless you know where you started from. That is the importance of baselines, both for project managers and for evaluators. Baselines provide us with perspective. They are often most effective when they reflect trends. Single points are dangerous. These may reflect temporary highs or lows. Baselines may come from inside organisations, or from outside. They are essential to setting good impact objectives. Impact objectives will be truly useful only if they are SMART. They will be arrived at only by interrogating the needs that lie behind them, and then by ensuring that the final objectives are specific and time bound.

The importance of baselines

You may indeed arrive at your destination, but if you don't know where you started from, you'll never know how far you've travelled. That much is obvious, but it is a message that is frequently disregarded. Understanding the baseline from which an improvement or achievement is being sought is just as important for those who are carrying through a project or activity as it is for an evaluator attempting to make sense of it. So when an evaluator forces the issue and demands solid baseline data it should serve as a timely reminder about the principles and practices that should be considered routine planning disciplines.

Ideas of what constitutes a baseline can, of course, differ. In marketing, we find definitions as various as:

- A line that is a base for measurement or for construction. A datum used as the basis for calculation or for comparison.

(Wiktionary, Creative Commons Attribution/Share-Alike License)

- An imaginary line or standard by which things are measured or compared.
  The back line at each end of a tennis court.
  Any horizontal line in a plot, graph, or diagram, or on a visual display in an
  electronic device, used as a reference point to which other values are referred.
  (GNU version of the Collaborative International Dictionary of English)

For us, there is nothing imaginary about baselines. We look for the value or the trend line that will show us the amount of improvement we will have to generate in order to achieve our targeted impact. The relevance and value of the baseline will depend both on its solidity and on its timeliness. The time issue becomes crucial in two sets of circumstances.

The first is when a baseline is being defined by a trend. This is always a good idea, if the data is available, because it avoids establishing baselines on the basis of false peaks or troughs. A trend line will show up these pieces of exceptional data. It will also show whether the situation in question was already improving, or was getting progressively worse.

The second is when there is a risk of the circumstance changing that underlies the baseline data, and therefore completely altering in significance.

This might occur, for example, when the time taken to complete a process (and possibly, as a consequence, its cost) is targeted for reduction. In a case like this, if broadband speed, which is not a direct aspect of the planned improvement, were to improve radically during the lifetime of the project, it might have a significant impact on the overall results. Any baseline for the overall impact target that was established on the assumption that the original, slower, broadband speed would remain in operation, would be deceptive. It might be taken to suggest that the project was far more successful than was actually the case.

So the baseline data that we need for evaluation is that which tells us clearly the status of the key metrics *before* the project or intervention started, and which is sufficiently detailed to draw our attention to significant changes in its underlying content *during* the project's life.

Baselines must provide perspective

The whole point of baselines is to put objectives and subsequent performance into perspective. If they fail in that, they have no real value. The *Oxford Dictionary*'s definition of perspective includes 'the art of representing three-dimensional objects on a two-dimensional surface so as to give the right impression of their height, width, depth, and position in relation to each other.'

The key words are 'to give the right impression of their . . . position in relation to each other.'

So, if we have an objective 'By the end of the year the number of complaints will have been reduced from an average of thirty-two per month to an average of ten per month', it is very helpful to gain perspective by understanding how much improvement this might require, and what kinds of improvements will be tracked.

We might find out that the baseline data from a single point in time (previous month) for this objective referred us to:

- 1st-level complaints: 24, which were closed within less than 1 hour and by one person only.
- 2nd-level complaints: 6, which were handled by one person, have required input from one other and were closed within 24 hours.
- 3rd-level (top level) complaints: 2, which required senior-level involvement, and are likely to require compensation.

In order to measure impact in this case we would need to know how the data had changed in terms of each of these three levels of complaint. But more importantly, a good understanding of the baseline data would help us to refine our objectives at the start. We might decide to focus on reducing the complaints that escalate to 2nd and 3rd level, in which case closing more complaints at the 1st level might turn out to be a more effective use of resources than attempting to reduce the overall number of complaints. Closing more 1st-level complaints would have the effect of reducing the numbers at the 2nd and 3rd levels. Better data on our baselines might prompt us to go back and change our original draft objectives.

This is helpful, but offers only part of the perspective we need. It tells us where we are now, but it doesn't indicate whether or not a baseline was already on the move. If we go back, say, a year, we may find that 'One year ago, there were 55 complaints in the month and the response time for 1st-level customer complaints was on average 14 days.'

This would tell us that there was already a downward trend. That is important information because it suggests that other efforts have been, and probably still are being, made elsewhere to bring down response times. Without any further intervention they might cause the situation to improve. This makes us see our target differently: it appears to be more reasonable and achievable than might otherwise seem to have been the case. It might also suggest that just doing nothing (at least for the moment) could even be better value, if only in order to find out if the factors already influencing a reduction in complaints continue. They might do the job on their own, without further expenditure. It would also alert us to the fact that when we come to apportion credit for getting this processing time down, we will need to give some to those who have been making the effort over a period of time.

Perspective comes from looking for trends, not just single data points

Perspective can also come from looking at averages. Imagine a hypothetical issue of complaints in a relatively new business. There is no great history of dealing with customer complaints, but there are a number of different branches or work units each servicing similar complaints, but with varying results. One unit takes an average of four days to respond, another an average of six days and a third an average of seven days. Our target is to make sure that we hit a two-day target. If we want to give perspective to this baseline data, and get a better idea of the viability of the target, we need an extra piece of information: the number of complaints that each of those units was dealing with. This turns out as shown in Table 4.1.

TABLE 4.1

	Number of complaints	Average time to respond (days)
Unit 1	80	4
Unit 2	15	6
Unit 3	20	7
Overall average response time per complaint		4.9

So, by adding this perspective we see immediately that the unit that services the most complaints is best at completing the process rapidly. So long as there is no evidence that it is achieving this by compromising on the quality of what it does, this ought to provide the most realistic baseline for improvement. The best operators should be able to teach the rest how to match their performance. They will all then have to find a way of shaving another day, on average, from the time the process takes.

We may also need to understand what the definition of a complaint is. Is it just a verbal indication of dissatisfaction? Must it be written? Must it be recorded on a helpline? Has the nature of complaints changed? What is meant by a response? Is an acknowledgement a response, or must it be something more constructive? We need to know.

Baselines may come from inside or outside organisations

Organisations that are determined to plan and track impact need to develop their own baselines for their key impact targets. As a start, they need to know their most important operational, financial and strategic organisational data:

- income data: including planned against actual
- profit/margin levels: again, planned against actual
- cost data: planned against actuals, including cost of process, cost of service, cost of materials, staff, attrition rates, staff sickness and absence
- output/productivity data: planned against actuals
- customer data (new, repeat): planned against actuals, customer attrition rates
- key quality indicators: complaints, waste, rework, customer satisfaction, quality of user benefits (better patient outcomes, increased educational outcomes)

- external perception data: brand perception, rankings as providers, trustworthiness
- internal perception data: staff satisfaction, engagement, good place to work
- innovation: new products, new processes, new markets

But organisations without existing baselines and lacking the consistent data to create them, and organisations embarking on activities that are quite new to them, are all likely to need to look elsewhere for relevant baseline data.

The significant word is 'relevant'. Only they can be sure that a piece of baseline data derived from an external source is appropriate to their context. And they will know that only when they examine it in sufficient detail. They will need to decide how close a match is provided with the source and its context. Growth rates of 20 per cent may be relevant to one organisation in one market or region but not to another where the characteristics and conditions of the organisation may be very different.

Remember, baselines help us to establish *why* we have decided to take action in the first place. They also help us to make sure that the impact objectives we ultimately set are relevant, and likely to be realistic and achievable.

Baselines and accountability

One of the strongest messages we get from those who plan and measure effectively and regularly is that the process transforms attitudes to accountability, and provides a powerful basis for delivering it.

The early activity of identifying and setting baselines is one of the most important factors in this. This can work as shown in Figure 4.1.

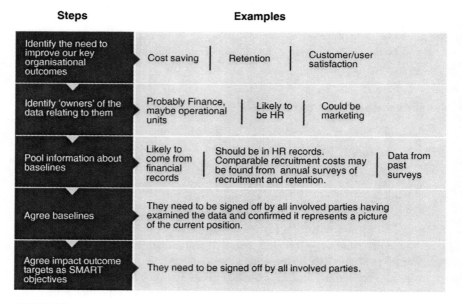

Steps	Examples		
Identify the need to improve our key organisational outcomes	Cost saving	Retention	Customer/user satisfaction
Identify 'owners' of the data relating to them	Probably Finance, maybe operational units	Likely to be HR	Could be marketing
Pool information about baselines	Likely to come from financial records	Should be in HR records. Comparable recruitment costs may be found from annual surveys of recruitment and retention.	Data from past surveys
Agree baselines	They need to be signed off by all involved parties having examined the data and confirmed it represents a picture of the current position.		
Agree impact outcome targets as SMART objectives	They need to be signed off by all involved parties.		

FIGURE 4.1

Using baselines intelligently

Finally, any baseline that's going to be used needs to be checked at regular intervals to ensure that it remains current and credible. Credibility depends mainly on two factors: *solidity* and *stability*.

Solidity requires a baseline to be built on data that is consistently collected using the same methods or tools – the baseline needs to relate to the same issue and the same population.

Stability requires any piece of data to be proof against significant change – sometimes data is reported on the basis of only partial information and estimates of what the rest of the information will reveal. A good example of this is the quarterly report we get of our national Gross Domestic Product (GDP) figures. For each quarter, they are reported during the following quarter, but they are based on only about 40 per cent of the information required to know how the UK has fared economically. The remaining 60 per cent of the data is collected over a period of about 12 months afterwards. There are two problems here. One is that the estimates are large and frequently turn out to be wrong. The second is that the UK appears to be poor at this form of estimation, so our subsequent revisions can be large enough to make the initial estimate useless for practical purposes.

We suggest that you analyse all your items of baseline data using a grid like the one shown in Table 4.2.

TABLE 4.2

Baseline data item	Do you know where this data is recorded?	Are there any plans to change it within the next 6–12 months?	How frequently is it collected?	Is it in current use?	Do you have access to it?	Does it have a standard monetary value in the organisation?	Who 'owns' or is accountable for it?

Planning for results

The next challenge we face is setting good, strong objectives that will enable us to do two things at the same time:

1. communicate relevant and attainable impact targets to an active audience of those who will try to ensure that they are achieved
2. inform a less active audience of stakeholders and other interested parties.

This is among the most critical tasks in the planning of any project or programme. If key objectives are omitted or poorly set, any project will become more difficult to execute. Its impact will be very hard to measure and communicate in any reliable or transparent way.

When impact objectives either are not set at all or are set poorly so that they cannot be measured, projects tend to be reported not in terms of their outcomes, but in terms of the inputs made to them.

So we might read, 'Five events were successfully mounted, and the planned activities were all carried out.' This tells us something about the effort and resource that have been put into the project, but nothing about what resulted from it. There is no mention of impact.

Projects may be planned with what their participants believe to be good process. But if this is not complemented by professional objective setting, the activity – the process – is all that will be reported. The key to ensuring that this does not happen is to use the thinking behind Theory of Change to move from inputs-focused, supply-sided plans into measurable objectives informed by clear needs – plans that are demand-sided. Planning is everything. It is rare to discover that too much time has been spent on planning. Commonly, too little time has been spent, or the time has been poorly focused. This is frequently seen in the planning of human capital projects.

- They fail to clarify their most crucial priorities, or, if they have done so, fail to ensure that the investments in question are properly aligned to them.
- Their managers encourage or allow a supply-sided culture, investing in suppliers, contractors and activities, rather than the results they want them to achieve, then repeating investments simply because they have been well regarded in the past.
- They perpetuate a culture of tracking inputs (money spent, activities undertaken), not outcomes (results achieved, net improvements consequent on results).

Impact objectives that you can measure

Objectives that are non-specific are relatively meaningless. In fact they are no more than expressions of need or general aspiration. The conversation in Figure 4.2 follows a pattern with which we are very familiar.

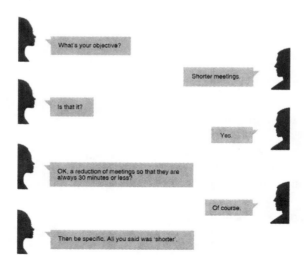

FIGURE 4.2

Apply this principle to the 'Shorter meetings' objective in Table 4.3, and sharper and better objectives will result. The rest of the table reflects the same thinking applied to four other common themes for objectives.

TABLE 4.3

Examples of non-specific and/or non-measurable objectives	*Specific, measurable versions*
Shorter meetings	As from the beginning of quarter 2 all meetings will be completed in 45 minutes or less.
More effective marketing	Sales leads will increase by 20% in the next quarter, and 30% over the year.
	The number of qualified leads will increase by 40% in quarter 1 and 50% over the year.
	The average time taken to qualify a lead will be reduced from 4 days to 2 days by the end of the first quarter, and that will be sustained over the year.
	Numbers of new customers spending more than £1,000 in the year will be 15% up on last year.
	Profits on these sales will improve from £30,000 in the last full year to £55,000 in the next full year.
Reduced expenditure on travel	Travel expenditure in the next 12 months will be reduced by 15% as a result of better advance planning.
Larger audiences at our exhibitions in the next 12 months	We will attract a further 2,000 visitors to our exhibitions in the next 12 months.
Improvement of overall patient satisfaction levels over the current 65%	Our overall patient satisfaction levels will improve from 65% to 75% in the next 6 months.

Judging by the sloppy and confused nature of many of the objectives we read, most people find it hard to define measurable objectives, at least until they become very practised. But there is a wealth of advice available to help us once we have made the effort to do the thinking we've outlined in the previous chapters.

Once we have made that effort, we will have formed clear explanations of need, which might be in the form of opportunities or problems, or a mixture of both. As soon as we look at them we will see that they fall under one, or sometimes more than one, of these seven generic categories:

1. saving costs
2. saving time
3. increasing output
4. improving quality
5. improving internal climate
6. improving external climate
7. innovation in terms of products, processes, policies.

Planning outcomes in a global project

A programme to build employability skills in developing economies has been an important global initiative for an international development agency. It seeks to promote the development of skills and innovation by encouraging closer links among educators, employers and policy makers. With a range of other partners and donors, the organisation needs to be able to demonstrate that it is achieving its objectives. However, the programme is implemented in a variety of countries and is tailored to fit the specific needs of each of them.

For example, a national conference in a Middle Eastern partner country brought together key stakeholders from other parts of the Middle East and from the UK to explore ways of addressing skills shortages in the financial sector. It resulted in an international partnership between UK colleges and learning providers in the partner country.

In another example, a culinary contest in a North African partner country was organised with local partners to raise the awareness and importance of technical education and to build the technical skills of apprentice chefs.

The international development agency's Skills for Employability team finally identified five projects from a cross-section of low- and high-priority countries to be evaluated against six targeted outcomes, each with specific success indicators:

1.   'improved knowledge and understanding of effective approaches to skills development'
2.   'application of the newly acquired knowledge and experience in skills development in the participant's institution/organisation'
3.   'relationships established or sustained with ministries, key skills agencies and employers'
4.   'the piloting of new approaches to skills development'
5.   'raising the profile of enterprise and skills development with governments, employers, practitioners and young people'
6.   'enhancing the UK's reputation as a source of expertise and partner for skills development'.

However, the levels of impact at which each project will be measured will depend on its own circumstances.

SMART

Many people find good objectives hard to frame. In truth there's nothing theoretically difficult about them. It's just hard to get them right in practice. The old slogan 'Rubbish in, rubbish out' certainly applies. If objectives are only as good as their content, their form does matter, and the accepted standard is SMART.

SMART objectives

In his 1981 *Management Review* article, 'There is a SMART way to write management's goals and objectives', George T. Doran differentiates between goals and objectives. Goals are usually continuous and long term, and 'represent unique executive beliefs and philosophies', while objectives 'give quantitative support and expression to management's beliefs'. Objectives provide managers with direction and allow them to focus on the problems the organisation needs to resolve.

Clearly defined objectives are statements of the results that need to be achieved. Dr Doran goes on to suggest the now popular SMART acronym. 'Specific – target a specific area for improvement, Measurable – quantify or at least suggest an indicator of progress, Assignable – specify who will do it, Realistic – state what results can realistically be achieved, given available resources, Time-related – specify when the result(s) can be achieved.' Other meanings for SMART have since been used, such as Ken Blanchard et al.'s 'Specific, Measurable, Attainable, Relevant and Trackable', as well as Paul Meyer's 'Specific, Measurable, Attainable, Realistic and Tangible'.

Source: Blanchard et al. (1985); Doran (1981); Meyer (2003).

SMARTER

In the way of these things, some users have now proposed that SMART isn't enough, and that SMARTER is better. The E stands for 'extending', and the R for 'rewarding'. The point of this is that it is meant to recognise the importance of individual engagement. Those who are executing the actions behind the objectives should have their capabilities stretched (they should find the objectives extending), and the achievement of the objective should be rewarding to both the individual and his or her institution. This SMARTER formula will be picked up in the next chapter, where we look at performance and behaviour objectives.

A further refinement of SMART is that some suggest that the acronym refers to two ideas, and is better applied in a different order: MA/RST. The point here is that Measurable and Achievable relate to preconditions for drafting the detailed objective, whereas Realistic, Specific and Timebound define the elements of an objective that render it effective.

If it helps, that's good. But it does lose the power of the punning acronym.

SMART-est

How can we apply these principles to impact objectives? How do we move from the demand-sided needs we've now discussed at length to SMART objectives?

The first step is to understand the nature of impact objectives themselves. They are the descriptors of demand. They define the ultimate results against which the success of any investment is going to be judged.

If they seem to be hard to frame, it may be because so many of us are uncomfortable describing process and impact in real detail. Process may seem to be easier, though when we get to the next chapter we'll see that it is, if anything, more demanding to describe well than impact. It is certainly a challenge to come up with objectives that are both robust and acceptable to key stakeholders.

What is impact? It is variously described as:

- achieved operational targets (including efficiency)
- improved financial performance
- successful and sustained innovation
- achieved organisational compliance
- enhanced reputation (internal and external)
- attributable legacy.

In the example in the box below, the objectives were set in terms of operational targets and enhanced reputation.

Setting impact objectives for a training programme in a luxury hotel

An image, style and talent development academy was contracted to provide training in an East Asian luxury hotel. The hotel aimed to provide the perfect 5-star luxury experience by giving each guest a highly personalised service. Although it is consistently voted the World's Leading Business Hotel in the World Travel Awards, it embarked on further initiatives to enhance its brand and image. This included a five-month renovation programme and a training programme, Interact with Customers. This programme had two modules 'Maintain Professional Image' and 'Offer Customised and Personalised Service'.

The 'Maintain Professional Image' module was selected for evaluation so that the hotel could determine whether it was receiving value for money for its training investment. Around 200 service staff were scheduled to attend the training and, once they successfully completed it, would be awarded a statement of achievement within a nationally recognised qualification framework.

The business impact needs were to improve workplace performance in guest satisfaction and the repeat guest ratio. The impact objectives, SMARTly written, were:

a. Increase overall guests' satisfaction from 75% to 85% in the first year
b. Increase repeat guest ratio from 50% to 85% within the first 6 months.

In this instance it was very clear what results the academy wanted. But often projects are launched with a far more general set of ambitions, and no very clear notion of how to pin them down.

A university's degree offer

Another example is a university that decided to amend and reform its engineering degree programmes. The project manager to whom the pro-vice chancellor assigned the job of developing and implementing the changes asked us for help. It was recognised that the quality of the knowledge and skills of the graduates was not good enough, and this was having an impact on the reputation of the university and its ability to attract students. The project manager began developing a new curriculum and recruiting new teachers. She wanted to measure its results.

But when we asked what these results needed to be, she was unable to be specific. We suggested that she pause in her busy activities to reflect on what they were really trying to achieve.

Our first question was, 'What is your evidence that there is a need for improvement?'

We suggested she look particularly at trends in examination scores and at market needs for qualified engineers. We asked what data the university collected on the employment patterns of graduates, on graduate experience in seeking work and on graduates' experiences in their early years of employment. We also asked her about the university's competition, and how competitors compared in terms of graduate attainment and employment.

We asked what the university knew about the factors that influenced its reputation among potential students, taking in secondary schools, parents, employers and influential institutional decision makers such as higher education officials at the Ministry of Education. We suggested that before embarking on changes to curriculum and staff, she needed to gather better evidence about the problems the university faced (using educational scores, employers' needs and graduates' employment needs) as well as the opportunities that any improvement might be expected to help them take advantage of.

The immediate response was that she wasn't ready to produce specific impact objectives. She just did not have the baseline data to be sure what was most needed, what was most feasible or what would ultimately be to the university's greatest advantage in its need to compete more effectively. More research was needed.

Interrogating needs

To produce consistently strong objectives for impact, we have to be able to interrogate, or examine, the expressions of problem or opportunity that we have identified. We can use the answers to those questions to define useful and usable objectives.

Here are some examples of interrogations (Figures 4.3 to 4.6).

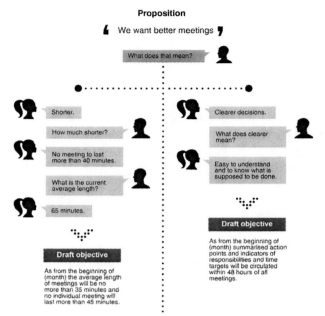

FIGURE 4.3

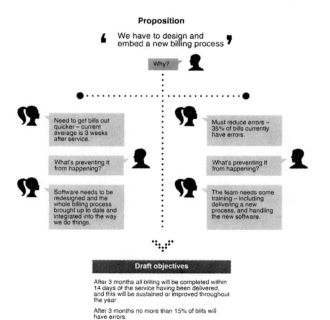

FIGURE 4.4

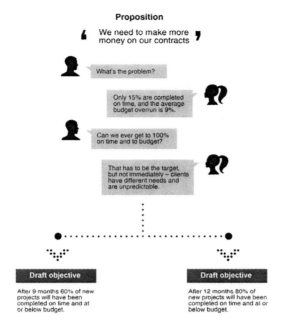

FIGURE 4.5

FIGURE 4.6

Far too often we are tempted to rush into developing objectives for our activities before we have carefully sorted out the needs that lie behind them. This may result in objectives that are only partly effective. It frequently results in no true impact objectives at all.

Time spent thinking through every aspect of *why* something is important is *never* wasted (Figures 4.7 and 4.8).

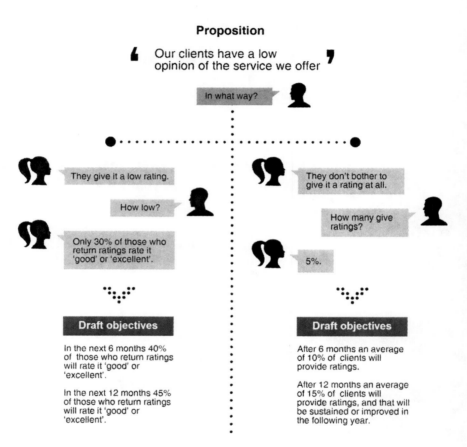

FIGURE 4.7

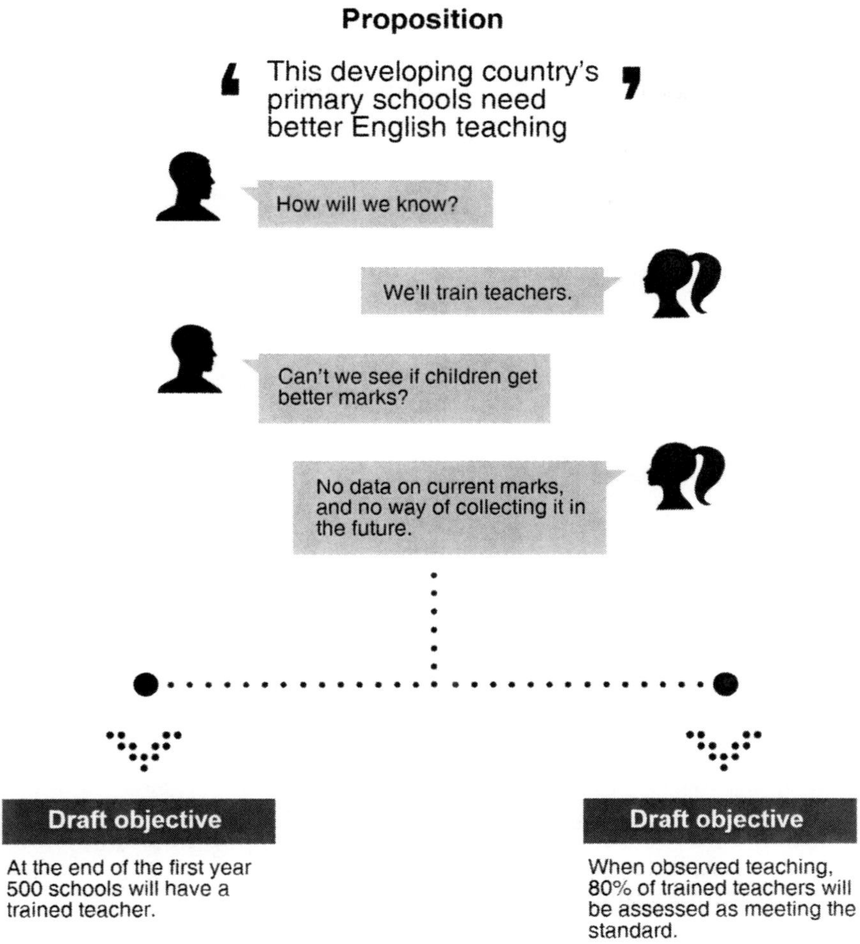

Proposition

" This developing country's primary schools need better English teaching "

How will we know?

We'll train teachers.

Can't we see if children get better marks?

No data on current marks, and no way of collecting it in the future.

Draft objective

At the end of the first year 500 schools will have a trained teacher.

Draft objective

When observed teaching, 80% of trained teachers will be assessed as meeting the standard.

FIGURE 4.8

5

STAKEHOLDERS

Evaluators have to understand the roles and responsibilities of all the key stakeholders in the projects and programmes they are tracking. Those who design projects and programmes need to have understood them too, and set objectives for them where appropriate. Stakeholders can present barriers to success. They can also be crucial enablers of success. Identifying and understanding stakeholders can be made easier by using some simple tools that help to categorise them and that help to present a clear view of their potential influences on outcomes. Stakeholders may not only need objectives for the actions they take; it may be necessary to ensure that they have the knowledge and capability to act, and to confirm that they are engaged and committed to play their part.

The importance of stakeholders

Most of us, most of the time, work in some sort of collaboration or relationship with others. Little that we achieve, however individual it may seem, is done in isolation. In our working lives companies and organisations routinely place us into interdependent structures: teams, extended organisations, partnerships, less-structured networks. These may well include a mix of colleagues, managers, associates, clients, funders and even regulators.

When we look at these through the perspective of the processes, projects, programmes or activities we want to evaluate we can see them all as potential stakeholders. We can then begin to specify their responsibilities, trace the linkages between them and see the influence we expect them to have on results.

'Stakeholder' is a slightly cumbersome term. But it is useful because it is widely used and understood, and, since it is very general, it should immediately prompt us to ask precisely what that stake or interest is. As evaluators we have to understand the roles and responsibilities of these stakeholders. And we must be clear about this as quickly as possible. This is because, if they fulfil their roles and tasks, they will massively improve the prospect of success. If they exceed expectations, success may be greatly enhanced. But if they underperform, fail to take actions for which they are responsible or, at worst, actually obstruct the work of the project or programme in question, they can profoundly endanger or even wreck any prospect of positive results.

Attempts to change performance, practices or behaviours can be undermined by a colleague's failure to provide a small but vital piece of support or to provide it at the correct time. How often do we hear people saying that a good idea has come to nothing because a line manager or senior colleague 'didn't really like it', or 'didn't give it priority'? As Kotter has noted so often, the majority of change management projects fail. One reason for this is that often *all* those who need to be engaged and committed have not been fully identified at the start and their roles neither thought through nor implemented.

Any stakeholders who positively oppose or obstruct a change they dislike will almost certainly have a disproportionate influence on its prospects of success. It is well known that those who feel that their interests are threatened by change are likely to be much more active in their response than those who have reason to believe they will benefit from it. This is one among several reasons why it is so hard to accomplish change.

It follows that the involvement, or the lack of involvement, of key stakeholders is among the most common contributory reasons to the underperformance – even failure – of human capital investments.

We constantly see instances where:

- colleagues or line managers claim not to have been informed, or not to understand the relevance of new skills acquired by others, and so fail to make use of them
- colleagues or line managers actively or passively obstruct change
- key supporters of a project claim never to have been fully informed of their responsibilities, and so perform them late, or not at all
- the fact that any of the above has occurred will inevitably have a negative influence on others.

Here are two simple examples.

1. A teacher-training programme aims to train teachers to change the way they teach their classes so as to make them more engaging to students by involving them more actively in learning. A key stakeholder is the school inspector, who needs to be actively committed to the new teaching approach. Another key stakeholder is the education ministry official responsible for publishing updated teaching standards. If the updated standards are not communicated to the inspector, and as a result teacher improvement is not properly recognised, those teachers who have been inspected will ask why they should bother to learn if their improvement is ignored. Other teachers who hear of this will attach less importance to the course.

2. A new customer service standard requires everyone to deal with complaints. Instead of each one taking an average of five working days to process, each should either be resolved within one day or be passed to another level. A key stakeholder is the line manager, who sets a personal example, monitors and gives feedback on progress. Customer service staff who find that they receive no line manager feedback, or who receive it only intermittently, will get the message that it does not matter that much.

Stakeholder analysis

Stakeholder identity and function should be a key aspect of the planning of any project or programme. And it is always part of the Theory of Change process.

> Identification and analysis is the first of eight components of stakeholder engagement identified by the International Finance Corporation (IFC), World Bank. It is a crucial part of stakeholder engagement because it can help prevent negative outcomes by involving the right people at the start of the project.
>
> During this process a full list of persons and/or groups with an interest or concern in the project is identified. Brainstorming sessions with experts can be useful in identifying stakeholders. Experts may be those in the front line of a service or project beneficiaries and are not always those higher in the hierarchy or considered to be 'in the know'.
>
> When considering who can be included as stakeholders, it can be helpful to identify persons and/or groups who must be engaged by law, those who may be adversely affected by the project, those who can help enhance or promote the project, as well as those who strongly support and oppose it.
>
> *International Finance Corporation (2007)*

We advise approaching stakeholder analysis via three deliberate steps.

1. *Step one*: Clarify who your stakeholders are.
2. *Step two*: Understand their roles, functions and influence.
3. *Step three*: Be clear about the nature of the contribution you need from each of them if they are to support, and not hinder, what others do.

Step one: identifying stakeholders

This could often be done sooner, and be done better. A telecoms organisation that was in the process of embedding a culture of impact measurement reported a project that had achieved good results, but which it believed could have been better. This was a leadership development programme for sales managers. It reported an ROI of 265 per cent. In addition, the attrition rates of sales managers who had participated in the programme were almost 10 per cent less than for those who had not. However, the results of the evaluation also showed that improvements would have been better if the sales managers had had more support from their line managers, the regional sales directors, to help them apply their new knowledge. This involved both moral support and resources and systems in place. The line managers who had signed off the approval and release for the training should have provided pre- and post-training discussion about the expected changes, including support, resources and systems. An environment needed to be created to ensure that new practices not only were not hindered but were actively supported and encouraged.

It is crucial to understand that those carrying out the evaluation also become important stakeholders. And not simply because of the significance of the final conclusions and recommendations that they will produce, but because of their important role in reporting early data that can be used immediately for improvement.

We can take account of these considerations by applying some simple process. We first use the following four headings to list as many potential stakeholders as possible, dividing them into four groups.

1. The *users* of services and other outputs of your project. They may be clients, attendees at events, partners.
2. Those who *choose* content and method, who take the decisions about policy and operational matters, who commission work.
3. Those who *pay* the direct and indirect costs of developing and delivering the activity or the service in question.
4. Those who *benefit*, including immediate – perhaps intermediate – beneficiaries and the wider range of those who may benefit in the longer term or from the legacy of the activity.

These can then be arranged visually into quadrants (Table 5.1). It may be apparent that some stakeholders can belong in more than one quadrant. The main purpose of this piece of discipline is to identify each one's principal interest. Once this has been done it is equally valuable to note any secondary or less important interests they may have.

TABLE 5.1

Who chooses?	*Who uses?*
Who pays?	*Who benefits?*

For instance, in the hypothetical example of the telecoms company above, our grid will help us do a first analysis of the roles and likely influences of the stakeholders. The first draft might look something like Table 5.2.

TABLE 5.2

Who chooses?	*Who uses?*
Regional sales directors	Sales managers
Sales training lead	

Who pays?	*Who benefits?*
Training budget holders	The company
Finance department	Sales directors
	Sales managers
	Sales teams
	Customers

Step two: understanding roles, functions and influence

To understand the roles and functions of stakeholders, we must have understood the 'process' to which they are making a contribution. This can sometimes be a challenge for external suppliers of services, including evaluators. They will fully understand the context in which they are working only if they take the time to conduct a thorough analysis. Such an analysis should be part of the 'requirements' collection phase of any project plan, but all too often it is forgotten or insufficiently considered.

A food manufacturer: stakeholder analysis

One of the lean management tools used by a major international food manufacturer is 'practical problem solving'. This is being embedded into its global network via Practical Problem Solving Workshops. The aim of these workshops is to enable all employees to follow standardised procedures using a problem-solving tool to ascertain the root cause of a problem and then find suitable solutions. The workshops are conducted over three days in the classroom and include working through a practical business problem. The senior management team has already completed the workshops and therefore the next group of learners are the line managers, who will then be followed by the other levels of employees. Although the workshops have been well received, it is important to ascertain whether they are returning value for money.

A key part of applying the abdi recommended ROI approach is stakeholder analysis, followed by an analysis of what each stakeholder or stakeholder group needs to do in order to ensure that the sum of the parts works together (Level

3: Performance, practice and behavioural change needs), followed by a quick check on whether each has the know-how and knows what to do (Level 2: Know-how and know-what needs) and, finally, commitment and engagement needs (Level 1: Engagement) (see Table 2.1). Identifying the key stakeholders and engaging them at the design stage of an initiative, i.e. establishing the needs and objectives, is crucial for its success. For this Practical Problem Solving Workshop, the stakeholders were identified and analysed as shown in Table 5.3.

TABLE 5.3

Who chooses?	*Who uses?*
Plant manager	Operators
Production manager	Production manager
Engineering manager	Engineering manager
Shift manager	Shift manager
Food safety officer	Food safety officer
Safety manager	Safety manager
HR manager	Team leaders
Team leader	
Operators	
Who pays?	*Who benefits?*
Plant manager	Operators
	Production manager
	Engineering manager
	Shift manager
	Food safety officer
	Safety manager
	Team leaders

Experienced project and programme commissioners and evaluators immediately recognise certain more or less 'typical' structures and processes:

- *projects,* where there may be promoters, funders, managers, team members, external associates, clients, customers, patients or beneficiaries and those applying what has been learned to other projects or activities
- *simple training and application of learning processes,* where there may be funders, trainers, learners, colleagues and line managers, and clients, customers, patients or beneficiaries

- *more complex 'cascaded' change management structures*, including training of trainers, quality circles and lean leaders
- *marketing and sales activities*, where there may be internal clients and managers, sales and marketing staff, customers and clients
- *events and conferences*, where there may be event sponsors and funders, event organisers, attendees and those to whom attendees pass on the benefit of what they have gained and learned.

Many organisations have their own ways of doing systems, situation and process analysis when building up their requirements. Our experience, however, is that this is too infrequently done, and poorly carried out in many cases.

The NHS Institute for Innovation and Improvement[1] came up with a useful list of what it termed '9Cs', and suggested that healthcare organisations should use it to help identify their stakeholders:

- *Commissioners*: those that pay the organisation to do things
- *Customers*: those that acquire and use the organisation's products
- *Collaborators*: those with whom the organisation works to develop and deliver products
- *Contributors*: those from whom the organisation acquires content for products
- *Channels*: those who provide the organisation with a route to a market or customer
- *Commentators*: those whose opinions of the organisation are heard by customers and others
- *Consumers*: those who are served by our customers: i.e. patients, families, users
- *Champions*: those who believe in and will actively promote the project
- *Competitors*: those working in the same area who offer similar or alternative services.

This list can be applied to very many organisations, not just those providing healthcare services.

Once the list of stakeholders has been generated and their broad roles and influence have been established, it then makes sense to analyse their specific areas of power and influence more closely. This will begin to clarify the respects in which their interests may be affected by the activity in question. It will also highlight the ways in which their actions, or their lack of action, can support or may obstruct the targeted result.

Again, a quadrant can be useful, but labelled differently from the first one we used. This sees the relative levels of power and influence of stakeholders in relation to the projected high- and lower-level outcomes of the project or activity (Figure 5.1).

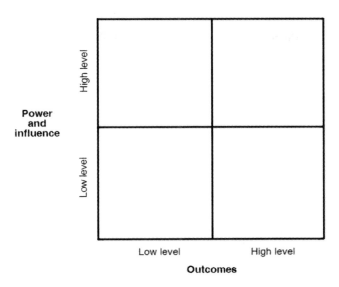

FIGURE 5.1

Using the example of the telecoms company from the beginning of this chapter, this grid might be constructed as shown in Figure 5.2 (note that the trainers have been added to this grid).

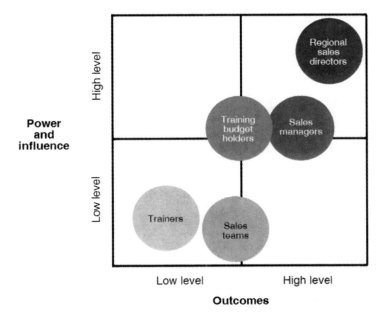

FIGURE 5.2

From this it can be seen that the trainers have the lowest levels of power and influence, and have responsibility for the results of the training only. That is not to say that the training is unimportant. It is crucial. But its results do not in themsleves constitute an impact outcome for the company. The regional sales directors, on the other hand, have the highest levels of power and influence, and their relationship is with the highest level of results: the value for money which the company gets from this investment in training.

We can also infer a good deal about the kinds of communication that will be essential if these stakeholders are to do their jobs effectively.

- The trainers will need to know about the results of the training, as well as the attitudes of the sales teams to it and their buy-in to the purpose of the training.
- The sales teams will need to know how they did in their training, and will also need constant feedback on how effectively it is being applied.
- The training budget holders need results data, including all costs and, especially, evidence of the training's impact on the organisation's operational objectives.
- The sales managers will need to know the initial (low-level outcomes) and much more detail of how the training is being applied and the impact on the business.
- The regional sales director will need to know about the impact on results, from revenue and margin increases to customer satisfaction and retention, and about the value for money of the whole exercise.

To be effective, this needs to be done with awareness of the distinct phases of the project or activity's life:

- the pre-phase: securing approval, planning and inception
- the action phase: participating, supporting others, exploiting results and lessons as soon as they are available, contributing to analysis and exploitation of final results
- getting the message out: planning consequential actions and initiatives, and securing the legacy.

Even at this early stage, this reflection is greatly strengthened if it takes into account the nature of the communications that each of the stakeholder groups will need to receive if they are to function as required.

These pieces of analysis, which need not take a great deal of time, are best done in consultation with at least with some of the stakeholders. As a result, it will be possible to complete a highly practical stakeholder analysis grid, which can then be shared widely. It will become a key project management tool.

The categories used in the example in Table 5.4 are fairly generic. But everyone will have their own appropriate categories and definitions.

TABLE 5.4

Type of stakeholder	Function and influence					
	Planning	Monitoring	Improvement during project/ activity	Future applications	Future policy	Contact details
Policy makers						
Management						
Colleagues						
Clients/beneficiaries						

Step three: ensuring stakeholders support our activity and do not hinder it in any way

Our priority is always to bring the key stakeholders out of the shadows, so that their tasks and their performance and behaviour are visible. Then:

- we set clear objectives with them and for them
- we can see how to support them
- we can discuss and negotiate changes and improvements with them
- we can track what they do and use that to build a picture of what has contributed to our final results.

The World Bank

The International Finance Corporation (or World Bank), has identified eight components of stakeholder engagement:

1. Stakeholder Identification and Analysis
2. Information Disclosure
3. Stakeholder Consultation
4. Negotiation and Partnerships
5. Grievance Management
6. Stakeholder Involvement in Project Monitoring
7. Reporting to Stakeholders
8. Management Functions

Source: International Finance Corporation (2007)

Gathering good data on stakeholder behaviour can be hard work, but it is essential if we are going to build a useful picture of what has happened. In many evaluation models this is not even attempted until after the action has been completed. Stakeholders of all kinds may be asked to trawl their memories. Why did this happen? Did so-and-so help or hinder the result? Why did that not happen? Was so-and-so negligent or inefficient?

This will give rise to two problems. The first is that invariably this will involve questions about things that have happened (or maybe not happened) weeks or months before. Memory is both fallible and selective. The resulting information may not be very good. The second is that often these post-activity questions contain prompts to make value judgements. These are generally not helpful: they can colour the evaluation and can result in opinion being represented as fact.

It is also worth noting that all interviewing, and especially this kind of post-project interviewing, is relatively expensive to carry out, and as expensive again to analyse and report. In many ways it is a poor substitute for timely data collection.

This timely collection of data is what works best, but it is possible only if the stakeholder analysis has been used to frame clear objectives against which the data can be collected. This setting of objectives for key stakeholders, as well as for the front-line deliverers of projects or activities, is often the key to good performance. It recognises that clear understanding of accountability leads to good allocation of responsibility.

Two examples will help to illustrate this.

An international project

In this example (Figure 5.3) it is obvious that if we are to be sure that the project is proceeding to time, to cost and to plan, we have to know that the project manager and the team members are completing their tasks. But if the HR manager and the finance director have not properly discharged their accountability the direct project workers will be powerless to deliver their responsibilities.

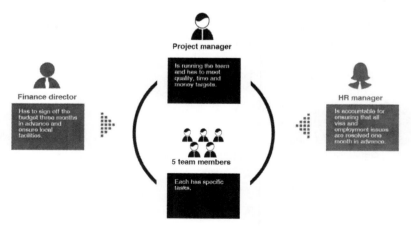

FIGURE 5.3

A hospital runs a hygiene course for non-medics

In the example illustrated in Figure 5.4, again there are principal groups with responsibilities, but the facilities manager, the HR and finance managers and the audit team staff are all accountable in different ways for ensuring that the culture of good hygiene is maintained and widely communicated.

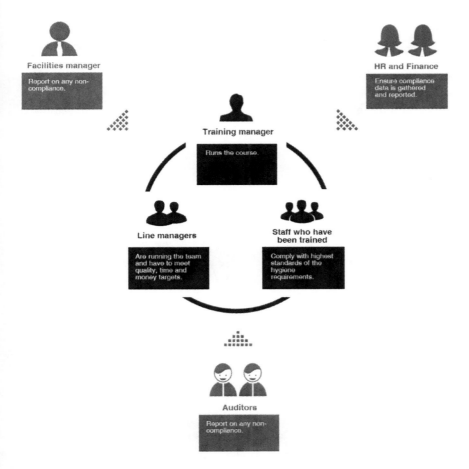

FIGURE 5.4

Stakeholder accountability

At the start of our courses we ask participants to reflect on the differences between responsibility and accountability. We ask them to list the main things for which they are responsible (where the buck starts with them) and those things for which they are accountable (where the buck finally stops with them).

The answers sometimes betray the fact that they have previously given too little thought to the difference between the two words. A dictionary definition of responsibility is: *the obligation to carry forward an assigned task to a successful conclusion,* whereas the definition of accountability is *the obligation to report or justify something.*

As can be seen from the two straightforward examples above, the timely exercise of accountability can permit those with operational responsibilities to complete their tasks, and the neglect of the same accountability can render their efforts worthless.

The problem is that by the time we have found out whether or not key stakeholders have discharged their accountability, the good or the damage has been done. So, both as evaluators and as project and operational managers, we need to know not just what it is that someone was expected to do, but also what the expected outcome is, that a record of outcomes is an integrated part of the systems and processes and whether the individual has been informed and believes that they are accountable for the outcome.

The purpose, of course, is to move from the state of unaccountability illustrated in Figure 5.5 to the state of accountability shown in Figure 5.6.

FIGURE 5.5

FIGURE 5.6

Stakeholder knowledge and competence

If you have tasks that you need your stakeholders to perform, or if you require them to behave in a certain way, it is your responsibility to be sure that they are *able* to comply.

We can never assume that stakeholders already have all the skills and knowledge that we need them to deploy. So once we have established what we want them to do, and to what standard, we must find a way of confirming that they *know what to do* and *how to do it*. In most circumstances, supporting stakeholders don't need to be formally trained. But they may very well need instructions and background information. You and they should be determined to confirm that they know precisely what is expected of them; when, or how often, they are supposed to do it; and if there is a standard they are expected to meet. A simple check-list at the end of every project meeting, a couple of structured questions noted at the end of a phone call, and a straightforward report template which everyone confirms they can complete and sign off may be quite enough.

But in some cases the skills of supporting stakeholders either may need to be extended, or they may need them checked, and if necessary refreshed. It is useless to discover this after the activity or project has been completed. It needs to be investigated and dealt with in advance.

Stakeholder engagement

Stakeholder knowledge, skills and attitudes are important. So is the question of whether they are sufficiently bought-in to the importance of the activity to be inclined to make the effort you expect from them.

Stakeholder engagement

During the planning stage of the project concerned with the prevention of falls amongst elderly people (see pp. 26–7), the team identified the impact needs (the number of falls, where and how they occurred, the number that required ambulance services, number requiring hospital services etc.), what and who needed to change their practices and behaviour, as well as how to provide the needed skills and engage extremely busy front-line staff in the need to improve. It also recognised that a crucial element in its planning was the identification of its stakeholder groups and the responsibilities of each group. This is shown in the grid below.

(Continued)

(Continued)

Stakeholders	Responsibilities
Quality framework assurance	Produce data in relation to operational assurance on compliance at Level 3
Governance and risk team	Produce data in relation to incidents, claim data (relating to costs) and provide advice on KPIs in this area
Workforce business unit	Produce workforce data set (classified by department, staff group, hourly costs, travel expenses, etc.)
Workforce development unit	Negotiate the new training programme content, as well as programme evaluation (from engagement of training providers to demonstrating ROI)
Trainers and participants	Participate in the programme and complete relevant documentation
Senior executive managers	Endorse changes to the programme, as well as provide clarity in communicating expected performance indicators
Education manager	Manage the project, coordinating the information needs, expectations and priorities of these stakeholders

In the planning, it was realised, when consulting with the hard-pressed healthcare community staff, that they had not previously been provided with data on over-60s falls within their work areas. This was a revelation to many. Moreover, once the timing and locations for consultations and training in managing the pathway were built around their working day, recognising their clinic and home visiting and travelling patterns, almost all staff were fully engaged and committed to improving falls levels in their area of work.

Five important messages about stakeholder engagement

1. We must confirm that they think the whole activity is a good idea. Do they see it as being in their interests to do all that they can to help it succeed?
2. We must know that they believe that the tasks they will perform, or the behaviour they are expected to exhibit, will make a difference to ultimate success.

3. How often have we heard the remark, once an initiative has been seen to fail, 'If they'd only bothered to ask me of course I'd have done . . .'? They must be asked.

4. Ask them directly, 'How important is this?', 'How important is it to you that it's a success?', 'What do we need to do to help you engage and commit?', 'What might prevent your full engagement and participation in achieving this change and improvement?'

5. Sometimes colleagues find that they have difficulty asking direct questions about the buy-in of very senior or very important stakeholders. Our view is that there must always be acceptable ways of asking these questions. We deal with this in much more detail in Chapter 8.

Note

1   The NHS Institute closed on 31 March 2013. A number of key resources were transferred to the NHS Improving Quality's website.

6

WHO NEEDS TO DO WHAT, TO WHAT STANDARD?

The good manager must know what good looks like – the right performance, the right behaviour. This means articulating performance and behaviour descriptors, understanding the factors that make performance or behaviour exceptional, acceptable or unacceptable. The focus needs to be on activity: activity-based costing, activity-based management. These are the routes to understanding clearly how things work. From that we can understand the key elements of change, how to balance efficiency with effectiveness, how to identify and work with key barriers and enablers to change, how to deal with compliance issues, and to set and manage behavioural expectations.

In the run-up to the 2012 London Olympics, Sir Clive Woodward, who was responsible for developing the performance of the elite athletes who were likely to be selected for Team GB, was asked what his medal target for the team was. He replied that he didn't have one. His target was that everyone should do a personal best on the day. Then the medals would take care of themselves.

He summed it up. Impact is driven by performance, and few business leaders would say anything other than that their ultimate success hangs on the performance of their managers and their teams. They, like Sir Clive, would be delighted if their teams consistently turned in personal bests. The problem is that in many working contexts no one knows what a personal best, or even good performance, might look like.

No problem for Sir Clive, but how do we measure it in a bank, a doctor's surgery, a bus depot, a toy manufacturer, a pharmaceutical research laboratory or a not-for-profit? What does good look like in their contexts?

And, of course, we don't have to think for too long to come to the conclusion that while Sir Clive was right about the importance of the search for optimum behaviour and performance, the example of the single-minded, obsessively focused athlete may not work for all contexts. In teams, the search for excellence is as important, but the individual 'personal best' may not always help the team to do its best. In combat, the individualist soldier may make the difference, may win a medal, but may also get himself and everyone else killed. In most working contexts today, the work is performed by teams and, when looking at performance, it is important to consider not just individual roles but the processes and dynamics within the team. This means that the good manager needs to understand 'what good looks like' both in respect of individuals' performance and in respect of the team, when all those individuals come together with a single purpose.

Performance and behaviour descriptors

It's not always as easy as it might seem to come up with a description that can be objectively observed. While many organisations have a set of competency descriptions for jobs and job families, few are provided to line managers in a form that enables them to observe objectively whether performance and behaviour are meeting the expected standard. Some argue that it is the line manager's job (rather than the job of HR, Organisational Development or L&D) to specify the performance and behaviour criteria for each directly reporting staff member. Our experience over the years is that this rarely happens. Few managers use more than the job and competency descriptions as a reference point when they assess performance and behaviour and propose ways in which performance can be improved and processes and procedures developed. For HR, OD or L&D, who are not in direct contact with the staff doing the day-to-day work, it is difficult to establish appropriate performance and behaviour indicators. To be useful, these need to be recorded in a way that can be used by managers to observe, objectively and fairly, the performance and behaviours of the staff.

If there is a single lesson we have learned about human capital investment, it is the importance of well-articulated, unambiguous descriptors of the expected standards of performance and behaviour. We have yet to come across an organisation where anyone believes that the performance appraisal and management system works as effectively as it should and could. And the most important reason for that is that few managers have those clear descriptors of what 'good' looks like in their staff.

Competency descriptions are very helpful when establishing what someone must be able to do, exhibit and know. They need to be derived from descriptors of performance and behaviour standards. Competency descriptions built over the years to establish occupational profiles for jobs and job families are of necessity generic. They are useful, but only when someone has bridged between the generic experience they reflect and the actual work someone is asked to do in a specific context. This means creating descriptors: what can be observed that is unacceptable, acceptable and exceptional in practice.

So, when an investment is made to achieve an impact outcome, the questions to follow are:

- What is the current state of performance and behaviour?
- Does it meet the standards required?

If it doesn't meet the required standard, will meeting the standard influence the required improvement in the impact outcomes? If it does meet the current standard, what improvement or change in the standard is needed to influence the impact outcomes?

In other words, who needs to do what better or differently?

Using descriptors to rate performance and behaviour

Our recommendation is to use a four-level rating scale, and for managers to complete descriptors at each level for key tasks and for the most important behavioural standards.

1. *Unacceptable*: Includes all behaviours and/or ways of doing the work that are not compliant with regulatory requirements, pose risk to the individual, others and the business, failure to meet even the most basic standards.
2. *Progress towards acceptable*: The individual is observed to be doing some of what is required to an acceptable standard but not everything, or meets the standard sometimes, but not consistently.
3. *Meets acceptable*: The individual consistently behaves and performs to the expected standard: no errors and no failures to comply.
4. *Exceptional*: Generally, behaviours that go beyond what is expected, someone does more than the acceptable standard, introduces innovations, demonstrates what tomorrow's 'acceptable' standard should look like. Not always used: innovation may post risk or deviate from a regulatory requirement.

Let's look at a simple example of a clear process to be followed. Good performance in first aid involves following the process laid down by St John Ambulance. At its simplest, the first contact with a casualty involves four process steps. Consider the descriptors that might be used to observe whether an appropriate standard was achieved at each step.

1.   *Check for further **danger**, to the casualty or yourself*

Acceptable performance

Checks for immediate danger pathway
Considers and checks potential danger/risks (hidden traffic, inflammable liquids near fire), checks risk to casualty such as falling material.

The added factor that would make this exceptional performance:

Alerts others to assist in avoidance of further danger.

Unacceptable performance

Fails to check for any danger, runs into pathway of danger, does not stop to look for any likelihood of danger or risk to self, casualty or bystanders.

The replacement that would signal progress towards acceptable:

Alerts others to assist in avoidance of further danger.

FIGURE 6.1

2. *Look for a **response** by talking to the casualty, or by touching on the shoulder*

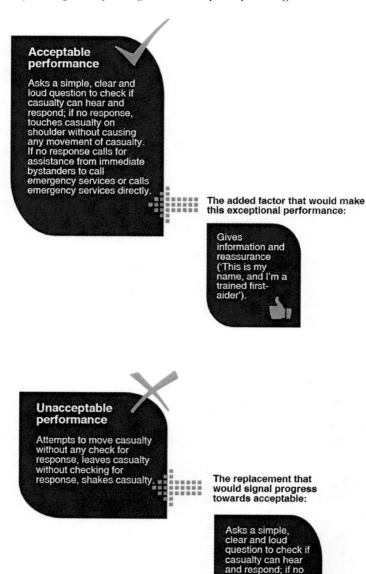

Acceptable performance

Asks a simple, clear and loud question to check if casualty can hear and respond; if no response, touches casualty on shoulder without causing any movement of casualty. If no response calls for assistance from immediate bystanders to call emergency services or calls emergency services directly.

The added factor that would make this exceptional performance:

Gives information and reassurance ('This is my name, and I'm a trained first-aider').

Unacceptable performance

Attempts to move casualty without any check for response, leaves casualty without checking for response, shakes casualty.

The replacement that would signal progress towards acceptable:

Asks a simple, clear and loud question to check if casualty can hear and respond; if no response, touches casualty on shoulder without causing any movement of casualty.

FIGURE 6.2

3. *Ensure that the **airway** is not blocked, and if it is, take steps to ensure that it is open*

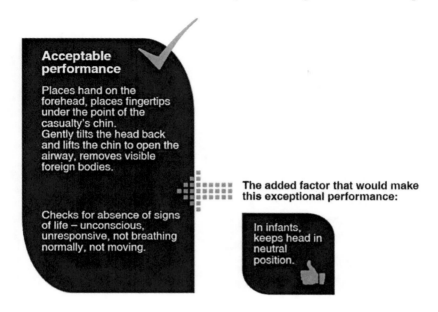

Acceptable performance

Places hand on the forehead, places fingertips under the point of the casualty's chin.
Gently tilts the head back and lifts the chin to open the airway, removes visible foreign bodies.

Checks for absence of signs of life – unconscious, unresponsive, not breathing normally, not moving.

The added factor that would make this exceptional performance:

In infants, keeps head in neutral position.

Unacceptable performance

Uses excessive force, blocks the airway with hands.

The replacement that would signal progress towards acceptable:

Tilts the head back and lifts the chin to open the airway, removes visible foreign bodies.

FIGURE 6.3

4. *Check **breathing**, and if necessary, begin resuscitation*

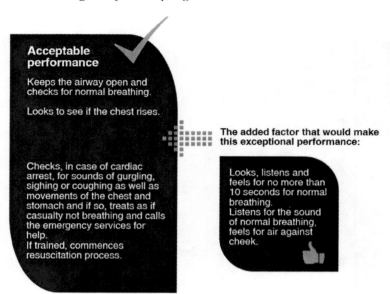

Acceptable performance

Keeps the airway open and checks for normal breathing.

Looks to see if the chest rises.

Checks, in case of cardiac arrest, for sounds of gurgling, sighing or coughing as well as movements of the chest and stomach and if so, treats as if casualty not breathing and calls the emergency services for help.
If trained, commences resuscitation process.

The added factor that would make this exceptional performance:

Looks, listens and feels for no more than 10 seconds for normal breathing.
Listens for the sound of normal breathing, feels for air against cheek.

Unacceptable performance

Fails to keep the airway open and check for normal breathing. Fails to listen for normal breathing. Commences resuscitation before checking breathing or blocked airway. Delays calling the emergency services.

The replacement that would signal progress towards acceptable:

Keeps the airway open and checks for normal breathing.
Looks, listens and feels for no more than 10 seconds for normal breathing.
Looks to see if the chest rises.
Commences resuscitation.

FIGURE 6.4

(Please note that the St John Ambulance advice in every case combines what we have listed under 'Acceptable performance', and 'The added factor that would make this exceptional performance'. The illustrations are ours entirely. No one should follow this advice without referring first to St John Ambulance (www.sja. org.uk). We advise all organisations to ensure that they have sufficient staff trained by St John Ambulance to ensure that emergency aid can be given in all working settings.)

In this case the objective is clear: to try to ensure that the casualty is alive, out of danger and as comfortable as possible until emergency services arrive on the scene. There is a process to follow and we have provided descriptors to help the observer in assessing how the first aider has performed. We, including the first-aider, will be able to record whether the process was followed, to what standard and what might need improving. St John Ambulance has set out clearly what good first aid involves, and a manager or other observer can fairly and objectively assess whether the standard has been achieved. The aim is to check both what might be called 'verifiable behaviour'; in other words, following the right steps in the right sequence and doing so in the correct manner, or 'attitude or approach' where we are dealing with 'perceived behaviour'; in other words, does the first-aider stay calm, act in a way that is mindful of the casualty's anxieties and the need to act swiftly and not go beyond his or her competence?

In a way, looking at clear examples where a process or a piece of compliance has been laid out in detail just underlines the problems that we all face when we attempt the same exercise with an activity for which the process is not clearly 'described on the packet'.

When we ask people 'what good looks like' in a project or process they've described to us, they invariably struggle. You can see them asking themselves how they should approach what seems to be a rather simple question. Is it a trick? No, it isn't a trick, but in order to address it we need to abandon some assumptions that we may have and look at the activity as if it were for the first time.

We need to take it to pieces as if it were a piece of machinery, identify its key moving parts and then understand how they act on and with each other. We will then be in a position to see how the process needs to work if it is to be efficient and effective. The process will be laid bare.

But even this still doesn't get us there. Merely understanding what has to be done will not tell us enough about what 'good' should look like. For that we need also to understand quality requirements – standards, if they exist; expectations, if they do not. Once we have done that, we will have understood performance, timing and sequencing. These will each have a bearing on whether a quality standard has been met or missed. They will also be important factors in demonstrating what has to be done to repeat good performance, or to rectify and eliminate poor performance.

This approach to thinking ourselves carefully into the element of activity or process in question would have been recognised by Frederick Winslow Taylor, the prophet of time and motion and scientific management. Much of his thinking may now have been superseded, but careful analysis of the component parts of an activity is an essential step in understanding it. It does not imply that the activity will then be managed in the authoritarian and somewhat mechanistic manner that characterised Taylorism at its most rigid.

Taylorism

Production efficiency methodology that breaks every action, job, or task into small and simple segments which can be easily analysed and taught.

(www.businessdictionary.com)

Activity-based costing (ABC)

Activity-based costing – costing the activities such as 'planning' and 'reporting' that make up projects and processes, rather than generic cost headings like 'travel' and 'HR' – became popular in the 1980s. Then many organisations were unhappy that they were unable to fully understand the value contribution that certain activities made to an organisation's performance. It fell out of favour again in the 1990s, but has regained popularity in recent years. For some organisations it has always been valued as a means of sharpening understanding of the true cost of products and services and of gaining insights into how can they be made as efficient as well as effective as possible.

In order to put a cost on each activity carried out in the organisation, we must have a detailed view of the time taken to perform it to the required standard. We must understand the process steps followed, and who has contributed to each activity. This is neither a simple nor a quick task, especially in complex operations. But we see the benefits that colleagues realise when they arrive at a real understanding of what their organisations spend on the processes they follow from day to day, as well as on the key elements of the projects they design. They understand actions, as well as inputs. They get more accurate pictures of their human resourcing requirements.

They see capacity and capability requirements more clearly and, as a result, are better able to decide the additional investments they need to make. It becomes easier to see the balance between financial investment and the improvements in performance and behaviour that may or may not influence impact outcomes such as revenues, profitability and customer and client satisfaction.

Activity-based management (ABM)

Activity-based management (ABM) is a method of identifying and evaluating the activities that a business performs using activity-based costing to carry out a value-chain analysis or a re-engineering initiative to improve strategic and operational decisions within an organisation. ABC establishes relationships between overhead costs and activities so that overhead costs can be more precisely allocated to products, services or customer segments. ABM focuses on managing activities to reduce costs and improve customer value.

Recent work by Robert Kaplan (considered by many to be the father of ABC[1]) and Michael Porter has demonstrated the benefits of using time-driven activity-based costing (TDABC) to understand the true cost of healthcare and to demonstrate how the deployment of TDABC can deliver significant improvements in efficiency and effectiveness, leading to much greater value from healthcare costs.[2]

We have borrowed the lessons from Kaplan to demonstrate the huge benefit that can come from a better understanding of workplace activities (process, performance, behaviour), how they deliver impact outcomes and at what cost (value) and to make the link between outcomes at Level 3 (performance and behaviour improvements) and Level 4 (organisational impact outcomes). The starting point is to review existing process, performance standards and behaviours. Teams within organisations review who does what, how and to what standard and at what cost. They examine the evidence to support the findings: this evidence needs to be based on actual current practice (not how things are supposed to be) – in other words, on the 'as is'. During this process (which may include stakeholder analysis and Root Cause Analysis (RCA) techniques), the 'as is' can be compared to the 'supposed to be' and, using TDABC, the true cost of both as is/supposed to be can be calculated. The review of actual process, performance and behaviour and their associated cost provides the basis for reflection on potential efficiencies and improvements in effectiveness, most specifically how changes in performance and behaviour can influence outcomes. The result is a 'new to be' which sets out the performance, process and behaviour standards for all involved. The quality of the 'new to be' will of course depend on the quality of the analysis and evidence base, including the assumptions made. Monitoring and evaluating the results helps to identify what is working well and where improvements can continue to be made.

Providing all involved with a clearer picture of the relationship between current performance and behaviour and impact outcomes and future performance and behaviour and improved impact outcomes provides a powerful rationale to engage stakeholders in making the changes proposed.

Changing the way people do things is hard

The most important function of evaluation in a business or organisational context is to gather evidence to drive improvement. That's why organisations make the effort and spend the money.

But changing the way in which people do things is very hard to accomplish. There is a bias in most organisations and most settings towards doing things as they have always been done. This is driven to a significant degree by inertia, caution about attempting anything new and unwillingness to expend effort and take risk – poor planning. It is also made inevitable in many organisations by a lack of support and encouragement for any form of change on the part of managers.

This last cause – lack of support – is very often the more important. Why is this so important? Just look at six of the more important reasons why support is so necessary:

1. to provide clarity about the reasons for change and agreement about the process, practice and behaviours that will comprise the change
2. to map the systems and stakeholders that need to be engaged in the change process and that will themselves need to change
3. to frame SMART objectives for changing behaviours and practices so as to achieve change
4. to assist in monitoring of the achievement of these objectives
5. to provide feedback on what has been achieved, and how it can be embedded and further improved
6. to show how this is making an important contribution to a team or to the organisation as a whole.

If managers cannot, or will not, do these things, it is easy to see why change is hard to achieve and sustain.

Police drivers' refresher courses

A police force that was concerned to reduce the numbers of complaints about police driving standards and behaviour set impact targets for reducing the number of refresher courses that had to be delivered, reducing public complaints about poor driving and behaviour in police vehicles and reducing the spend on damaged vehicles.

The behaviour and performance objectives that were set included:

*   All managers to carry out checks on police vehicle log books immediately following each shift to ensure that standard operating procedure has been used.
*   All managers to provide written feedback to officers in relation to adverse drinking reports within two working days of receipt, and ensure that a SMART action plan for improvement is created and agreed to address causes.

- All officers and staff to drive police vehicles at all times in line with National Standards.
- All officers use the signing in and out Force vehicle standard operating procedure on every occasion, following training.
- Vehicle Maintenance to report all instances of police vehicle damage to the next available Performance Board meeting using the agreed format.
- Customer Services and Professional Standards Department to report all driving incident complaints to the next available Performance Board using the agreed format.
- Performance Board to advise line managers of report details within two working days of board meetings.
- Performance Board to publish a communication on the intranet to all staff on driving requirements and standards expected by August 2013.
- Performance Board to establish and communicate to Fleet Manager, Customer Services and Professional Standards Department by August 2013 the procedure, format and due dates for reporting behaviour complaints.

Understanding how it works

As evaluators of human capital activities, we need to display many of the instincts and interests of the engineer and the inventor. Most importantly, we must develop a fascination with how pieces of process and activity actually work and where improvements can be made.

Let's take the example of recruitment. The following may help to illustrate the point.

A non-governmental organisation (NGO) is finding it difficult to attract and retain really high-quality project team leaders. As a result, projects are delayed and fail to achieve the planned objectives and the NGO is finding it difficult to get funding renewed. An analysis suggests that there are excellent job candidates in the market, that other NGOs are able to recruit and retain them and the problem is not related to pay, which is similar across the sector. Exit interviews provide little useful data but suggest that the employee leaving feels that the fit with the organisation is wrong and not what was expected and has sought and found a 'better' offer. The organisation decides that it needs to improve the interviewing skills of the HR team, but a sensible voice suggests that before commencing the development of a training programme, more analysis might be useful.

The process of recruitment seems straightforward. Agree the job description, competency requirements and remuneration. Advertise the job, short-list candidates, interview, offer to the selected candidate, negotiate the final terms and the candidate starts work on the agreed date, receives an induction and stays in post for a minimum of five years, doing the job to a high standard.

An analysis of the process and the development of a stakeholder map identifies the problem and shows that it lies in two points in the process: the job description does not reflect the actual day-to-day work in the role and, consequently, the discussions at interview do not reveal the experience and competence of the individual with regard to the specific tasks they will be expected to undertake.

By identifying the points in the process, the HR team can work with the projects team manager and members to examine the actual tasks, required performance standard, expected time that tasks take and processes involved (especially those processes that involve others) and can then revise the competency requirements. Using this information, the interviewers can be provided with questions that can elicit whether the candidate has the required competency and experience and the candidate can have a much clearer idea of what is expected in the role.

Clarity about the elements of change

Just as the first questions that need to be asked about any potential investment in a project or programme are, 'Why? What's the problem or the opportunity?', the next set of questions must be about the operational or process change that's required to address that problem or opportunity.

Operational change can be understood only through the answers to four questions:

1. *Who* needs to drive it?
2. *What* will need to be done in order to achieve it?
3. *When*, or on what timescale, will it have to be done?
4. *What standards* are essential to success?

Establishing observable criteria

The work of Taylor, while largely dismissed as unacceptable in today's world, is nonetheless visible in Business Process Improvement, and in recent years is a requirement when building and implementing Enterprise Resource Planning (ERP) systems.

Table 6.1 shows an example of this questioning process at work in managing absenteeism.

TABLE 6.1

Who	What	When	Why	Standard of performance expected
HR manager	Will benchmark absenteeism rates, identify overall internal patterns and propose target time and level for improvement	By end of month 1	To establish SMART objective for absenteeism	Report delivered on time, at least 3 other organisations in similar sector benchmarked, absenteeism rates of 100% of staff by team and department reported
All line managers	Will analyse own team absenteeism data	By 5th working day of month for previous month	To identify patterns and sources of absenteeism that need to be addressed	Monthly summary in team meeting minutes: graph shows absenteeism rates month on month and summary of findings and where actions needed
HR	Will complete collation by department and team	By 3rd working day of month	To provide information to line managers	Reports reach all line managers by close of business on 3rd working day of every month
Line managers	Will add item on absenteeism to weekly team meetings and share data	At least one meeting in every month	To discuss, record and get agreement on reasons for absenteeism with staff/agree no action required	Item discussion to be recorded in minutes of one meeting per month
Line managers	Will request teams to identify at least one way to reduce absenteeism	At first meeting and then if/when required or once a year if sooner	Where actions required, to propose at least one absenteeism reduction action and who will be responsible	Action reduction proposals to be recorded in minutes of one meeting per month

(Continued)

TABLE 6.1 (Continued)

Who	What	When	Why	Standard of performance expected
Line managers	Will discuss proposals from team members with HR and senior managers	Within one week of team meeting	To agree reduction actions that can be implemented and supported	Proposals presented to HR/senior management team must be SMART
Team members	Will implement agreed actions	Commence within 1 week of sign-off by HR/senior management	To reduce number of absences	Commenced and completed on time as proposed
Line managers	Will request team members to report on implementation and provide guidance	Weekly team meetings	To maintain focus and engagement	Request and update in minutes
Senior management	Will communicate in writing the proposed team actions and successes	On commencement of implementation and once every 6 months	To maintain focus and engagement	At least 3 communications per year which clearly explain reasons for the need to address absenteeism and describe successful actions

Through this bit of process we've done three things.

1. We've clarified, for those taking part in it, what we mean by the activity of (in this case) absenteeism management.
2. We've demonstrated what we believe are the elements of what 'good' should look like in our context.
3. We've given the senior manager, HR, line managers and their team members a clear sight of what needs to happen between them.

Balancing efficiency with effectiveness

A working definition of efficiency: the lowest amount of inputs achieving the greatest amount of outputs. It will do, but behind it lie two important issues:

1. whether or not we can show that what we have achieved has really been done with the least amount of inputs, including time and energy, or just with what we have grown used to believing are the least amount of inputs;
2. and, if this is so, whether in doing so we have sacrificed any unacceptable degree of quality, or any important professional, ethical or legal standards: we should always balance efficiency with effectiveness.

Acceptable standards are indispensable. Reducing inputs may very well have some impact on quality. Of course, this requires that we have a clearly established standard of quality that can be objectively observed. Anything that reduces the benefit and value expected by the service user or customer and risks breaking the 'relationship' needs to be carefully considered in the balance. In some instances, a small reduction in quality is an acceptable price to pay for lower costs or more rapid working. But it's crucial to know how much quality can be lost before the apparent efficiency savings become illusory.

In the end, we need to be able to answer in the positive when we ask ourselves: 'Are we doing the right thing?' In other words, are we solving our problems, making the most of our opportunity and achieving our objectives to the expected standard?

Barriers and enablers

The most common error in planning for performance, and in tracking whether it has been realised, is to forget entirely the crucial influence of what are rather impersonally called 'barriers and enablers'.

They may, of course be impersonal. A fair wind will literally speed a boat towards its destination. A favourable change of rules may allow a process to be completed far more rapidly than before. A new law may prohibit a procedural short-cut, or limit the time or conditions under which someone may be allowed to work. Extreme weather may prevent travel.

But often 'barriers and enablers' are highly personal. One of the most common explanations for failure to apply some clever bit of technique picked up in a training course is, 'The boss wasn't comfortable with it'. In other words, because it was new it wasn't the way the boss was used to doing things, and he or she wasn't going to have workable good practice upset by someone who'd just been on a course.

This is all very understandable. It's also serious. The fact is that the boss was one of the most important stakeholders in the success of that course. It cost money, and it took time, which cost even more money. If that money was to be well spent there needed to be a line of communication to the boss to ensure that he or she understood what was being taught, bought into its importance and relevance, and committed to playing an enabling role in making sure that what was learned was used.

Essential in the planning stage is examination of the drivers of and impediments to changing practices and behaviours with the richest source of information, in other words the employees and beneficiaries who are expected to make the change. In the data collection stage, it may not be necessary (or efficient use of evaluation resources) to revisit the barriers and enablers unless there is evidence that performance, practices and behaviours have not changed.

Dealing with compliance

Massive amounts of time and money are now devoted to ensuring that individuals and organisations are compliant with laws, rules and prescribed processes. The compliance and mandatory training that result affect virtually every worker in some way or another. At its least extensive, compliance training involves basic information on health and safety and on acceptable (or, more to the point, unacceptable) workplace behaviours. At its most sophisticated it takes in legal, financial and medical compliance that is a statutory and mandatory part of the training of any professional with duties of care.

Evidence suggests that compliance/regulated training has little or no impact on expected outcomes.

There is little evidence that it delivers behaviour change.

There is equally little in the way of reliable data to confirm that the behaviours that compliance training is intended to influence are actually aligned to the problems that are deemed to result from failure to comply, such as breaking the law, increasing capital risk and avoiding litigation.

This is partly due to the sheer rapidity of the growth in statutory and mandatory compliance training over the last twenty years. The true purpose of compliance training has too often been disregarded in favour of a box-ticking approach. Frequently, all that ticked boxes tell us is that we have spent many millions of pounds on compliance training that participants have attended.

The problem with this is easy to spot. The fact that people turned up to a training course provides no assurance that they learned anything. Neither does it tell us that they subsequently practised what they were taught. Since attendance on compliance courses is not, by definition, likely to be voluntary, merely being there does not even confirm that attendees agreed that what they were supposed to be learning was relevant, nor that they had any intention of applying it in practice. Again, evidence suggests that non-voluntary training is the form of training that is least likely to deliver any impact and value.[3]

So, compliance based on attendance is no more than a fig leaf that covers very little by way of risk or liability.

Setting behavioural expectations

'How' work is performed is just as important as 'What' is achieved. Behavioural objectives can be included in a performance plan.

The Personal Development Review (PDR) provides both supervisor and staff member the opportunity to establish and/or revise performance expectations and give feedback on how work is performed throughout the year. Behavioural expectations can be included in performance objectives where they relate to the staff member's key positional responsibilities.

Notes

1. Kaplan and Anderson (2007).
2. Kaplan and Porter (2011).
3. Bassi (2011).

7

KNOWING WHAT, KNOWING HOW

In organisations much of the learning is informal, or non-formal, as opposed to formal. Organisations invest in their people's learning for a wide variety of reasons. Sometimes, the investment in ensuring that everyone knows what to do and how to do it isn't obvious. The assumptions behind the planning of learning are often unrealistic – it makes practical sense to begin by checking what individuals on a project are expected to do, and our assumptions about what they already know and are able to do. This will help to decide what form of learning is likely to be the most suitable and effective. Too often broad learning needs are used in place of good learning objectives. These may be about 'know-how', 'know-what', attitude or confidence. Learning in organisational settings must be measurable. Tools like Bloom's Taxonomy and the Dreyfus Model of Skill Acquisition are important.

We start this chapter looking specifically at formal learning within organisations. But we know that many readers will not be planning or measuring formal learning projects and programmes. The later sections of the chapter consider the less formal, but no less important, acquisition of the 'know-how, the know-what' and the confidence essential to planning, conducting and achieving impact outcomes from projects and programmes of all kinds.

We all know that much of the 'learning' that takes place in organisations is not formalised. But whether it is formal, non-formal or informal, if it requires resource inputs (e.g. time normally deployed on daily work tasks, research reports, tools), and if it is expected to influence performance or behaviour change outcomes, it should be planned and measured.

Why do organisations invest in formal and non-formal[1] learning? A selection of responses might include:

- To make sure that people have the skills to do their jobs.
- To ensure that the organisation has the quality of human resources it needs.
- To learn new techniques.
- To keep ahead of the competition.
- To improve and maintain quality.
- To ensure that succession planning is in place.
- To ensure that employees and potential employees have the opportunity to develop and enrich their knowledge and skills to develop new working experiences.

What you won't hear so often these days is:

- Because learning is a good thing.

There are, however, some individuals, especially in HR and L&D functions, who see this as the main reason for investing in learning. But in today's world the investment in learning for learning's sake does not usually come from employers. They generally have an end in mind. Or they should do.

So it is no surprise that sometimes the word 'learning' sits uncomfortably in business or organisational contexts. Used in the 'personal' sense, it successfully captures the fact that knowledge and skills are being acquired, but provides no clear insight into the type of knowledge or skills in question, nor into the manner or context of their intended use.

But still the word 'learning' is frequently used, often in the title of the function that is tasked with providing it: learning and development. So how well do we understand what it means to organisations?

Most L&D professionals no doubt feel that they understand it well enough. But the more we look at the way people plan and then monitor the effects of learning in work-related settings, the more we wonder if that can be true.

We have already observed that far too much of what is called learning in organisations is supply-led, whether the 'supplier' is an internal HR or training department or an external provider of learning and related services. This is neither inspired by the individual's pure desire for knowledge or skills, nor planned in response to operational or strategic organisational needs.

But if we begin from the demand side, we are accepting that all learning (whether formal, informal or non-formal) should be recognised in organisations and planned with an end in view. This immediately leads us to think more critically about the nature of the learning we are talking about.

In order to make sense of what needs to be learned, and how, we must understand the working contexts in which knowledge or skills will have to be put to use. Only then can we be confident of being able to frame strong and useful learning objectives.

We can broadly categorise the function of 'learning' into three groups:

1. innovation and improvement, creative thinking, experimental exploration
2. performance of existing tasks, application of required techniques and compliance with agreed processes
3. a set of attitudes or values associated with the required standards of behaviour.

Of course the groups overlap. Many tasks and functions – management is an example – may involve all three.

But it is helpful to appreciate that each of these three groups relates predominantly to one of three types of knowledge:

1. Innovation and improvement planning, thinking, experimental exploration is largely driven by factual knowledge or information – relates to what might be called *know-what*.
2. Performance of existing tasks, application of required techniques and compliance with agreed processes – relates to *know-how*.
3. A set of attitudes or values associated with the required standards of behaviour depends on a mixture of awareness, *self-knowledge* and interpersonal facility – these relate to confidence and *mindfulness*.

Know-what is learned through the absorption of information, sometimes taught, sometimes acquired by independent study or knowledge sharing, often through a mixture of the three.

Know-how is acquired through a mixture of study, practice and experience. Information and techniques that are explained frequently then need to be tested and practised before it is possible to be sure that they have been embedded.

Self-knowledge and mindfulness require practice, so are commonly acquired through review of experience, simulations of scenarios or rehearsals of events or activities (role-play).

Knowledge types and knowledge building

Philosophers do not agree on what knowledge is; however, there are three main types of knowledge:

1. Knowledge *about* something – e.g. a person can have knowledge about driving and can describe the process and activities involved; they know *what* to do. This has been called by other names: descriptive, declarative or propositional knowledge.
2. Knowledge *of* something – e.g. a person has the ability to drive and therefore can both describe the procedures and actually drive; they know *how* to do it. This is sometimes called procedural knowledge.

3. Knowledge *by acquaintance* – e.g. being directly acquainted with a person, place or thing. This is also called personal knowledge.

Interestingly, Benjamin Bloom and his colleagues identified three major learning domains, which in adult education have been summarised as knowledge, skills and attitude:

1. Cognitive *knowledge*, can be linked with knowledge *about*, it is the recall or recollection of knowledge.
2. Psychomotor *skills*, can be linked with knowledge *of*, they are the ability to carry out a physical skill as a result of the learning.
3. Affective *attitude*, this is dealing with the 'changes in interest, attitudes, and values, and the development of appreciations and adequate adjustment' (Krathwohl et al., 1964).

The theory of knowledge building is a description of what a community of learners need to accomplish in order to create knowledge. The creators of this theory, Carl Bereiter and Marlene Scardamalia, see learning as an almost unobservable process resulting in changes of beliefs, attitudes and skills, while knowledge building is seen as creating or modifying public knowledge. Therefore, 'students see themselves and their work as part of the civilization-wide effort to advance knowledge frontiers' (Scardamalia and Bereiter, 2006). Knowledge building is a process that involves the creation of new knowledge resulting from group discussions and the synthesising of ideas by employing a range of knowledge-building components, such as goals, strategies, resources, evaluation of results etc.

Sources: DePoe (2013); Koedinger and Corbett (2006); Krathwohl et al. (1964); Scardamalia and Bereiter (2006); Shields (2001).

Planning learning

So, when we plan learning in organisations or look at a project plan and consider how to ensure that all those who are key to its success know what is expected and are able to do what we have planned for them, the first question we ask ourselves is what they might need to know about and/or be able to do.

We often make assumptions that are unrealistic or fail to recognise a gap in our analysis. All too often we assume, without digging deeper to check if our assumption is correct, that someone knows something or how to do it.

For example, we may have detailed the expected learning outcomes from a course and be able to assess whether our participants have acquired some new knowledge. But can we also assume that they will be able to use this knowledge and reconstruct it into their workplace tasks and immediately apply it to the standard we expect? Is this likely, given that our course is only a few hours and provides little or no opportunity to practise? We are assuming that participants can go back to work and now 'do it' to the expected standard. We may also be assuming that their line managers know what they are learning and how to support them most effectively to apply it at work. But do they? Our experience is that line managers may have only a general idea of what someone in their team might be learning and do not necessarily expect to have to support them in applying it directly at work, or know how best to do it.

So it makes practical sense to check the roles that everyone who can influence outcomes will be asked to play, and then to look also at their learning needs in terms of the tasks they are likely to need to perform, or the behaviours we expect them to demonstrate.

One way of doing that is to divide them into six groups.

1. *Planners*: involved early, drawing information and evidence from other sources, establishing needs, building learning objectives and how these will be formatively and/or summatively assessed, designing activity and learning support.
2. *Overseers*: signing off decisions on policy and practice, holding key people accountable, setting out monitoring and evaluation requirements.
3. *Managers*: planning and leading performance implementation and behaviour standards, supporting staff, problem solving, managing relationships.
4. *Operators*: performing allocated tasks.
5. *Disseminators*: reporting progress and achievement, passing on learning from both good and bad experience.
6. *Future policy makers*: receiving reports and assessing their content for valuable information, data and insights.

A first rough guide to the types of learning that each of these might need to acquire or reinforce could look as shown in Table 7.1.

TABLE 7.1

	Know-what	*Know-how*	*Confidence*
Planners			
Overseers			
Managers			
Operators			
Disseminators			
Future policy makers			

The second question we ask ourselves is, 'How are they most likely to acquire the learning they need?' There are many options, and it's essential to narrow them down as rapidly as possible:

- classroom learning
- self-study
- study visits
- online or distance learning
- information sessions
- simulations and role playing
- social networks
- action learning
- meetings
- research
- blended learning combining some or all of the above.

Table 7.2 provides a useful matrix for helping planners to reflect on the kinds of learning that can be delivered through the various learning media.

TABLE 7.2

	Know-what	*Know-how*	*Confidence*
Classroom learning			
Self-study			
Study visits			
Online/distance learning			
Information sessions			
Simulation and role playing			
Social networks			
Action learning			
Meetings			
Research			
Blended learning			

The third, and very necessary question is, 'What is feasible?'
Feasibility is likely to depend on some or all of:

- *Time*: a crucial consideration from two points of view: the deadline by which the learning must be successfully achieved, and the amount of time that can be devoted to acquiring the knowledge, skill or confidence.
- *Available expertise and capacity*: may be a limiting factor, but it may also be the consideration that dictates whether learning takes place in-house, or is entrusted to an external supplier.
- *Learner preferences*: always important because, generally, people learn best by methods they find comfortable. Some are quite happy to be lectured to. Others are very unhappy unless they can learn in a highly participative way. Some are adept at self-learning. Some love online learning and some are intimidated by it.

Having said that, in most organisations most of the time, *cost* will be a determining factor around which the commissioners of learning and its users will need to make compromises and provide assurances.

Ultimately, though, we need to be realistic about the changes we can expect to see in knowledge, skills and attitudes. Consider Bloom's Taxonomy (see below). Where are they starting from? Where do you expect them to get to? Is it realistic within the time and from the resources invested?

The difference between learning needs and learning objectives

Needs are derived from two requirements: what the learner already knows and can do, and their performance and behaviour gaps and how these two are related. Understanding *why* someone is unable to perform to standard or needs to do something differently, or *why* someone's behaviour fails to meet expected standards should in the first instance lead us to ask:

- Do they lack the knowledge?
- Do they have the required standard of skills?
- Do they have the right attitude with regard to the behaviours expected of them?

Until we understand the relationship between our desired performance and behaviour and the knowledge, skills and attitudes that are required to achieve them, we cannot begin to understand learning needs. We must then factor in the potential learner's existing knowledge, skills and attitudes before we can reach a conclusion about what is required.

Moving from needs to objectives

When we commission a piece of software, we first build our requirements. We analyse what everyone needs to do and, alongside that, what they currently are doing and what they are able to do. Then a software specification is developed, including the objectives that will be achieved once it is implemented. It will also describe in detail how the software will operate.

Analysing our performance and behaviour needs and our learning needs creates the equivalent of a requirements document. Our specification will express our learning objectives, and how these will be met.

We cannot frame objectives until we have clarified our needs. These express the gap between where we are now with regard to knowledge, skills and attitudes ('the current position') and our desired 'future' position. Once we have defined these two positions, we can establish our objectives in detail.

Needs are very different from objectives. SMART objectives set out precisely the standard and condition of achievement that need to be met.

Setting good learning objectives

An aspiration such as, 'Everyone must learn the new client care process', provides little guidance to the learner in terms of the learning outcomes expected. It does not tell us what content we need to provide so as to fill the learning gap.

Nor does it tell us anything about the standards we need to see achieved. Do we require knowledge of every step of a process? Must this include knowledge of why the process has been developed? Must we see confirmation of ability to follow the process unsupervised and unaided?

It does not tell us if there is a time deadline by which this needs to be done – say, within one month. It does not tell us if there is a mandatory requirement to demonstrate specific knowledge and skill standards prior to being signed off, or if everyone must demonstrate the same standard on every learning outcome criterion.

A good learning objective fully clarifies the criteria that will be used to assess the learning outcomes. This includes the standard required, any time issues (particularly important with regard to self-learning), and any conditions that relate to the achievement of the criteria. An example might be: *Every staff member must be able to complete the process in the correct sequence within five minutes of receipt of their instructions with no errors or rework.*

It is vital to understand that a learning objective that says, 'Everyone must complete the course', is not a learning objective at all. It is a statement about physical presence. It neither suggests nor confirms that anyone has actually acquired any knowledge, skill or has changed their attitude.

Learning objectives, if they are to be of any value, must tell us not only that knowledge and skills have been increased, but also that the learner can perform the required role or task to the standard expected and/or demonstrate an awareness of and behave in the expected manner.

Know-how

Learning objectives are useless unless we can measure their achievement. Take the very common example: to improve leadership skills. What exactly does this mean? It is certainly not measurable. Do we mean evidence of some specific knowledge about a theory of leadership? Do we need evidence that certain behaviours can be demonstrated, that some recommended processes consistent with good leadership models are understood and can be followed?

Demand-led training and setting clear objectives

A regional health service team is responsible for the development and delivery of education and training for more than 150,000 staff. It organises a range of events including annual meetings, conferences, consultations, training and workshops. With only a small 'events' team in place it realised that it needed

(Continued)

(Continued)

to reduce the number of non-training events on its schedule and ensure that colleagues from other departments planned more of their own events, especially the smaller ones.

The head of corporate communications required that each event was justified by clear objectives, that there were ways of measuring achievement and that the impact of events was measured. But it was clear that colleagues did not have all the necessary skills and knowledge to plan and manage events. So the communications team set clear objectives at Levels 1 to 4 and then developed and delivered Event Management Workshops for their colleagues.

The Level 2 learning objectives were:

- Staff must know and be able to implement the range of communication methods available to them.
- They should know and be able to explain the organisation's policies and procedures for organising events.
- They should be able to organise 'an effective event' in line with the recommended processes set out in the organisation's models.

What we have learned about adult learning and workforce and workplace learning

All adults have experienced their education 'systems'. The earliest and the largest proportion of their formal learning will have been experienced through the education system.

These education systems have been developed over thousands of years of accumulation of bodies of knowledge. These bodies of knowledge are constructed around specific knowledge domains, e.g. mathematics, English language, chemistry, history etc. As we acquire basic knowledge, we build on this. Some knowledge may be an essential requirement or threshold that has to be achieved before we can add to it and develop a more comprehensive understanding of the subject domain in question.

Educational courses are not, of course, generally constructed according to what we want someone to do, but according to the knowledge we want them to acquire: constructing and reconstructing how they understand and 'know' that subject.

However, the development of vocational systems over many decades has shown that learning to perform a task to standard, and to work in a specific way, may not require a deep knowledge of the subject in question.

The process of constructing the support for learning at work has to begin from what we expect someone in a job role to do, and how we want them to behave.

This recognition of 'start from the role/job family' has led to the development of competence profiles and frameworks, built around job families and occupational standards. Competence standards do not exclude the expectation that someone needs a body of basic or threshold knowledge. Without threshold knowledge of mathematics, no one can learn to be an electrician. Threshold knowledge of anatomy is essential for a surgeon. When we build objectives for work-related learning we must always frame them against a clear understanding of what it is that we want learners to go on to do specifically with their new skills or knowledge.

However, as occupational standards (usually national) have been developed sectorally with input from employers as well as domain experts, there has been an understandable focus on creating generalisable standards applicable to all those working in the same or similar roles in different organisations and contexts. Moreover, in the drive to professionalise occupations outside the traditional fields of medicine, engineering or accounting, competence profiles have been extended to cover roles such as customer service, management and cleaning.

The value of these competence profiles is that they offer those investing in L&D and workforce planning a strong basis on which to define their human capital requirements. However, they are generic and are intended to be applied widely. They also take a significant amount of time and consultation to develop; often years, by which time some areas of work may already have changed. Then updating these profiles requires the whole cycle to commence again.

Competence profiles serve as a useful reference point for establishing learning needs and for building learning objectives. This is especially the case either if there is a requirement to achieve a recognised professional 'qualification' or if the learner wants formal recognition of new knowledge or skills.

Competence profiles are attractive to education and training providers because they offer the opportunity to build courses for large numbers, delivering economies of scale. This is consistent with the growth over the past two decades of the idea that learning is a product that can be commoditised. The difficulty is that once you deliver a single standardised product, it requires an intermediary to help the learner apply the learning in context. This, of course, assumes that the intermediary has a deep knowledge of the job, work area and learning content. Otherwise the learner must have the self-efficacy to adapt the generic learning to his or her specific needs.

Longer terms of employment (lifetime jobs) are gone. Few employers expect to invest in and develop their staff over years and decades. Today's more flexible labour markets and the growing expectation of 'lifelong learning' imposes an even greater requirement that the learning needs of participants be regularly assessed and mapped to job performance and behaviour needs, and that learning objectives then and only then be defined. These objectives can then be referenced against existing course and programme provision, or can be used to define the customised requirements that will ensure that the learning objectives for each specific job role are achieved.

A learner may be permitted to assume a job role only after having achieved the relevant professional qualification. But if there is a mismatch between the learning outcomes specifically required for the job and the learning outcomes offered in the learning programmes delivering the 'qualifications', whoever is commissioning the course will need to ensure that any learning objectives required for the job are added to the existing qualification course provision. A decision on whether or not to select a course may then be based on the proportion of course content that is not required for the job in question. It is possible that the purpose of some of it may be to furnish the basic or threshold knowledge required to enable the learner to acquire the full range of knowledge and skills needed for the job.

Good learning objectives make clear and transparent links between learning and application. Troubling and puzzling examples of poor linkage turn up frequently in projects and programmes that are concerned with better process and direction in the middle ranks of organisations. It is often not at all clear what specific, practical skills the learning objectives are intended to develop.

'Improve the leadership skills of supervisors' is thoroughly representative of a poorly defined learning objective. It is seductive. Instinctively we are inclined to nod and agree that it represents a worthy aspiration. But what leadership skills are meant? Why are they important? What is their acquisition supposed to achieve?

That final question leads us to the means of addressing and resolving the problem.

Leadership, performance management and teamwork skills have become talismanic features of what the effective, talented manager is expected to offer. But, in the main, they acquire meaning only in the context of the organisational tasks they are meant to support.

'Know-how' and 'know-what' outside formal education and training

Looking beyond formal learning and development, every project and initiative requires that those involved have the information they need. They must know what is expected and know how they are supposed to perform. Projects and programmes often include internal managers and staff members or partners from different organisations, all working together to achieve their planned impact outcomes. They all require the know-how to carry out their tasks and roles. Too often, individuals and teams assume that everyone involved is informed, and knows how to carry out designated activities, complete required tasks and implement agreed actions. Sometimes they will need to become more aware of how they should change the way they currently do things.

As noted in Chapter 5, every project or initiative needs a stakeholder analysis at the planning stage. And then agreement as to who will do what. An assumption that when someone offers or is allocated responsibility for some action or task they will know what they are supposed to do and how to do it to the required standard is not borne out by experience.

Any project, initiative or programme must articulate clear learning objectives to ensure that achievement of the planned activities, tasks and behaviour change are within the skill, knowledge and confidence compass of the core team and stakeholders. The achievement of these learning objectives can be confirmed only by good data, whether the learning has been formal or not.

Assessing learning needs and setting learning objectives

One of the most helpful ways of getting people, even those with no previous experience of learning assessment, to consider what learning outcomes are needed and the 'dosage' required to achieve these outcomes is to expose them to the discipline of Bloom's Taxonomy. The relevant cognitive domain is illustrated below at six levels, starting from the basic level of 'knowledge' and ending at the highest level, 'evaluation'.

Bloom's Taxonomy

Benjamin Bloom led a group of fellow college examiners in classifying educational objectives for assessing the performance of students. In their research, they found that most learning objectives set by teachers could be classified in one of three major domains – cognitive, affective and psychomotor. In adult education these have been summarised as knowledge, attitude and skills, respectively.

The cognitive domain was the easiest to classify, since most educational objectives are located here. Cognitive domain objectives are those that cover 'the recall or recognition of knowledge and the development of intellectual abilities and skills.' The examiners classified this domain further into six areas: knowledge, comprehension, application, analysis, synthesis and evaluation (Figure 7.1). These are in a hierarchical order from knowledge to evaluation, where each level builds on the previous level. Teachers/trainers can assess learning using a variety of options.

The affective domain was not as easy to classify, since it dealt with 'changes in interest, attitudes, and values, and the development of appreciations and adequate adjustment.' This domain is focused on the emotion of the student/trainee and has been further classified into five hierarchical areas: receiving, responding, valuing, organisation and internalising values. Testing someone's attitude is still difficult today and is sometimes done by pre- and post-attitude/motivation questionnaires.

The examiners did not further classify the psychomotor domain; however, other researchers have contributed to the discussion by adding their classification of this domain. One popular sub-classification of the psychomotor domain is from Elizabeth Simpson. Her hierarchical sub-classification includes perception, set, guided response, mechanism, complex or overt response, adaptation and origination. Testing can be done in a variety of ways, since the educator is interested in whether the student/trainee can carry out what is required.

Sources: Bloom et al. (1956); Krathwohl et al. (1964); Shields (2001); Simpson (1966).

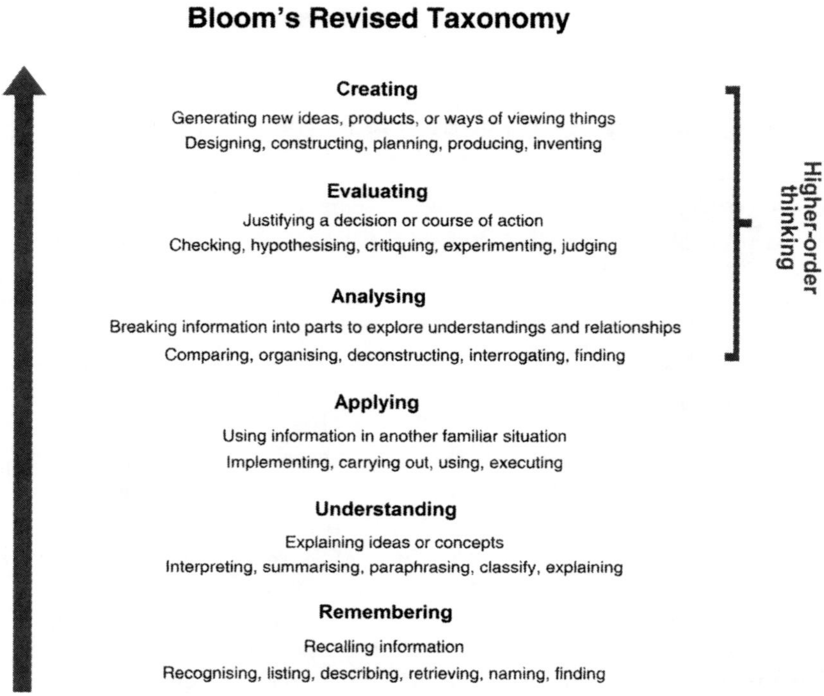

Bloom's Revised Taxonomy

Creating
Generating new ideas, products, or ways of viewing things
Designing, constructing, planning, producing, inventing

Evaluating
Justifying a decision or course of action
Checking, hypothesising, critiquing, experimenting, judging

Analysing
Breaking information into parts to explore understandings and relationships
Comparing, organising, deconstructing, interrogating, finding

Applying
Using information in another familiar situation
Implementing, carrying out, using, executing

Understanding
Explaining ideas or concepts
Interpreting, summarising, paraphrasing, classify, explaining

Remembering
Recalling information
Recognising, listing, describing, retrieving, naming, finding

Higher-order thinking

FIGURE 7.1

Source: Adapted from www.utar.edu.my/fegt/file/Revised_Blooms_Info.pdf.

This straightforward structure, once understood, can help operational and learning professionals to debate and agree on the extent and depth of knowledge required for particular tasks in specific contexts. If the operational requirement for a piece of knowledge were to be defined as, 'Comprehend this thoroughly and be able to apply it wherever required', we could be pretty sure that the 3rd level (application) in Blooms Taxonomy should provide us with the basis for developing our learning objectives. Simply being able to recite the process to be followed (1st level) would not be sufficient. Understanding why the process should be followed (2nd level) wouldn't do either. It would be essential to go to the 3rd level.

A good example of this, which we come across frequently in our work with clients in health and social care organisations, is hygiene – most commonly, hand washing. There is no guarantee at all that people who can simply recite the hand-washing instructions given to them (1st level) will ever observe them. Comprehending why thorough hand washing is required, and the risks associated with failure to wash (the 2nd level) is certainly likely to help. But if infections are to be controlled and lives preserved they need to demonstrate what is meant by 'thorough' hand washing (3rd level). We can see that they then know what, they know why and they know how, and we have some confidence that they can apply personal hygiene knowledge in any setting they are likely to encounter.

Bloom's Taxonomy is equally helpful with another common workplace task: completing performance appraisals.

- Bloom's level 1

  Managers are able to recall what actions need to be taken, what forms are to be used and when they are to be completed. This simple information could be provided as a job aid and you can assess this very simply by asking some simple closed questions.

- Bloom's level 2

  Managers know why the process is needed and the reasons why the form and processes have been structured as they have. They are able to summarise the benefits that doing it well will bring to them, their department, their teams and their organisations.

- Bloom's level 3

  Managers are able to complete all the steps in the process in the correct sequence and exhibit behaviours that demonstrate the values of fairness, objectivity and transparency. They complete the form comprehensively in language that is both appropriate and consistent. Their completed results, when standardised, align broadly with the range reflected by other relevant populations.

- Bloom's level 4

  Managers are able to cross-reference, compare and reflect on differences across appraisals that they have carried out and identify where improvements in the process, their objectivity and approach and their recording of results can be made.

Another valuable tool, the *Dreyfus five-stage model of skill acquisition,* is described on pages 106–7.

The two examples above relate to common forms of compliance activity (sometimes statutory, often mandatory). One of the most disquieting aspects of the design and delivery of a great deal of compliance training is that it is done largely by what is scornfully described as 'sheep-dipping'. The term also says much about the process and suggests how trainees are apt to view such settings.

So the important considerations behind these knowledge or know-what objectives are, first, that they are set at all, and second, that they are set in a way that directly reflects the nature of the demand that prompted them in the first place.

It is in the provision of learning and the setting of learning objectives that the difference between supply-led and demand-led activity has to be thought through and visible.

Supply-led learning tends to produce objectives that imply no clear context, that recognise few imperatives other than that of completing a course or an activity. Demand-led objectives have been derived from a specific set of performance and behaviour requirements for those whose know-how, know-what or confidence needs to be improved; what they need to learn and to what standard; and by when they must learn it in order to become operational.

Attitude

For many organisations, in order to bring about the desired changes, most especially behaviour changes, the need is not for knowledge or skills but for a change in attitude. Developing mindfulness, a caring mind-set, placing the customer first, deep concern for their teams' well-being and engagement, a belief in the values and vision of the organisation are very often what someone really wants from their intervention.

Bringing about these changes is always called 'changing hearts and minds'. Unfortunately, too often the 'solution' is to focus on participants' knowledge, repeating information they already know, running the same programmes and initiatives again and again.

If it is a question of behaviour change and participants already know what they are expected to do, or how they are expected to behave, and they don't change, then it is fairly evident that the training is not effective. Therefore, the starting point is to analyse what behaviours (in observable and objective terms) are current and why, and to consult widely about what behaviours are desirable and appropriate. Poor behaviour in employees is unlikely to be solved by telling them something they already know. They may well be imitating or responding to the behaviours of their managers.

Behaviours change only if people are mindful of their current behaviours. They need to recognise the impact that those behaviours have on others. They must believe that their behaviour can be changed. And they have to wish to change it. It has to be clear that it will benefit them and their peers.

Analysing learning needs and setting learning objectives requires consideration of knowledge, skills and attitudes, establishing how these will be assessed and developing content and learning approaches that are focused on the measurable achievement of these objectives.

Confidence

The least considered and most elusive aspect of learning in working contexts is the generation and boosting of confidence.

Confidence is the X factor that convinces selection panels and senior managers that people can deliver. It's the 'can-do' factor that overcomes awkward circumstances, deals well with the unexpected, copes with upset or angry colleagues or clients and enables its possessors to address the unknown. It's that extra quality that enables people to operate well under pressure, because they are convinced that they can.

At all levels in most organisations you find people who have been held back because, although they have knowledge and skills, they lack the 'it' factor that convinces others that they can cope under all circumstances: that they can react actively to events.

It is summed up as 'confidence', but it is more complex and multi-faceted than that.

Self-confidence (the French say of someone who is self-confident 'il est bien dans son peau', *comfortable in his skin*) may involve:

- comprehending and then operating within the extent and limits of one's capacity and ability
- presenting oneself positively
- allowing others to shine without feeling the need to compete for attention.

But self-confidence may be required to be demonstrated situationally, showing that one is able to:

- deploy skills comfortably within boundaries set by others, or dictated by specific settings or sets of rules
- be unafraid of applying skills in previously untested situations.

Confidence is closely bound up with attitude and mindfulness. It may be required in the context of testing interpersonal encounters:

- explaining and giving instructions with authority
- criticising without causing hurt
- reinforcing the confidence and skills of others
- providing support without appearing patronising
- communicating bad news.

These definitions themselves are all personal, and though most people would come up with many that are similar, they might express them differently. This is what makes it difficult to set objectives for attitude change and development of confidence, and equally difficult to teach and assess it. The challenge is to move it from the abstract to something that can be observed and measured.

Confidence is most commonly, and most effectively, measured by requiring someone to demonstrate it in a simulated setting. Driving instructors are requiring their pupils to demonstrate know-what, know-how, mindfulness and confidence when they drive for the first time on a busy road. A trainee HR manager is similarly challenged when subjected to a demanding piece of role-play, conducting a simulated redundancy interview with an emotional soon-to-be-ex-employee. A trainee hospital manager is in the same situation when confronted by a colleague acting out the role of a stressed and irate father of a child who has been made to wait three hours in Accident and Emergency while more urgent cases are dealt with.

What is important is that mindfulness and confidence are recognised as crucial aspects of learning and are measured regularly and systematically.

Learning in organisational settings must be measurable

Finally, if learning in organisational contexts must be demand-led to be *justifiable*, it must be measurable if it is to be *justified*.

This applies only the same standards of evidence of effectiveness, quality and efficiency to learning as are routinely applied to other investments that organisations make, and other services they contract. However, the primary purpose of measurement is to improve. So measurement provides the data that can help in continuous improvement, including, often, recognising when outcomes are not achieved or not achieved to the expected standard.

So these principles present those responsible for learning development, hopefully in partnership with those responsible for supporting its monitoring and evaluation, with a challenge.

They should be able to frame measurable objectives for all learning activity. If they find that they cannot measure results for whatever reason, it is simply unacceptable to continue with the investment. Learning investments are made by organisations for the express purpose of achieving outcomes that benefit the organisation. If a learning investment cannot demonstrate learning outcomes, why would anyone continue to put resources into it?

Life can, of course, be complex. Those who are responsible for learning development may find themselves left with vague and general learning objectives conceived by others, without thought of their measurement. The objectives may turn out to be unusually difficult to measure, possibly because the learning has already taken place. In this case, those in the position of responsibility have a duty to the present, and to the future. In the reality of the present, they will need to do everything they can to identify and deploy measurement tools capable of supplying at least some useful and indicative data within a reasonable budget. For the future, they need to be prepared to state the partial and inadequate nature of what they are able to report. They also need to articulate clearly what they will do to ensure that the value and cost of learning are never taken so lightly again, and that no learning is in future commissioned without clear, measurable objectives related directly to demand and linked to expectations of subsequent behaviour and action.

Dreyfus five-stage model of skill acquisition

In 1980, Stuart and Hubert Dreyfus described their model of the normal directed skill acquisition process in their paper 'A Five-Stage Model of the Mental Activities Involved in Directed Skill Acquisition'. In their paper they argued that 'skill in its minimal form is produced by following abstract formal rules, but that only experience with concrete cases can account for higher levels of performance.' Their original model comprised the five stages of Novice, Competence, Proficiency, Expertise and Mastery. However, these were later changed to Novice, Advanced beginner, Competence, Proficiency and Expertise. These are described below.

1. *Novice*: a learner who is provided with context-free features of a task, which has been broken down into its component parts, that is recognisable by the learner. S/he is given rules that determine actions based on the features of the task and is observed, to check for conformity to the rules.
2. *Advanced beginner*: the novice gains experience coping with real situations and develops an understanding of the relevant contexts in which the task can be applied, while also learning to identify meaningful aspects of the situation.
3. *Competence*: the advanced beginner learns to devise a plan to determine those elements of a situation that are to be treated as important and those that can be ignored while completing the task.
4. *Proficiency*: the competent learner develops proficiency if, and only if, experience is assimilated in an embodied, atheoretical way. When completing the task, s/he sees the point and the important aspects of the situation and falls back on the rules to help decision making.
5. *Expertise*: the proficient learner becomes an expert when s/he is able to subtly make refined discriminations that allow her/him to make an immediate intuitive, situational response when completing the task.

Understanding these stages is essential to designing projects/programmes that require acquisition of skills. During implementation of these projects/programmes, it is important to identify the stage(s) that the learner has acquired and the stage(s) that he is in a position to attain, providing suitable assistance where necessary.

Sources: Dreyfus (2004); Dreyfus and Dreyfus (1980).

Note

1 'Formal learning is always organised and structured, and has learning objectives. From the learner's standpoint, it is always intentional: i.e. the learner's explicit objective is to gain knowledge, skills and/or competences. Typical examples are learning that takes place within the initial education and training system or workplace training arranged by the employer. One can also speak about formal education and/or training or, more accurately speaking, education and/or training in a formal setting. This definition is rather consensual.

'Informal learning is never organised, has no set objective in terms of learning outcomes and is never intentional from the learner's standpoint. Often it is referred to as learning by experience or just as experience. The idea is that the simple fact of existing constantly exposes the individual to learning situations, at work, at home or during leisure time, for instance. This definition, with a few exceptions (see Werquin, 2007) also meets with a fair degree of consensus.

'Mid-way between the first two, non-formal learning is the concept on which there is the least consensus, which is not to say that there is consensus on the other two, simply that the wide variety of approaches in this case makes consensus even more difficult. Nevertheless, for the majority of authors, it seems clear that non-formal learning is rather organised and can have learning objectives. The advantage of the intermediate concept lies in the fact that such learning may occur at the initiative of the individual but also happens as a by-product of more organised activities, whether or not the activities themselves have learning objectives. In some countries, the entire sector of adult learning falls under non-formal learning; in others, most adult learning is formal. Non-formal learning therefore gives some flexibility between formal and informal learning, which must be strictly defined to be operational, by being mutually exclusive, and avoid overlap.' (http://www.oecd.org/edu/skills-beyond-school/recognitionofnon-formalandinformal-learning-home.htm.)

8

ENGAGEMENT

Do they get it?

Only people can deliver outcomes. We have to know whether the people who we need to deliver actions feel as we do about the importance and practicality of what we are asking them to support and do. We need to understand the level of their engagement or buy-in as early as possible. Then, if there are problems, we can address them. We can find this out at the end of an event or a training course. Many professionals say they do this through 'Happy Sheets'. Conventional Happy Sheets do not work because they ask questions unrelated to buy-in and intention to act. Many factors influence buy-in, and almost all of them relate to the individual's expectation of benefit to them personally and how its importance is perceived within their working environment. A few short questions around engagement or buy-in objectives should be set. Most questions need to be rated for the best and most useful results. They need to be framed in ways that make a firm link with the actions expected of the respondents.

Unasked questions

Remember, the whole of this approach concerns practical delivery of services and achievement of impact outcome objectives. Only people can do these things, and we focus on them throughout our work of planning, monitoring and evaluating.

Is there a single one of us who, at some time or another, has not told a sad tale of a goal under-achieved, a target missed or maybe an appointment or a deadline missed, only to receive a response from a more experienced colleague along the line of, 'I could have told you that would happen, they were never signed up for it in the first place'?

Few responses are more annoying than these, 'I told you so's'. But, if they are correct, they are important. They point to information that should already have been known, probably at the start of the process or activity in question. They suggest that in order to find out, we probably only needed to ask.

This chapter is simply about *asking*. *Asking* whether our colleagues, partners or stakeholders feel as we do about the importance and practicality of whatever it is we're spending money and effort on. Thinking about it, nothing could be more important at the outset of any venture. And, generally speaking, nothing could be much easier to do: take an opportunity when everyone knows what they are expected to do and has had a chance to form a view of its importance and practicality, and *ask* them what they think.

Engagement or buy-in can be described as the emotional connection or commitment of stakeholders for an initiative's or an organisation's success. When people are engaged, it is more likely that they will be intellectually and emotionally committed to the initiative and/or the organisation. Employee engagement is becoming increasingly important and a key element for the HR practitioner. Research shows that there may be a link between the 'engaged employee' and organisational performance. Employees' enthusiasm and motivation for their work can drive better individual performance and may result in improved organisational performance.

Sources: Kotter and Whitehead (2010); MacLeod and Clarke (2009).

Need to know

Nothing happens unless we want it to happen. Whatever the task, whatever the situation, the first indicator we ever get of whether people are likely to take action of some sort is an indication of whether or not they want to do it (Figure 8.1).

FIGURE 8.1

We ask these familiar questions informally all the time to reassure ourselves whether the she and he in question are at all engaged in whatever concerns us. If the answer in any case is 'no', we wouldn't expect much to happen. If it's 'yes', then it might. Nothing certain, but at least the first hurdle has been crossed. The people who need to do something have at least told us they are ready to act.

This readiness to act is just as important in any kind of working or business activity as it is in a family or a social setting. In the family or social setting we busily process the data informally, and often share it with others to confirm our view of its validity or to check out what others think should be done as a result of it. Do we, as a family or social group, really sign up to take those exercise classes, or do we only do it because we are forced into it or reluctant to say no? Will we stay the course? Only if we recognise that we are not as fit as we could or should be, consider it important enough and are emotionally and cognitively engaged in the steps we need to take to achieve an improved level of fitness and have no genuine barriers to participating in the activities that will lead us to be fitter.

International development: engaging partners

An international development organisation carries out a number and variety of cultural relations initiatives across the world. It is partly government funded and therefore actively seeks partners worldwide to enhance its grant support. For each initiative partners are sought who have a shared vision with the organisation. It is therefore crucial that partnership organisations are fully engaged and completely bought-in to the aims and objectives of an initiative.

The organisation's team in one country embarked on a mobility project with funding from the European Commission under the Lifelong Learning Programme. This is linked to the parent organisation's existing programme aimed at providing participants with international learning and networking, as well as creating partnerships across the private, public and third sectors. The project aims to connect participants with host organisations in the UK, both charities and NGOs. The participants visit their hosts for a two-week period to improve their knowledge and understanding of social enterprise concepts, as well as to learn how to develop social enterprise projects.

The project's success is dependent on each partner playing its part: the organisation ensures that it understands the level of the stakeholders' engagement – particularly asking for their opinions on the importance of the work, and for their plans for implementing their own roles.

Formally, at work, we should be doing the same thing: looking for the first evidence we are likely to get that our project outcomes may or may not be achieved. If we come to the conclusion that key people's buy-in and engagement to key tasks and processes are weak, we can expect the results to be poor. We can use this as an opportunity to try to do something about it while we still have time.

Nothing could be more important to any enterprise or activity, and yet only a minority of managers do it at all, and many of those do it so poorly that the information or data they collect is barely usable.

The conventional way of collecting data at Kirkpatrick Level 1 is a questionnaire, often referred to as a Happy Sheet, asking about attendees' reactions to an event. However, as we have already noted, as generally used, the Happy Sheet provides little or no evidence to help to answer questions about the potential for achievement of outcomes.

The curse of the Happy Sheet

What does the typical Happy Sheet ask, say, for an away-day or training course? Probably:

- How satisfied were you with the meeting?
- Was it well prepared?
- How would you rate the facilities?
- How would you rate the facilitator?
- How would you rate the surroundings/refreshments/parking etc.?
- What is your overall level of satisfaction?

This is important information for those who *arranged* the venue and *delivered* the event. Almost none of it is of prime importance to whoever *commissioned* the event. She or he had a result in mind. The comfort and satisfaction reported by the attendees may have bolstered their enthusiasm to perform the roles and tasks expected of them. But these responses tell us nothing about whether they believe the effort being asked of them is worthwhile, and whether they expect and commit to making the changes that the training or away day was intended to stimulate.

So why are so many project managers, trainers and team leaders apparently satisfied with the level of information they get from Happy Sheets? We offer three answers:

- They rarely, if ever, read them.
- They may not set clear learning and subsequent performance objectives in advance, so they have no other questions to ask.
- If the above is true, the away day or training course was a classic supply-sided event (a good idea without a clear focus).

The final answer is crucial. Those who come from the supply side need only to know how their clients reacted. Would they want to buy the experience again? Did they enjoy it? What did they think about the trainers? Those who come from the demand side need most urgently to know the extent to which attendees are engaged and are committed to applying what they have learned so as to perform their part in achieving the results that prompted the investment in the first place. If objectives have been set for the desired level of active engagement, we can see that the conventional Happy Sheet is not going to be fit for purpose. Good engagement information, on the other hand, is a key performance indicator.

The importance of buy-in

We can't ask our car if it believes it is a good or bad idea to travel, say, from Birmingham to Liverpool. Neither can we ask it if the route selected is appropriate, or whether it knows what it will do to ensure that its engine starts and keeps going until we arrive safely.

Our car is a machine. It simply responds to commands. It won't break off halfway to Liverpool and decide to divert into Derbyshire and visit a stately home.

But if we set the driver the task of *driving* the car on that journey, it will be highly relevant to check in advance if she or he might be inclined to travel slowly or divert the journey. It will be relevant to check if the driver believes the journey is sensible and desirable. If there are any reasons to suppose there might be difficulties in the journey, we need to know in advance.

The car has already been bought – it is passive. The degree of active buy-in of the driver is what tells us if the journey is likely to be a success.

So we *must* always know that people on whom we have spent money, and on whom we depend to play active roles, are fully signed up to perform them. If they are, they may do what we require them to do. If they are not, they may not do it all, or they may fall far short of what is needed in terms of efficiency and quality. At worst, they may appear to offer passive support, but actively sabotage the attempt to make the change.

The responsible manager must have this information. It focuses attention directly onto the most powerful but unpredictable part of the project plan: people. Early data is always powerful, and this is the first data we can usually collect that will confirm or deny our chances of reaching our final objectives.

PICU: stakeholder engagement

Hospital X is one of the biggest private medical centres in the Middle East. Although it has a paediatric department, it does not have a Paediatric Intensive Care Unit (PICU). This means that when children require this service they have to be stabilised and then transferred to other medical facilities. Not only does this affect the quality of care that the patient and their family receive, it also affects the hospital's image as a fully equipped medical centre, as well as the revenues earned. To address this need, a PICU is being established within the paediatric department.

The stakeholders for this project include top managers (department heads), the paediatric team, patients and their families. Engaging these stakeholders and keeping them committed throughout the project is essential for the success of the project. Therefore, measurable data indicating their active engagement and commitment have been established:

1. top managers signing off the project proposal
2. construction report signed off by the construction staff and approved by the top managers

(Continued)

(Continued)

3. development, communication, and implementation of the clinical practice guidelines, each approved and signed by the related physicians,
   nurses and the interdisciplinary committee chairman
4. the equipment quotations and purchase orders signed by the purchase
   director, unit director and top managers
5. minutes of all the meetings signed off by all the members
6. signing off the project proposal by the heads of the paediatric, laboratory,
   radiology, pharmacy, IT, HR and reception departments
7. training plans signed by the education director, unit director, director of
   nursing and the trainees (registrars and nurses)
8. data from the marketing campaign relating to engagement of marketing
   staff, the public and parents.

What influences buy-in?

If we're honest with ourselves, high on the list of considerations when we decide
how enthusiastic and committed we are to some project or course of action or
learning is our own *self-interest*.

It may not always be the most important factor, but it can have a strong positive
and/or negative influence on what we do. This includes how hard it will be to
learn what we are being asked to learn; how hard it will be to make the changes
that are asked of us. We will be considering how far these will ask us to move from
our current 'norm'. We will be asking if the benefit to us is likely to warrant the
effort.

Then there will be the even more complex *interests of the group or organisation*
we work in.

In a large organisation, the interests of a division or a local branch may be as
important as the more distant interests of the whole. Many individuals may show
immediate interest in learning something new or changing the way things are
done, but putting a head above the parapet, stepping outside the norms of peers
and colleagues, may act as a strong deterrent. And of course, if the processes, culture or dominant message in the group suggest that something is of low importance, or is not likely to work, then it probably won't be feasible.

Most of us prefer things to be seen to be done properly. We will not be willing
to buy-in strongly to something that we and our peers believe to have been poorly
set up, launched or taught. So we look for *appropriateness* in the things we are to
learn or are being asked to change, and their connection with the tasks we need
to perform. Moreover, we may or may not believe the evidence of the need for
change. We may doubt the source, the rationale or the motivations of those who
are proposing it. All of these will influence our engagement.

Whatever we think about the principles of a given situation, project or opportunity, we are pragmatic animals. We like to buy into things that have a chance of working, so we expose the objectives set for us to the test of *realism*. Our judgement of what is realistic will be based on comparing our current state and practice against what is proposed. Experience of similar initiatives or projects will also influence our views. If something has worked before, unless background factors have visibly changed, it may work again. If we are inclined to believe that it is achievable, what evidence is there to support this?

Finally, we react strongly to the fact it has been thought important to make an investment in us and our skills. It tells us a lot about how we are regarded. It confirms that what we do is important. But, even so, we will be cautious and will want confirmation that the full requirements have been taken into account. We will weigh up whether we have been given the time, equipment and other resources that we need to make a change, and to make it work.

These boil down to five essential factors, each with its own implications, each one with questions that need to be asked in respect of it (Table 8.1).

TABLE 8.1

Key factors in buy-in	Implications – think about	Questions to ask
Self-interest	Own role Relationships with colleagues Pressures and influences on our room to make decisions	How important is this to your discharge of your own role and responsibilities? Do you have the freedom to decide?
Interests of the organisation or group	Collegiality KPIs	How important is it to the organisation/team/group as a whole?
Appropriateness	Demand-led Current processes and practices	Have I learned or acquired something useful and new? Is it something that can and should be applied?
Realism	Connection to possible action Known barriers and enablers Past experience	Do I know what I'm going to need to do next? What is the evidence that demonstrates this can be achieved?
Quality and status	Expectations Past events and activities	How would I rate the whole experience of the course/meeting/event I've just taken part in? Would I recommend it to others? Have I got the resources and support I need to take the next step?

The five strong areas

How do we assure ourselves that we have appropriate levels of buy-in and positive engagement from those we are preparing for activity? The short answer is that we do it by asking them. It is surprising how reluctant many are to ask direct questions. But there is no substitute, and five questions will serve in most cases. The first three are directly about relevance.

1. Is it important to the organisation and its objectives?
2. Is it relevant to the situation or role of the person who is being asked to do it?
3. Would the person who has completed this preparation, and is therefore in a privileged position with regard to understanding the usefulness of what has been provided, recommend it to a colleague?

Then we may need to check the efficiency of the approach to ensuring that knowledge, skill and confidence are present.

4. How much of the information provided was new to them?

Finally, we need to know about intention to act, and to act quickly.

5. Can they identify and explain the actions to be taken in order to start to apply this information to the task in hand?

Just signing up or showing up won't do

It's amazing how many people and organisations assume that they have an assurance of commitment just because someone has turned up for a meeting or attended a training course. To that someone, time may be cheap, so attendance means very little. For some, time is expensive and valuable. In their case attendance may be such an important symbolic action that it does indeed confirm engagement and buy-in. But this is rare. A minister or chief executive who prioritises one meeting over another might be confirming engagement. But not necessarily. Turning up may be for other reasons: to be with colleagues, to show the face, to avoid loss of face.

Engaging stakeholder organisations

Engaging stakeholders within an organisation is challenging. It can be even more challenging when trying to engage or get the commitment of a number of different organisations. This is due, in large part, to the variety of organisational cultures, structures, visions and missions. However, when the key objectives of an initiative are shared, getting buy-in may be easier.

A university working with a pharmaceutical education and training group collaborated with several NHS Trusts to develop an e-learning training programme for Aseptic Processing. The purpose was to create a standardised curriculum that covered the basics of Good Manufacturing Practice (GMP) in Aseptic Processing. The programme utilised a variety of formats, namely an online workbook, interactive computer-based learning, CDs, as well as printed material.

In this setting, each stakeholder could easily commit to the programme because they shared the vision of improved quality of care for patients. Importantly, they shared the view that using the medium of e-learning to share the basics of GMP in Aseptic Processing was a good opportunity for users, internal and external to the NHS. The stakeholders worked together to assess the viability of this training solution using our evaluation approach.

Generally, all we can infer from someone's attendance is just that: they were there. But were they actually listening and taking part? Were they signalling an intention to take the action hoped of them? There's no immediate way of knowing unless you ask. They may have been 'resting their eyes' in anticipation of some demanding task on the near horizon. They may have come for the coffee. They may have been busy texting and e-mailing throughout. In some cases, they may not even know why they were there: they were told to go!

In other words, we have to ask for evidence of engagement or buy-in. Signing up and showing up are, except in rare circumstances, weak indicators. We have to ask directly whether people are really committed to joining us on our journey to achieve planned outcomes.

Setting the right objectives

Understanding the need to check engagement and buy-in is only the first step in what for many is both a step-up in practice and a culture change. Both of these hit home when it comes to setting realistic and measurable objectives.

The step-up in practice proves difficult in many organisations where engagement and commitment are taken for granted, and the assumption that everyone subscribes to them is seen as part of the ethos. The error here is in assuming that generalised statements of commitment also indicate buy-in to specific projects, activities or desired behaviours. We may be passionately committed to an overall organisational strategy and approach, but feel that a particular plan or required process is counterproductive, even wrong. So the step-up in practice is not about *gauging* general commitment, but about *measuring* specific attitudes to defined activities or behaviours.

The culture change is required particularly when the same questions to measure buy-in need to be asked of the most senior person involved as well as of the most junior, and of everyone in between. This is about acknowledgement of shared accountability. It connects directly with the data we will later gather about performance, which will differentiate between tasks, and therefore between levels of seniority. But at the level of engagement, surely everyone is equal. If it is important to ask an administrator how important on a 1 to 5 scale a project is to the organisation, is it not even more crucial to put the same question in precisely the same terms to a director, who does fewer hours of work on the project, but whose capacity to influence its success or failure may be far greater?

Six questions should always be asked of all the key stakeholders involved in a project or activity (Tables 8.2 to 8.6).

TABLE 8.2

Interests of the organisation or group	Type of target	Measure	Sample objective
Is it important to the department or organisation (or community or family or peer group) and its objectives?	Strong affirmation in most contexts (80–85%) shows a high level of importance. In cases where safety is involved, or where strict compliance is required, 100% is likely to be the required level of buy-in.	A 4- or 5-point scale is the best measure to use. Some people will never use a 5-point scale because they feel it encourages everyone to opt for the middle point. We think that decision is driven not so much by the number of points as by the way the question is asked, the time provided to answer the question and the seriousness with which the facilitator explains the question.	On a scale of 1–5, how important is this course/ activity to your department's operational goals?

TABLE 8.3

Self-interest	Type of target	Measure	Sample objective
Is it relevant to the situation or role of the person who is being asked to do it?	Strong affirmation in most contexts (80–85%) shows a high level of importance In cases where safety is involved, or where strict compliance is required, 100% is likely to be the required level of buy-in.	A 4- or 5-point scale	On a scale of 1–5, how important is this course/activity to your job and role?

TABLE 8.4

Appropriateness	Type of target	Measure	Sample objective
How much of the information provided was new to them?	In most instances of training or knowledge acquisition, a high (60%+) level of new knowledge is an indication that the course or activity was worthwhile. In a refresher course, participants are likely to encounter information they covered previously. In this case, it is useful to check whether the refresher has helped to deepen comprehension or enabled participants to develop skills through practising them in the refresher. In cases where participants show large differences in this measure, it is right to ask whether the same course or activity was suitable for all of them.	We suggest a question graded: 0–30%, 31–60%, 61–100% or similar.	How much of the information provided was new to you? If it was not new, how much of what you already knew was reinforced or practised to improve your skills?

TABLE 8.5

Realism	Type of target	Measure	Sample objective
Do they have a clear idea of the important things to be done in order to start to apply this information to the task in hand?	Everyone should know what he or she now needs to do as a follow-up	Use action plans if they are part of the training or project team activities. If not, ask for a minimum of three actions that will be taken within, say, the next 1–3 weeks. Early actions are good indicators and are likely to be easier to track.	Note at least three actions you will take in the next 1–3 weeks to apply what you have learned on this course/activity.

TABLE 8.6

Quality and status	Type of target	Measure	Sample objective
What overall quality rating would attendees give to the event?	Strong affirmation	Rating on a 1–4 or a 1–5 scale	On a 1–5 scale, how would you rate the overall quality of the event?
Would they recommend it to a colleague?	Everyone agreeing	Yes/no question	Would you recommend this course/activity to others in a similar role?

Why is it so important to get Kirkpatrick's Level 1 right?

1 The direct relationship with behaviour and actions

People's belief in the appropriateness of what is planned, their confirmation that they understand their roles and responsibilities and the fact that they have plans for what they will do to deliver results are all immensely powerful. Collecting and then reporting good engagement data provides the first confirmation you will get either that your investment is on course or that there are issues you should address.

2 The opportunity to intervene

Evidence of good buy-in is no guarantee of success. But any lack of it is an early warning of possible, or even likely, failure *unless* something is done rapidly to put things right.

Discovering that five people in a group give low ratings when asked how important an initiative is to their organisation provides an opportunity to speak to each one of them, to find out why they give it a lower priority and importance rating than you think they should and to consider the reasons for this. You can then work on how to overcome or go around any barriers.

3 Risk

The linkage of all this to your calculation of risk is obvious. Any weakness in the buy-in of key stakeholders puts any activity in peril. As well as the risk of weak engagement, the added risk of finding that out too late to take action compounds the danger of sub-standard performance and results. The overall risk of weak engagement can be illustrated quite easily (Figure 8.2).

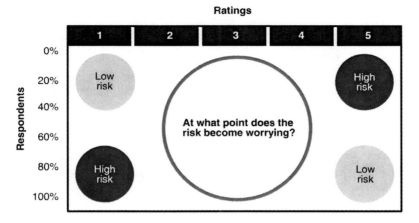

FIGURE 8.2

If more than 80 per cent of your participants give you a rating of 3/5 or less on, for example, relevance to role, then you really need to investigate why, as a matter of urgency.

Here are some possible reasons.

- The project aims or course content are not relevant to their work. This begs the question, why were they selected?
- The way the project or course was communicated in advance was inappropriate and led to the incorrect selection of participants.
- The way the project was communicated or taught in the classroom failed to make reference to its direct relevance to the participants' work.
- The content was insufficiently tailored to the day-to-day work and interests of the participants.

The data from the responses to your questions helps you identify if there is a problem to follow up. The next step is to investigate why, so that you can do something about it as quickly as possible to minimise the risk to the project's outcomes.

Use the data to enable early intervention to improve your chances of achieving your results.

4 Accountability

Many people who plan and track impact using this approach report that one of its most important effects is to extend accountability.

Accountability begins with buy-in. It starts with a clear, shared confirmation of the importance of a change of behaviour or process, and then is consolidated by the shared commitment to some relevant planned action.

The manner in which this is done is then crucial because a sense of personal accountability, whilst important, can be an intensely private thing, but an acknowledgement of shared accountability has a quite different resonance and importance. This issue of shared accountability is key to the practical usefulness of this approach, and Level 1 is the place to begin tracking it.

We frequently come across projects where there are a number of stakeholders with quite different status, roles and responsibilities. They are all key to the success of the project, and it is vital to know that they are committed to playing their roles and that they provide evidence of this. It will later become important to be able to track the degree to which they fulfil their own and others' plans and ambitions for them.

So, starting at Level 1, we need to view the most influential stakeholders as an extended team and then treat them as we would treat a team within a single organisation. This means that we must know that they share a view of the importance of the tasks to be undertaken and the way to approach the project or programme activities they are embarking on, and that they actually intend to do what is required of them. They each need to have engagement and buy-in objectives set for them. And the data needs to be collected to show that they have met the objectives. Otherwise, instead of being valuable partners, they are likely to form passive or even active barriers to the actions that others need to take at Level 3.

5 Benchmarking

This is particularly important where courses or activities are repeated over time. It is then vital, not just to understand how participants have responded to each one, but to be able to see if responses have altered, or appear to be in the process of altering. The use of a 5-point scale for all the questions about importance (to organisation and to individual job or role) provides the opportunity to capitalise on tracking data over time by setting benchmarks based on prior experience.

The bell-curve in Figure 8.3 shows the 5-point scale and a set of moderate expectations of the responses to the questions posed.

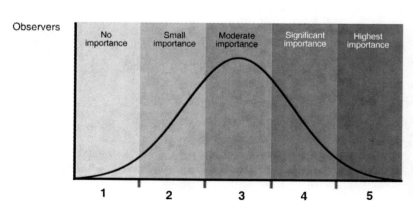

FIGURE 8.3

It is easy to see that the 5-point scale has the potential to provide much more nuanced information than could be done with a simple yes/no question. The bell-curve in Figure 8.4 shows this.

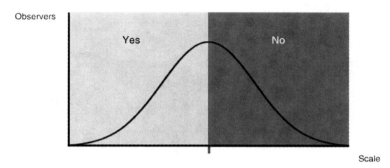

FIGURE 8.4

Once the nuanced data has been collected, it can be used to provide a degree of analysis at Level 1 that simply is not otherwise available.

The danger of averages

Averages, as we constantly point out, are useful for benchmarking, but they can be very dangerous when they are used on their own to report data. To put it quite simply, they conceal detail – which is what they are meant to do. They are useful when they summarise or simplify data so that it can be used for quick reference and to communicate an approximation. This is appropriate when the need is to signpost or validate plans. But averages are dangerous when they are used to report in a summarised manner data that is then going to be applied to conclusions or decisions concerning performance or achievement. Then the detail behind the average immediately becomes more important and valuable than the summary which the average communicates. Only the detail reveals results at the extreme ends of the scale (Figure 8.5): in an operational context these always need to be seen and understood, and often require action.

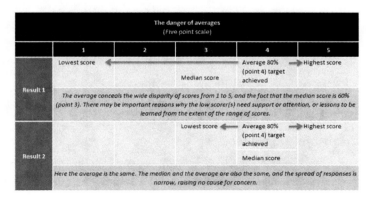

FIGURE 8.5

Put this information onto a bell-curve and it can be seen how far the averaged data (Figure 8.7) has moved the curve from the pattern of moderate expectations (Figure 8.6).

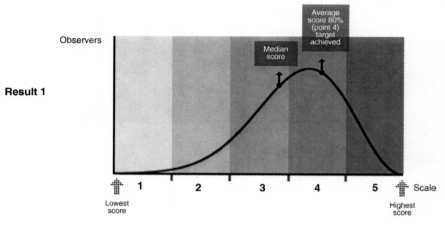

FIGURE 8.6

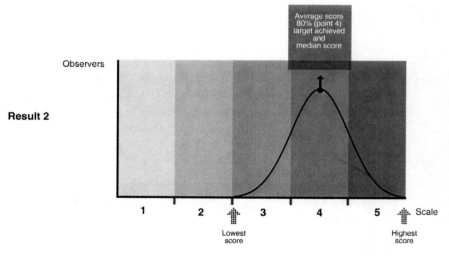

FIGURE 8.7

The relationship to application

The link between Levels 1 and 3 is clear. The direct link is through the planned actions that should show a clear alignment with our Level 3 objectives. If there are a clear set of actions at Level 1, they should be tracked at Level 3 and analysed for coherence with what was planned for our performance, implementation and/or behaviour change objectives. People confirm that they know what they should be doing, and then we can find out if they go ahead and do it. This is at its strongest where a formal process of action planning is integrated into the course or project work plan.

Getting Level 1 data from diverse settings: issues and options

The most common way of collecting data about engagement and planned actions is by survey or questionnaire. In our definition, a survey is comprised of closed questions, whereas a questionnaire may include both open and closed questions.

The advantage of surveys or questionnaires is that they enable you to ask the same questions in the same way again and again and again. This provides rich data of the type: 'Over the last 12 months our CPD events were scored on average 3.7 on a 5-point scale in terms of importance to the organisation.'

Advantages and disadvantages of surveys and questionnaires and ways to mitigate

Table 8.7 displays the most commonly mentioned advantages and disadvantages of surveys and questionnaires and suggests some ways of respectively benefitting from or mitigating these pros and cons.

TABLE 8.7

Advantages	Disadvantages	Ways to benefit/mitigate
Surveys are easy to distribute to a large number of people.	Closed questions limit the detail of data that can be collected.	Well-constructed questions with a range of answer options that can be correlated and cross-referenced can provide rich data sets.
Surveys are easy for a variety of people to respond to.	Surveys assume a level of literacy and cognitive ability.	When designing, consider the respondents. Use sounds, pictures, symbols and a variety of ways of communicating your questions and answers.
Surveys are extremely easy to collate and analyse.	Simplistic analysis can often lead to poor interpretation and misleading conclusions.	Design the collation tables, identify the questions you need to answer from the data. Before final sign-off, test the survey for its capacity to supply answers to all the questions.

(Continued)

TABLE 8.7 (Continued)

Advantages	Disadvantages	Ways to benefit/mitigate
Questionnaires offer the opportunity for richer and more considered and personalised responses.	Questionnaires can be difficult to analyse, especially where there are open, free-text responses. They can also be very time consuming and costly to analyse.	Consider your approach to data analysis when designing the questionnaire. Use reference statements, word or phrase identification and categories to support the analysis. Use open questions only when it is absolutely critical to do so.
Surveys, and sometimes questionnaires, can be low cost, enabling large amounts of data to be collected quickly and efficiently.	Analysis, design, development, testing and distribution costs can add significantly to the total cost.	Weigh up the balance between efficiency and effectiveness.
Surveys and questionnaires can be distributed again and again to provide large population data sets for analysis and comparisons. Repeating the same surveys again and again strengthens reliability.	When used for small populations and/or if not randomly sampled, they may suggest results that are true for only the specific respondents and cannot be considered valid to extrapolate for future planning, or to draw conclusions except for that specific population.	Try to generate responses from as close to 100% of the population as possible. Where this is not feasible, use random sampling. Check the potential margin for error based on the number of responses against the total population count. Always allow for a margin of error in your reporting.

You may decide that the direct use of a survey is inappropriate for certain populations. This occurs frequently when policy-related projects are being evaluated. Politicians and senior officials, even when they have attended briefing or demonstration events, often consider surveys or questionnaires inappropriate for themselves. This is fairly commonly overcome by conducting short, directed interviews, covering the same questions as those in a general survey or questionnaire. This can be effective, but the disadvantages are the time and cost involved in both conducting and then analysing the interviews, and so you should try to avoid open questions in order to be able to quickly and efficiently collate and analyse the data. That being said, once your questions have been answered it may be useful to take advantage of the opportunity to also collect individual personal observations.

Even simple paper-based surveys are sometimes too cumbersome in certain circumstances and would be difficult to complete, and liable to be ignored. This is rarely the case in courses, briefing sessions and conferences, but in other events it can be. For instance, in events where there is no opportunity to sit down and complete a survey, some other means needs to be found. Sometimes at exhibitions attendees might be asked as they leave to place their name badge or a business card in one of three receptacles: A – 'This event was very important to my organisation', B – 'This event was fairly important to my organisation' or C – 'This event was not important to my organisation'. Increasingly, people are being asked to communicate relatively simple Level 1 information via apps completed on tablet computers at the event or delivered to mobile devices.

Return to the unasked question

We began this chapter by referring to the important questions about engagement, buy-in and planned action that so often lie unasked while everyone worries too much about the housekeeping issues of whether or not everyone was comfortable and satisfied.

We end it by emphasising once more that this planning, monitoring and measurement approach is all about the human factor – tracking the progress of individuals and groups of colleagues as they try to achieve organisational objectives.

This can start only by collecting the data that confirms that they are fully engaged in the project from the start.

Motivation

The field of motivation has many theories and no agreement on a single phrase that defines the concept. However, there is some agreement that motivation includes the definition of principles that explain why people initiate, choose or persist in specific actions in particular circumstances. Therefore, statements about the needs and goals of the individual and the incentives in the environment are usually included in motivational formulations. There have been a number of trends in motivation research, including:

- *Experimental studies.* These are focused on the elements that drive behaviour, i.e. viscerogenic (e.g. hunger and thirst) rather than psychogenic (e.g. achievement and affiliative) needs, and have two main concepts: (1) hedonism (striving to increase pleasure and reduce pain) and (2) homeostasis (reaching a state of internal equilibrium).
- *Choice behaviour studies.* Since it is now generally accepted that living entities are always active, researchers in these studies are more interested in understanding what determines the direction of activity or choice. Some have proposed that choices are made as a result of evolutionary

(Continued)

(Continued)

theories, while others (expectancy-value theorists in particular) argue that an individual's choice is guided by what s/he will get and by the probability of getting it. The latter group focus on research that discovers the determinants of the expectancy of goal attainment and goal value.

- *Human motivation studies.* These studies focus on what is uniquely human, which is a desire to attain success, the pursuit of life goals and wanting to be judged as morally good, as well as focusing on individual differences in needs. The domain of 'achievement motivation' is an active area within motivation studies. It studies concepts such as self-efficacy (i.e. referring to beliefs about a person's ability to perform a task), intrinsic (versus extrinsic) motivation, mastery and learning (as opposed to ego and performance) goals, causal beliefs and achievement needs. Here, research suggests that having high self-efficacy, intrinsic motivation and mastery goals is desirable.

Studies of individual differences include the propensities to affiliate, aggress and attain power, as well as the more prominent need for achievement, anxiety and locus of control. Individuals with a high need for achievement are more likely to undertake achievement activities and particularly prefer tasks of intermediate difficulty. Anxiety is considered an inhibitor to motivation, while a belief that having personal control over events has been shown to relate to positive adaptation in stressful circumstances.

Studies that examine personal goals have found that pursuing a goal requires a constant inner representation of the goal pursuit (sometimes called 'current concern'). This directs a person's perceptions, emotional reactions, thoughts, dreams and behaviours toward the stimuli that are associated with the desired goal.

Goal-setting theory is an open motivation theory that involves limitless discoveries and integrations with other theories. Studies within this theory have shown that setting specific, high (hard) goals leads to a higher performance level on tasks than does setting easy, vague or abstract goals. There is also a positive, linear relationship between goal difficulty and task performance, as long as the individual is dedicated to the goal, has the required abilities to achieve it and has no conflicting goals. Having goals directs an individual's attention, effort and action toward goal-relevant actions at the expense of actions that have no relevance. There are four key moderators of goal setting:

1. feedback – to track progress
2. commitment to the goal – enhanced by self-efficacy and viewing the goal as important

3. task complexity – to the extent that task knowledge is harder to acquire on complex tasks
4. situational constraints.

Research has suggested that planning can facilitate self-regulation by transforming an abstract goal into more concrete actions for implementation of that goal. Recent research that probed the effect of goal distance and concrete implementation plans shows that when the goal distance is shorter, planning of concrete implementations may aid self-control. Therefore, making long-term goals appear shorter by breaking them down into smaller sub-goals and then focusing on achieving each sub-goal one at a time will be less daunting and distressing. Within education, a few studies have examined changes in goal achievement over time. They show that task goals tend to decline over time.

Sources: Hernandez et al. (2013); Locke and Latham (2006); Townsend and Liu (2012); Weiner (2000).

9

FULL COST

Even when there is no intention to report monetised benefits, there must always be a report of the full cost of any programme, project or activity. Any manager who does not understand the full cost of the activities for which they are responsible is not being completely accountable. An important part of this is the cost of people – the cost of their time. The fact that conventional accounting sees people in an organisation as a cost rather than an asset does not help with evaluation of the value of human capital improvement. But no list of costs is complete unless it includes the indirect cost of the time of those who have taken part in a course, an event or an activity. They are a cost to their organisation, and could have been doing something else productive. Reports of fully loaded costs are often a shock. They can be between three and ten times the direct costs of a course or activity. It is important to understand and plan for the key cost elements. Activity-based costing can make an important contribution to understanding and managing costs.

Full costs must always be reported

Unless we know what an investment has cost – the full cost of every input – any report of what it has achieved is incomplete. We will also have failed to place it in context. It is quite simple: without knowing full costs we cannot judge whether what has been achieved was worth it.

A definition of full costs

Total cost of all *resources* used or consumed in *production*, including direct, indirect, and *investing costs*.

Source: www.businessdictionary.com

The fact that we may often not be in a position to place a money value on the results we have achieved is not the point. Whatever we have achieved, whether we have been able to monetise it or not, we must always calculate, and be in a position to report, what it cost to achieve our results.

Let us say that we have improved the public estimation in which our organisation is held by a significant percentage. Are we to suppose that our colleagues in the organisation, no doubt thrilled with the improvement, will be so happy that they have no interest in what the achievement cost us? They will want to know if the cost was consistent with our strategic and operational goals or if it was so costly that it cannot be justified.

For a project or programme leader to fail to understand what a project or a programme cost is unprofessional. For an evaluator to fail to report full costs is simply unforgivable.

Imagine that you are evaluating a pilot project. You need to find out if it is worth replicating. If you cannot report full costs you will present an incomplete, and therefore misleading, picture of the results. It will be a faulty template for future planning. What will be the perceived benefits of projects if they hold out the prospect of replicating desirable results, but at a cost that turns out to be unrealistically low? This is especially important in social programmes and development projects. Here, some costs within a pilot are considered 'sunk'. We are told, 'This is what we do, so there is no need to add it as a cost'; or, 'The organisation already expects people to spend time on training so there is no need to include the cost of their time on this training.' We need to see the initiative, project or programme as an entity, and not as an extension of wider work or activity. At the outset we need a cost estimate. Later we need to know actual costs and who absorbed them, even if they were settled directly in cash or were represented as contributions in kind. Without this, we cannot offer any authoritative views on whether an activity should be continued, repeated or recommended to others as something worth doing.

This lack of realism is even further compounded when evaluators produce reports that compare incomplete costs with benefits that describe increased revenue. This is a cardinal error because it mistakes gross revenue for net value (gross revenue less the cost of achieving it). Net value may be called net profit, contribution or margin. Remember that different organisations use slightly different conventions for calculating their net value from operational activities.

To bring the example back to the issue of costs, consider an organisation that buys a training course for its sales staff for £10,000 and achieves increased revenues of £100,000 with profits of £20,000. This looks like a fairly good deal until the crucial indirect costs are taken into account, particularly the time of those attending the course. Assume that these indirect costs are at the lower end of the scale, and no more than three times the direct costs (£10,000 direct costs + £30,000 indirect costs = £40,000). This truer picture looks rather different, and is likely to raise questions about the feasibility of attaining a similar result without the expense of the face-to-face time of the sales force.

People as cost or asset

Perhaps one of the reasons why this principle has not always been, and still is not invariably, honoured is that, under accounting conventions, human capital does not appear on the balance sheet. It is seen as a cost rather than a benefit. It does not have an asset value, and therefore improvements to it, like increased levels of skill, are described as an expense.

This is controversial in many quarters. Two interesting approaches are worth noting.

- Hekimian and Jones (1967) suggested that a valuation could be arrived at through a bidding process. A department in an organisation would value its staff on the basis of what another department would be prepared to bid for each member. There are obvious links with the way professional football clubs value their players.
- Lev and Schwartz (1971) make their valuations based on future earnings, and do this through a formula that takes age into account.

It is easy to understand some of the objections to both approaches. In the case of the first, there is often real resistance to viewing people as a commodity. In the case of the second, many point out that employee earnings *are* a cost and that representing them as an asset is inherently illogical.

In the 1990s, there was an upsurge of interest in whether intangible assets, including people, could be included as an asset on the balance sheet. Much of this was driven by the dotcom boom and the value associated with many companies that were hugely in debt and showing no signs of becoming profitable. The bubble burst, and, with it, the apparent value of many of these firms. The debate receded and is raised from time to time in management literature and research papers, but there is little likelihood of change in the way people are accounted for by organisations.

In spite of the claim by many senior managers that, 'Our people are our greatest asset', staff remain firmly accounted for in the income and expenditure statements.

For something to be classified as an asset there are three key requirements:

1. it must be possible to identify future service potential
2. it needs to be measurable in monetary terms
3. it must be subject to the ownership and control of the organisation, or it is rented or leased.

The idea of rental and leasing is interesting because it comes closer than the bidding process above to recognising an organisation's relationship with its employees. It is also interesting that some organisations are now successfully recording the values of the leases of premises they do not own, but rent for their activities. However, people possess a characteristic that no building has: they have minds of their own, and can walk away. As we consider the cost of people as a part of our project costs, we need to recognise that they are accounted for on the income and expenditure statement and not on the balance sheet. We must also therefore note that, as a cost, they are accounted for in the time period in which we incurred that cost. Later in this chapter we will look at how costs can be spread over time and whether this should apply to the cost of people's time.

So, for the present, people remain a cost, not an asset. And in terms of our evaluation interests, while it remains often difficult to value human improvement, the cost of human time is one of the largest items in any project's expenses.

Finding the true costs

The World Health Organisation (WHO) estimates that about 284 million people are visually impaired, worldwide, with 90 per cent of them living in developing countries. Eighty per cent of all visual impairment is treatable or preventable. The goals of an initiative in sub-Saharan Africa have been to eliminate the main causes of avoidable blindness for 100 million people by the year 2020. This is a joint programme between WHO and the International Agency for the Prevention of Blindness. This programme is one of the initiatives working towards achieving this goal, facilitated under an international board.

The programme is a partnership initiative that seeks to *link* specialist or medical institutions in the UK with a training hospital or institution in the developing country to help build capacity for eye care in that country. The programme receives contributions to its funding from two international eye-care NGOs but has to raise the rest. Therefore, it is imperative that it can show the true costs for each link as well as the impact of these investments.

We worked with the team to establish a standardised way of collecting data across each link. During this exercise, the true cost of each link was estimated. The team identified that the full costs of each link included both direct costs (costs of administration and management travel, accommodation, evaluation cost etc.) and indirect costs (salary of participating teams such as specialists and trainees, use of hospital facilities for training for both parties etc.).

The shock of full costs

Managers and project leaders sometimes confuse budgets with forecasts of full costs. The difference between the two gets to the basics of reporting full costs.

A budget is a forecast of the money you will be obliged to pay out as a project or programme unfolds. A full cost forecast includes everything that is in a budget, but also reports the costs that will not be invoiced or necessarily appear on anyone's budget.

The most important, and generally the largest of these is the cost of the time of participants, trainees and managers.

Telecoms: calculating the full costs

A telecoms L&D management team designed the Sales Director programme for the most senior sales account directors in the organisation and senior sales professionals across the globe. The aim of the programme was to equip the team with the skills to develop and maintain executive-level relationships with target accounts. The team was trained on how to analyse its clients' overall business strategy, identify key business drivers as well as any potential for using the company's telecoms services to resolve clients' problems.

It was important for the Learning Management team to know if the programme was successful, and especially if it returned value for money, therefore it decided to undertake a full value-for-money evaluation. The evaluation showed an increase in gross revenues directly attributable to the programme. The project team leader consulted with the finance director to agree the contribution percentage from this revenue increase. The full costs (both direct and indirect) of the programme were calculated, including training partner development and delivery costs, programme management and evaluation costs, participants' travel costs, as well as the costs for participants' time. The L&D team reported conservatively and showed that the programme was indeed very successful with an ROI of over 150 per cent.

Sometimes, organisations working especially in social and economic development programmes receive benefit in kind; in other words, some of the costs of the project are provided by a government, donor or other partner. The fact that these costs have been contributed does not mean that they were not needed and so the financial worth of these costs *must* also be included in the project costs.

In organisations accustomed only to showing direct costs, finding out the full cost of projects can be a shock. The shock is likely to be most rude if there has been no serious attempt to estimate full costs in advance. Final full cost data will transform how the results are received by stakeholders.

This may reveal that the ratio of indirect to direct costs for projects is rather higher than the 3:1 used in the sales example above. It can go as high as 10:1. In an evaluation we carried out a few years ago, a leadership course for top managers in a very large organisation had a direct cost of £5 million. Once the indirect cost, including the significant management salaries, had been taken into account, the reported cost had risen to £20 million, a 4:1 ratio. This was a cost figure against which there was no robust evidence to show any organisational benefits or measurable operational, financial or strategic impact outcomes.

Defining costs

Table 9.1 shows how cost definitions relate to costs typically incurred in human capital projects and programmes. These definitions are useful both to enable project and programme managers to understand the nature of their costs and to equip them for communication and discussions with their senior managers and finance departments.

TABLE 9.1

Type of cost Classic definitions (from http://www. businessdictionary.com)	Comments on application to projects and programmes	Examples
Direct costs		
Expenses that can be traced directly to (or associated with) a specific cost centre or cost object (e.g. department, process, program or product).	In a project or programme these will include the fixed costs and many of the variable and semi-variable costs (see below).	Learning resources Trainer costs Evaluation costs Travel costs
Indirect costs		
Expenses incurred in joint usage (such as advertising, maintenance computing and security) and therefore difficult to assign to or identify with a specific cost centre or cost object.	In a project or programme these will be drawn in general from variable and semi-variable costs (see below). They include the cost of the time of workers and stakeholders taking part in training and preparation exercises. They may also include fixed research and development costs. For instance, if a number of programmes are being run that have been supported by common research and development work, it may be appropriate to apportion some of the R&D costs to each programme.	Hourly or daily employment costs of managers/ participants Research and development costs

You may find it helpful (or your finance department may require you) to define your direct and indirect costs more specifically, identifying fixed, variable and semi-variable elements.

Fixed costs		
Costs that remain more or less unchanged irrespective of the output level for goods or services of the organisation, often referred to as overhead cost.	In longer programmes, these may be spread over more than one year. But conventions differ from one organisation or financial regime to another. In some cases, it is practice to divide fixed costs equally between the years. In others, they are required to be loaded into the first year. One implication of this front-loading approach is that if a financial ROI is being calculated it will obviously be distorted, being much lower in the first year and rising in subsequent years.	Planning, research, evaluation, equipment such as simulation machines or computers for trainees

(continued)

TABLE 9.1 (Continued)

Type of cost Classic definitions (from http://www. businessdictionary.com)	Comments on application to projects and programmes	Examples
Variable costs		

Costs that change with the output level of the project.	Organisations often have their own rules about the apportionment of variable costs. If those don't exist it is important to decide on a convention, and to make clear what that is.	Participant time costs
		Consumables
		    including materials
		    costs

Semi-variable costs		

Costs that change with the output level of the project.	This definition can be useful when there is some limited flexibility. For example, the planned cost might be 1 manager to every 20 beneficiaries in a development project. In the case of a development site with 30 beneficiaries, there may need to be 2 managers even through the ratio to beneficiaries cannot be held to 1 : 20.	Room rentals
		Fees for trainers
		    or project team
		    leaders
		Administration costs

Cost elements

Many of the main cost elements are generic, but different programmes may also incur specific costs that need to be tracked (Table 9.2).

Some notes on cost categories

Research and planning. The time of those involved in identifying needs, building baselines, researching requirements, establishing scope and details, costing, agreeing main tasks and resources required, developing and testing tools, content, processes and everything else needed to start project implementation – all these need to be reflected. If they are not covered by salary costs that are already included, they must be noted separately.

Volunteers. Where individuals give of their own time with no charge to the project, there is no need to include their costs *unless* in future, in order to sustain the project, the same time would have to be paid for. In this case, the cost of the time should be included at the rate at which it would have to be paid for.

Facilities. Facilities costs may include: premises for meetings, events, learning and dissemination activities

Utilities (light, heat, communications charges). Again, any costs such as these must be included unless they are already included in the facilities or overhead charges.

Equipment. We need to include the costs of any equipment we buy. If we are using equipment already owned by the project partners, their depreciation may need to be taken on a fair pro-rated basis.

Transport, refreshments, accommodation, materials. All these are direct costs associated with our project and must be included.

TABLE 9.2

Some examples of cost headings and the types of projects and programmes to which they may apply

Training course	HR initiative	International development programme	Project	Marketing activity	Event, meeting or conference
Some specific costs					
Participants' time to attend Line managers' time to mentor new practice Backfill to allow participants to attend	Backfill to allow participants to attend Time for meetings, analysis of process for improvement, administration of activities Overhead contribution	Time of stakeholders who are not direct participants (e.g. officials' time and travel to attend meetings, or time costs when beneficiary participates in project instead of job role)	Backfill to allow participants to attend Time for activities that are specific to project	All time costs associated with activity, including research, analysis, communications, presentations etc.	Participants' time to attend Backfill to allow participants to attend
Refreshments/accommodation/travel etc.	Refreshments/accommodation/travel etc.	Refreshments/accommodation/travel etc.	Refreshments/accommodation/travel etc.	Refreshments/accommodation/travel etc.	Refreshments/accommodation/travel etc.
External or internal provider/facilitator costs	Project leader costs/costs of external experts/facilitator	Project leader costs/costs of external experts/facilitator	Project leader costs/costs of external experts/facilitator	Project leader costs/costs of external experts/facilitator	Project leader costs/costs of external experts/facilitator
Course, licence, equipment and exam fees	Licence/equipment fees	Participant fees, fees for use of tools, equipment costs	Licence/equipment fees	Licence/equipment/web-hosting fees	Conference/event fees

(Continued)

TABLE 9.2 (Continued)

Training course	HR initiative	International development programme	Project	Marketing activity	Event, meeting or conference
Some specific costs					
Administration, contribution to overhead, management information system costs		Other costs – applicable to all kinds of activities			
Some generic costs					

Evaluation

Share of unallocated overheads

Research

Planning and development

Facilities/equipment

Utilities

Materials

Travel and accommodation

Staff fully loaded employment costs

Value of time contributed by volunteers

Communications and publicity

Course and exam fees, legal and other fees. These are all direct costs that must be included.

Employment costs. One of the first surprises we had as evaluators was finding that some organisations had great difficulty in telling us what their employees' time cost. It's understandable that over time large organisations, in particular, develop complex structures. So you find people with job titles that suggest levels of status and responsibility – and therefore salary – that are not awarded in reality. The ultimate nightmare might be thought to be the Brazilian company Semco, which has no offices, no job titles, no organisational chart. Employees can choose their own salaries from eleven options. But as far as salaries go, Semco is transparent because everyone's pay is openly available online. Full employment costs may be more difficult to come by.

The point is that the enemies of gaining an accurate view of costs are complexity and lack of transparency. So often the evaluator will have to do some of the work her or himself.

Take note:

- the average working year should be used (for example, 220 days) unless particular contracts or conventions specify otherwise
- consider that a half-day programme usually involves a full day away from work, and what is being reflected here is the actual amount of time someone is away from their job when they could have been doing something productive for the organisation.

Backfill. In service organisations – public sector such as hospitals, private sector such as hotels and retail outlets – releasing staff for training is often only possible if backfill has been arranged. The cost of this backfill – the fully loaded employment costs of the replacement worker – becomes a part of the cost of the course in the same way as the fully loaded employment costs of all the attendees. Similarly, staff working on special projects which are not part of their everyday work may need to be replaced if they are not available to work. This may be the case for specialists working on volunteer or development projects such as the programme tackling blindness described on page 133. The clinician's employer may not be able to deliver patient services at home if the clinician is participating in such a programme and she or he may need to be replaced unless appointments are to be cancelled.

Calculating the full cost of training

A regional health authority running a major leadership programme commissioned an evaluation to determine the training's impact on service improvement using the abdi evaluation approach, which was already widely used across its region. This evaluation was required to include gathering data and reporting on the effectiveness, costs and value for money of the courses.

(Continued)

(Continued)

The evaluators identified the following direct and indirect cost categories:

- college course fees and registration and assessment fees
- the time for each of the participating organisation's programme managers to communicate, engage and support the participants and their line managers before, during and after the programme delivery
- the time of line managers to support and facilitate the participants to plan their learning, apply their learning and monitor and discuss the achievement of outcomes
- administrative support
- overhead allocation
- other consumables
- participant time (the participants attended face-to-face sessions in work time)
- participant travel costs (in some cases this was reimbursed by NHS Trusts)
- meals/refreshments
- venue costs for programme delivery
- health authority managers' and administrative time in planning, contracting, monitoring and reporting the pilot
- pilot evaluation costs
- the time for each organisation's programme managers to attend meetings with participating Trusts and the authority to plan, review and monitor the pilot programme
- managers' travel and subsistence costs for the pilot meetings and venue costs for hosting meetings.

As all those involved rapidly realised, these full costs had not been considered by most of the participating organisations before committing to any training programme, and the scale of the full costs was for many a great surprise.

Understanding and managing costs

As well as the resources we need to deploy in our projects, we need to consider when and how these costs are incurred and how we should treat them in our calculations.

Activity-Based Costing. One of the key benefits of understanding costs fully is to be in a position to use that knowledge to improve the way projects and activities are managed and resources utilised. This is greatly helped, however, by activity-based costing, which allocates costs to phases of a project, or to specific sets of tasks and activities within it.

Activity-based costing

The theory of activity-based costing (ABC) emerged in the mid-1980s to provide management with more detailed information about the costs of the activities involved in developing a product. The aim was to help managers make better decisions regarding the use of the organisation's resources by providing them with more reliable cost information. It was considered a more sophisticated approach when allocating overhead expenses to the activities and products that created these overheads.

The process involved tracing costs from resources to activities, then from activities to specific products or customers. Two types of costs were normally excluded – costs of excess capacity and research and development for new products. However, although the approach works well in limited contexts, it was often abandoned in large, complex contexts because of the costs and time required to implement it.

The concept itself is, however, very useful to managers as it provides a tool to help manage limited resources. Therefore, in an effort to encourage managers not to completely abandon the concept, the new time-driven ABC (TDABC) was developed in the late 1990s. Instead of assigning resource costs first to activities, then to products or customers, in TDABC the manager estimates the

1.   cost per time unit of capacity
2.   unit times of activities.

Previous capacity and activity levels can be used to generate these estimates.

The manager then calculates the 'cost-driver rate' by multiplying these two variables. This standard rate can now be assigned to products, customers or transactions. More complicated 'time equations' can be created to capture complex operations.

The information generated from this updated ABC helps managers to report costs of actual work activities and the time spent on each activity, as well as to identify how well capacity is being used. With time-driven ABC, reporting is on an on-going basis and so it also presents a more accurate picture of the organisation's performance.[1]

Activity–based costing as applied to a project or programme might, at its most basic, see costs forecast and then monitored against:

*   research and planning
*   set–up and inception
*   process and completing

- monitoring and reporting
- evaluation and next steps.

As the explanation above then makes clear, it can be used to dig further into the process of the activity to establish what it cost to repeat particular tasks and functions.

Since the whole of our approach to evaluation is based on planning and then tracking what people are able to do, what they actually do and the results they achieve from it, understanding the costs of the activities and the phases of activity they go through is entirely logical. ABC helps to plan the use of resources, and it helps everyone involved to understand how resources (including human resources) have been used, and how that might be improved.

We suggest that once a category-based cost forecast has been established, a parallel activity-based forecast is created. The graphic in Figure 9.1 shows how the costs might be allocated to activities.

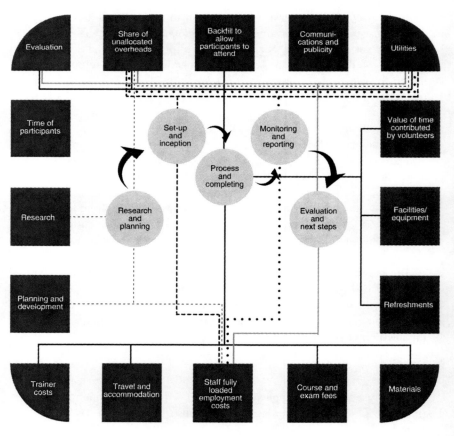

FIGURE 9.1

Allocating a proportion of unallocated overheads to a project

If you do not deploy TDABC, your organisation may not have a convention setting out the way in which unallocated overheads will be charged to various projects and programmes. Many organisations do, but, if not, it is easy enough to arrive at a formula.

Example: An HR department is managing a project which costs £50,000. The department has nine members (Figure 9.2).

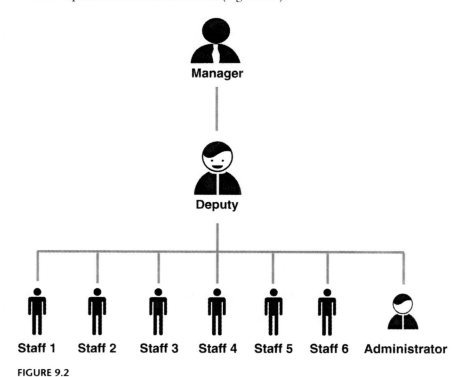

Manager

Deputy

Staff 1   **Staff 2**   **Staff 3**   **Staff 4**   **Staff 5**   **Staff 6**   **Administrator**

FIGURE 9.2

The full employment costs, including apportionment of fixed costs, are £495,000 a year.

The total of this overhead which has not been allocated to projects is £150,000.

In this case, it has been decided that, in addition to the £50,000 project costs, 8 per cent of the unallocated overhead should be attributed to it. The decision has been taken on the basis of the cost of the number of unallocated days available to the department (the total number of working days of all staff members not already allocated to specific projects) apportioned according to the value of each of the department's projects. In this case, that comes to £12,000 (8% of the unallocated overhead costs). So the full costs of the project are £62,000.

Treatment of fixed costs in projects

One of the issues which project managers and evaluators frequently encounter is that of allocation of fixed costs over the life of a project. This can obviously make a difference to the apparent value for money of the project.

Where these fixed costs are capital equipment, they will be treated like any other capital costs and depreciated over an agreed period. When calculating the ROI, the first year will include what has been allocated to that year, with the remainder on the balance sheet depreciating year on year until fully paid off.

However, some fixed costs will never be accorded a place on the balance sheet: in particular, human capital costs such as project planning and research time, materials development time and evaluation costs. These may be incurred before full project implementation. They will certainly be incurred in the first year. If these fixed costs are allocated to the first year, then any value-for-money (ROI) calculation will appear to be poor for that year, but proportionally better in subsequent years. The normal rule enforced by finance departments, and one to which we subscribe, is to record costs in the years in which they are incurred: in other words, when they are included in the costs that make up the income and expenditure accounts. If there are very large set-up costs, this can cause difficulties for the project team, who may feel that any value-for-money calculation in the very short term may show a loss. There may be a case for extending the period in which the ROI is measured (this is very common for projects such as IT investments).

Some other present and future cost issues
Benefit in kind

> 'The income from this training scheme was better than usual because we were lent the room, the lunches were free and the trainer was hired through a government grant. So we didn't incur any costs.'

How do we regard this statement?

The answer is that we disregard it.

First, the project needed these resources. These are necessary inputs. So whether they need to be paid for or not, they are still real costs to the project.

Second, some development projects have, in our experience, treated these contributions from donors and partners as income and, in doing so, believe that they have achieved an outcome by raising project investment. But income in kind of this sort is not a project outcome. It is a contribution towards offsetting costs.

Project teams need to know the equivalent cost of these contributions so that they can add those sums to the overall costs of the project in question. We then have an accurate view of the real cost of the activity. The fact that someone other than us paid the bill is neither here nor there.

Opportunity costs

We generally reject the idea of including the cost of potential lost revenue as part of the cost of, say, a training course. Why? Have you ever heard of a sales director saying, 'I'll reduce your sales targets so that you can attend training?' We certainly have not.

Some salespeople may disagree with us, but we all know that they have days when they sell little or nothing, and others when they make up a good deal of their monthly target. Who is to know which this will be? The fact is that they are expected to make up the loss, so adding lost opportunity costs in this case is not going to give a true picture.

Behind this lies our strong principle that evaluation should be based entirely on reality. So we neither deal in estimates of revenue lost, nor, when we come to calculate benefit, do we imagine what might have been gained. We measure it.

There may, of course, be some circumstances in which we should take lost revenue into account. For instance, if a motor mechanic takes a day away to train without backfill and there is a known throughput of cars for service it may be that fewer jobs can be accepted for that day and that week. That instance will represent a genuine loss for the organisation, and the value of those lost sales can be added as a cost. But – and this is a very important but – the loss to the organisation is not the total fees charged for the number of lost services. It is the margin or profit that would have been earned.

Note

1. Cooper and Kaplan (1988); Kaplan and Anderson (2004).

10

TRACKING

How to leverage data to improve the results

Active measurement ensures that evaluation is focused on improvement. This means that as we collect data, we report it and use the lessons to improve the activity we are evaluating. Level 1, buy-in data tells us if our key people are likely to do what we want of them. Level 2, learning and confidence data, tells us if they are able to do it. Level 3, performance and behaviour data, tells us if they are actually doing it in the way, to the standard and at the time required. Shortcomings in any of these may be able to be addressed, if spotted early enough. The chain of impact that is constructed from the data once the final impact outcomes have been measured provides what only this approach to evaluation can offer: data-led evidence showing how and why results were achieved (or were not achieved). This works only if data is collected and analysed at each of the levels.

Active measurement

Evaluation – measuring and reporting results – must be objective. But it cannot, in any kind of project activity, be detached from the need to drive constant improvement.

It's one of the oddities of working life that the attention given to collecting data for use in improving research, marketing, production and sales is rarely if ever matched by a similarly systematic concern with collecting and using data related to the improvement of human capacity and human capital projects. All too often there just isn't the data to support proposals and initiatives about how better to develop, organise and manage people.

In this, the public, the not-for-profit and the private sectors are equally lackadaisical.

Of course, huge investment and effort are put into human resource planning and improvement. But serial schemes, plans and tools, and their attendant expenditure, are generated, carried through and sometimes abandoned with little or no systematic reference to relevant prior data. Evidence of what went right or wrong in previous activities remains uncollected and unused.

Consider the checks we would routinely put in place if we deployed a new piece of kit or machinery. Less formally perhaps, the same would apply if, in our private lives, we purchased a piece of household equipment.

1. We have a clear idea of our needs and use requirement.
2. We would want to see the specification to ensure that it was apparently appropriate to our needs.
3. We would check that it was fit for the precise purpose and location we had in mind, and therefore was capable of doing the job for us.
4. Before we became irrevocably committed, we would need to see that it actually did what it was advertised to do.
5. We would normally consider one further option to compare the best value.

Only when we had seen evidence of all the above could we be confident that we were doing the right thing and could expect the result we wanted.

Once we had installed the equipment, we would consider whether it matched our needs and performed to our expectations. If not, we would complain or return it. We might realise we hadn't done enough good research and had bought something that didn't actually fit our needs or perform as expected.

That evidential process should be matched exactly in our management of projects, programmes, events, courses – all those initiatives and activities where the resource and/or the clients are people rather than machines or pieces of kit or software. Figure 10.1 shows how the type of evidence justifying a typical human capital investment compares to that which would relate to an investment in kit and machines. It is perfectly possible to collect hard data on both.

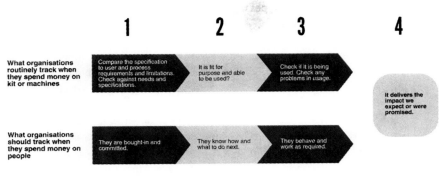

FIGURE 10.1

The simple illustration in Figure 10.1 suggests that we should think of our investment in people in much the same way as we think of our investment in kit and machines. But there is one respect in which we should think of it quite differently. Once we have bought a machine, we hope it will do what we intended of it. But we won't be able to do much to improve its performance or to make use of it in any context for which it wasn't designed.

We cannot easily remake and improve the machine once it is purchased and installed. But we can certainly do that with people, whether they are working independently or as part of teams.

We track and measure impact outcomes so that we can compare them to the money and effort we invested to achieve them. We gather data on the outcomes that create a chain of impact leading to final impact outcomes so that we can identify what went well and what did not. We can then ensure that we repeat the good and avoid repeating the bad. So a good evaluation collects real-time data about engagement, about acquisition and/or improvements in know-what, know-how and confidence and about behaviour and performance. We need data specifically relating to the population and context and we need to communicate this data immediately to those who can use it to improve the project's effectiveness and efficiency and improve our chances of achieving the ultimate impact outcomes.

Evaluation becomes a worthwhile activity when it becomes active – when it works for the positive outcomes that lie behind the investment or initiative that is being tracked.

Formative and summative evaluation

Evaluation can be defined as the systematic and objective assessment of an on-going or completed initiative (whether a project, programme or other type of intervention). It is carried out to determine the relevance, effectiveness and sustainability of the design, implementation and/or results of the initiative.

Although there are many types of evaluations, the two main types are formative and summative evaluation.

- *Formative* evaluation refers to evaluations that improve an initiative. It is focused on identifying and correcting implementation problems as the initiative is being carried out. Data collected during formative evaluation is used to monitor the progress of the initiative. Adjustments are made on the basis of the feedback received, which provides an early assessment of whether the desired outcomes are being achieved (or likely to be achieved). Formative evaluation improves the initiative's model and gets it stabilised and standardised for summative assessment.
- *Summative* evaluation is conducted upon completion of an initiative. It is carried out to determine whether to continue, expand or disseminate the

initiative's model. During summative evaluation, the model is tested to ascertain whether it produces the desired outcomes. It is also during this evaluation that observed outcomes are assessed as to whether they can be attributed to the initiative.

Sources: OECD (2002); Patton (2011).

This combination of process and impact evaluation in no way implies less rigour or objectivity. Quite the contrary; it places greater emphasis on the need to provide quality decision-making data so that improvements can be applied.

The chain of impact

We assemble that data in a chain of impact that follows the logic model and that is constructed to mirror the way in which people participate in the activities and journey that are their project. To understand fully what is going on with the chain of impact, all we have to do is imagine that we are setting a family member or close friend a daunting and demanding task. What is the first question we would ask?

Buy-in

Of course we'd find an appropriate way of asking if they were willing to take it on. If they didn't believe it was worth doing, there would be no point in pursuing the idea any further. We might want to test their commitment in a number of ways. They need to know and share the commitment to achieving the ultimate outcomes. They need to signal if there is any reason why they cannot or will not undertake the activities to achieve these results. They need to believe they can do it and be prepared to learn how to do it. And we need to know what might influence them to lose commitment or fail to carry out the tasks or activities planned.

We should behave in exactly the same way in any kind of business project or challenge. Before proceeding we should be clear that the key people involved are engaged and committed and have a clear idea of what they are going to need to do next.

If we find out that they are not, or not to the extent that we need, we have two choices.

1. We can take steps to bolster their engagement, maybe by emphasising the importance of our project or activity to them and their colleagues.
2. We can decide that they are not the right people to do this and either abandon the idea or find others who are more suitable.

If the data and information we gather from them is positive, or if we satisfactorily deal with their issues, we've assured the first link in our chain of impact (Figure 10.2).

Find out if the people who are important to you have bought in to what you need them to do.

If they have doubts about the rightness or feasibility these need to be addressed immediately.

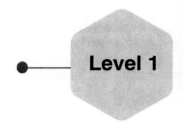

FIGURE 10.2

If, at this stage, we've decided to abandon our project, at least we have been able to do it early, without too much money wasted – far less, at any rate, than if we had pushed on and later discovered that failure was caused by a problem we should have been able to identify right at the beginning.

How might we collect our data on 'engagement'?

As the source of engagement data is the individuals that we want to ensure are engaged, we need to ask them!

We can talk to them face to face or by telephone and ask them some standardised questions to which we record the answers.

We can survey them through a paper-based or electronically delivered survey instrument.

The data–collection instruments don't need to be boring! But they do need to be developed in ways that ensure the collection of valid and reliable data. Graphics/images/sound/video and text can all be used in data collection.

The process of building the data collection method and instrument and the approach to collation and analysis need to be considered carefully and together. The steps in designing and developing, testing, distributing, collecting, collation, analysis and reporting need to be specified and the tasks allocated to those responsible. Those with tasks need to be selected for their skills and be provided with the know-how, and must know what to do, when and under what conditions and to what standard. A surprising number of people think that designing surveys is simple and can be done using 'common sense'. We can all look around and see shocking examples of poorly designed instruments that deliver responses that are neither valid nor reliable.

Know-how and know-what

Back to our family member or close friend. Our next concern would be whether they know what to do and how to perform their allotted tasks and/or behave as expected.

Again, the question in a business or operational context is precisely the same. And if we gather data and evidence that shows people do not have the know-how or know what to do at the expected standard or do not exhibit an attitude that gives us confidence that their behaviour will change, we have data that enables us to intervene immediately with what will be needed if they are to implement activities and improvements in performance and behaviours.

How do we collect evidence of changes in knowledge, skills and attitudes?

There is a vast body of literature and examples of ways to evidence changes in knowledge, skills and attitudes (KSA). Some approaches derive from traditional educational assessment. These tend to be more appropriate for knowledge assessment (exams, tests) and it is important to consider whether they are norm based (common in wider education systems) or criteria based. For human capital investments, and to evidence changes in adults' KSA, we should deploy criteria-based assessment. This means that our approach and associated instruments should be founded on explicit criteria which deliver evidence that people know something quite specific, can do something to a set standard and demonstrate an attitude within a context or circumstances that can be objectively observed (Figure 10.3).

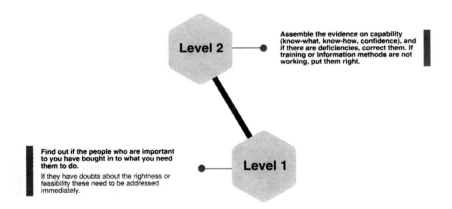

FIGURE 10.3

But a further vital check still needs to be made.

Implementation of tasks and changes in performance and behaviour in real conditions

Back to our family and friend example. We may know they're enthusiastic to perform this daunting task for us. We may be satisfied that they have the knowledge and the skills to get through it. But in the testing conditions they're going to meet, will they actually apply the skills that we know they have? Will something we hadn't thought of prevent them? How can we know that they are actually doing it?

Similarly at work, we need to be sure that our people actually do what we want them to do. After all, we designed our project. Resources have been devoted to making sure that they are prepared to do it.

When people go to carry out their tasks, implement change or behave differently, we need to comprehend what actually happens, if it happens in the way that we expect and to the standard that has been set. And if not, why?

People may simply not be applying enough of their knowledge and skill. The capability they showed in training may now be only partly remembered. We may have assumed they had the information they needed and would be able to recall it, but neither was the case. Or there may be other problems: uncooperative or ill-informed colleagues, poor equipment, unexpected barriers. These can all be addressed, at least to some extent, so long as data and information are gathered to reveal what happened.

This third link in the chain of impact is, in many ways, the most crucial (Figure 10.4). It looks early on in the project at task implementation, performance improvement and behaviour change and provides an opportunity to improve these as the project unfolds.

It is also generally the least well understood, and the least well done.

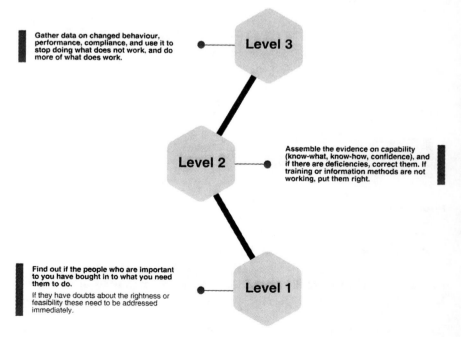

FIGURE 10.4

Data collection methods and instruments

Implementation data is often the most difficult to collect. As often as not this is because the descriptors of tasks, completion, performance indicators or behavioural standards have not been properly established and recorded at the planning stage.

Where the indicators and descriptors have been agreed and are SMART, recording is usually simply a matter of ensuring that the monitoring records are embedded within the project itself. For example, if you require someone to complete a task, you can develop a simple instrument or check-list to record that it has been done, and then capture the evidence. If you want someone to behave in a certain way, for example with customers, you can either calibrate the descriptors of behaviours with an existing instrument (for example a mystery shop-monitoring instrument) or use the descriptors to build an instrument that a line manager can use on a frequent and regular basis.

The most effective and efficient data-collection approaches at this level embed records of implementation, task completion and performance monitoring within the project plan at the start. If these already exist, you need to check that they are consistent with your outcomes. If they do not exist, you can build them so that they act as a performance support or job aid for whoever is expected to complete the task or undertake the change. Once the individual discovers that they are useful, he or she will use them as a reminder and record. You then need simply to agree when you will review the record and collect the evidence.

Existing systems may generate reports: 360 reviews and call monitoring are two examples. For projects funded from the public purse you may already be required to complete templates of work completed and to provide supporting evidence that it is to the required standard.

Tracking the implementation of a Funding, Monitoring and Evaluation Framework

A devolved government programme set out to reshape care for older people by shifting the balance of care from acute/care home settings into the community. As part of this programme, a change team in one area was obliged to provide evidence on the use of the change fund in meeting the objectives outlined in this change plan. It developed an integrated Funding, Monitoring and Evaluation Framework. This Framework would be made available to project leads who applied for funding from the health, local authority, third and independent sectors. The change team uses the framework to assess project applications, monitor progress and evaluate the success of each project.

The chain of impact can be tracked through the following levels.

(Continued)

(Continued)

- Level 1: the Framework is considered user-friendly by at least 80 per cent of project leads.
- Level 2: project leads and stakeholders wishing to apply for project funding are able to use the Framework to apply for funding and to provide monitoring data that meet the objectives of the change plan.
- Level 3: two months after implementation, 100 per cent of project leads are completing their applications and monitoring returns that reflect the Framework.
- Level 4: 100 per cent of projects adhere to the quarterly, six-monthly and annual monitoring plan outlined in the Framework.

Since monitoring is carried out quarterly, six-monthly and annually, the data it provides gives an early indication of the likelihood of the projects meeting their objectives, thereby giving project leaders the opportunity to implement changes, if required.

Of course, you can use other approaches: you can ask people about what they have done or changed. However, this is often very weak. It may not be possible to support statements with evidence. Ideally, if you do ask them, or their line managers or colleagues, you will want to seek supporting evidence. You can do this through one-to-one or group interviews, focus groups, questionnaires and surveys, assignment or action plan reports and portfolio 'books of evidence'.

Technology can assist greatly, as a job aid or performance support and also as a source of data. It can be used to organise, expedite and analyse surveys and questionnaires. And, as we have already noted, questions do not always have to be put through the medium of text. Visual images, as well as audio and video responses, can be collected. But the design, development and testing of these instruments must be done by professionals and accompanied by required additional templates, a step-by-step process and assignment of responsibilities. Timing must always be planned in advance.

Interviews and focus groups, while extremely useful to probe and deepen the opportunity for analysis, can be very costly and, most of all, need expert involvement: they are not for amateurs. We generally advise using them as a follow-up to the collection of data through some other means and to help explore and interpret the results.

Our experience overall is that there is a tendency to fall back on traditional methods such as questionnaires or surveys, which yield limited responses and, because the respondent does not see any benefit in completing, deliver unreliable data. We have found that when we suggest more creative and embedded ways to collect data these are seized on, though some are rightly cautious until they see that underlying rigour has not been sacrificed in pursuit of responder engagement.

But even at this stage there is still a further opportunity to collect more useful data, and to use it to improve our chances of overall success.

Early achievement

This may not be available in our family and friend example. We may not know the ultimate results of their mission until it has been completed.

But in the working world, experienced project teams will have taken the extra precaution of identifying 'milestones' that indicate progress towards final impact outcomes and arranging to collect data that will indicate if the project is likely to be on course to achieve its desired end result.

If these milestones are all met, then all well and good.

But if they are not, it may still be possible to take remedial, reinforcing or even evading action to improve the end result.

This provides the fourth link in the chain (Figure 10.5).

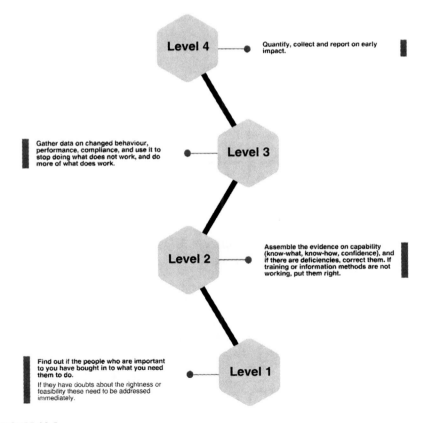

FIGURE 10.5

In an ideal world, no impact–outcome improvement objective will have been planned unless measurable data of achievement, including baseline data, already exists.

In different settings this might include:

- number of daily unit sales of product X
- number of customer complaints per month
- number of surgical procures in an operating theatre in a 24-hour period
- student grades in freshman year in a subject
- percentage deterioration in water quality year on year
- increase in brand awareness
- improvement in employee satisfaction ratings.

Where these outcomes are already monitored, data will come from the existing information systems.

In the next chapter, we look in more detail at the measurement of results when the agreed point for final reporting arrives. In the meantime, we recommend that these are monitored on a regular basis so that there are no surprises at the end.

We do not live in an ideal world and sometimes our objectives break new ground. We may be monitoring the number of citizens in a specific geographic area who willingly and intentionally die at home, rather than in a hospital or hospice. We may not have existing data on this. So, very early in our project we will have to collect 'baseline' data so that we can use the project to establish a new indicator to show whether or not there is any evidence of care being improved over time.

Another example. We may not have a rating on our customers' perceptions of the quality of our product. We may need to establish a baseline, again early in our project. This may involve us in asking product purchasers to rate our products against those of our competitors.

Although it is not strictly monitoring, building baseline data in the absence of existing indicators may be an essential milestone in the very early stages of our project. We will then be in a position to monitor any changes from the baseline. This may be imperfect, but it is sometimes a necessary step in the journey towards improving our overall measurement practice.

Using the chain

The following examples, composites from a large number of projects worked on by our students over a number of years, show the chain of impact as a reporting structure for data gathered from a wide range of contexts.

Example 1 (Figure 10.6)

We have 50 staff participating in a training course designed to get a team that interfaces regularly with the public to adopt a new web-based tool for managing responses to comments, requests and complaints. It is important because the current system is far too hit-and-miss, with the result that public perception of our operation has been growing more negative for some time. The tool needs to be secured on licence for each user. The costs of this, and the training to ensure that it is properly used, are fairly high but, if public perceptions become more positive, it will be justified. We've targeted an improvement of 5 points (from number 12 to number 7) in our rankings across the sector.

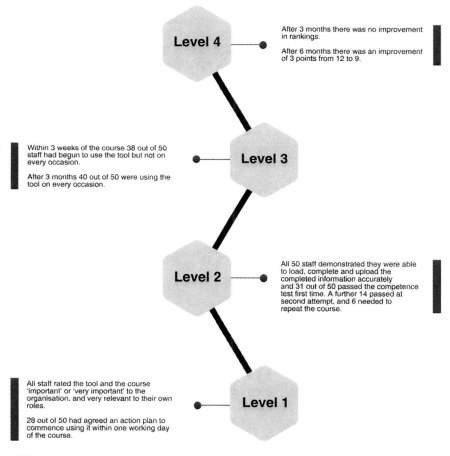

FIGURE 10.6

What does Figure 10.6 tell us?

1. We noticed a problem at the start, when 22 of the 50 participants had no commitment to commence using the tool. This should be investigated.
2. Many needed to sit the test more than once, and six had to repeat the course before they were able to load, complete the data record and upload the record into the system without error.

3. After three weeks 12 staff were still not using the tool. And even after three months 10 staff were still not using it on every occasion. This needed investigation.
4. So it wasn't a surprise when the three- and six-month public ranking changes were below expectation and suggested that we would struggle to meet our end-of-year target.

Example 2 (Figure 10.7)

This project piloted a new maths curriculum in early primary education which would ultimately be rolled out in five regions of a developing country. The pilot was in one region and its results were reviewed before any further activity. This took six months. The systemic change was Level 4 (legacy). This was a milestone towards the ultimate goal of improving student attainment in maths. It would be at least five years before improvement would be evident in scores. So a milestone was set for 80 per cent of participating schools to have at least one teacher delivering the new curriculum to the required standard after one year. This was used to monitor the potential for achieving the ultimate goal.

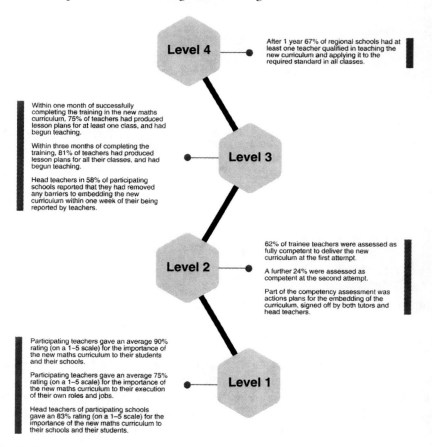

Level 4

After 1 year 67% of regional schools had at least one teacher qualified in teaching the new curriculum and applying it to the required standard in all classes.

Within one month of successfully completing the training in the new maths curriculum, 75% of teachers had produced lesson plans for at least one class, and had begun teaching.

Within three months of completing the training, 81% of teachers had produced lesson plans for all their classes, and had begun teaching.

Head teachers in 58% of participating schools reported that they had removed any barriers to embedding the new curriculum within one week of their being reported by teachers.

Level 3

62% of trainee teachers were assessed as fully competent to deliver the new curriculum at the first attempt.

A further 24% were assessed as competent at the second attempt.

Part of the competency assessment was actions plans for the embedding of the curriculum, signed off by both tutors and head teachers.

Level 2

Participating teachers gave an average 90% rating (on a 1–5 scale) for the importance of the new maths curriculum to their students and their schools.

Participating teachers gave an average 75% rating (on a 1–5 scale) for the importance of the new maths curriculum to their execution of their own roles and jobs.

Head teachers of participating schools gave an 83% rating (on a 1–5 scale) for the importance of the new maths curriculum to their schools and their students.

Level 1

FIGURE 10.7

What does Figure 10.7 tell us?

1. There were no apparent problems with regard to the commitment and buy-in of the teachers, or of their head teachers.
2. At Level 2 (learning, competence and confidence), the number of teachers assessed as competent on the first attempt was lower than expected, and even after the second attempt 14 per cent of those trained were still not seen as competent.
3. Three sets of problems emerged at Level 3 (application).

    a. The percentage of trained teachers beginning the embedding of the new curriculum after one month was lower than deemed necessary.
    b. The same was true after three months.
    c. It appeared either that the head teachers in some schools had encountered some unexpectedly difficult obstacles, or the priority they were giving to the embedding of the new curriculum had slipped.

4. At Level 4 (impact and legacy) the first year's target was missed. Was this by so much that the ultimate legacy target would have to be revised? Would changes in support for embedding have to be made? Was the training meeting the standard?

Example 3 (Figure 10.8)

We are reorganising our sales operation from a single department into five teams. This has proved hard to manage and has underperformed on revenue targets against plans by 10 per cent. Each will have a team leader answerable to a departmental manager. The individuals in the teams will have more responsibility than before and the teams will have a certain degree of autonomy within an overall set of plans and key performance objectives.

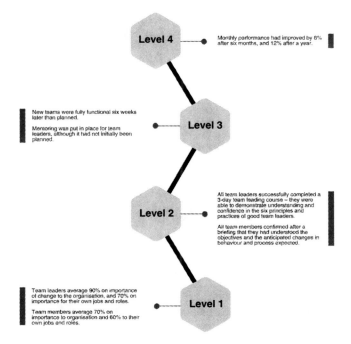

FIGURE 10.8

What does Figure 10.8 tell us?

1. We discovered at the end of the team leader training that although the team leaders saw the importance of the reorganisation, and had successfully completed the training, they were still uneasy about their own roles.
2. There was no evidence in the Level 2 data to conclude that they had failed to learn as expected. They had also been able to demonstrate confidence through role-play.
3. There was a delay (Level 3) in the full functioning of the teams. The introduction of mentoring seems to have been a response partly to insecure personal buy-in, and perhaps partly to barriers encountered in making behaviour and process changes.

Only the complete chain works

As these examples demonstrate, when data is collected throughout the chain, it becomes possible to begin to see the results of an investment or project in something approaching real time.

- Levels 1 and 2 provide evidence of buy-in and know-how/know-what more or less at the same time – generally Level 1 is collected as early in the intervention as possible, and possibly again over the early lifetime of the project in order to monitor early and on-going engagement.
- Level 3 provides – so long as SMART and appropriate objectives have been set – very early indications of task application, improvements in performance and changes in behaviour. If the results of, say, training are being tracked, then they should report settled behaviour. If some form of compliance or performance to a standard is being tracked, then the results focus on the quality and level of performance against a clear benchmark and might need to be monitored after some time has elapsed to see if sustained change has occurred.
- Early Level 4 results can show the first evidence of impact.
- But none of these can be interpreted on its own because it might lead us to the wrong conclusions.

Disappointing early impact results might be due to weak know-how, or unexpected barriers at Level 3. But it might also be worth investigating whether the assumptions about the connections between performance change and task implementation were correct and/or our timing expectations were over optimistic.

Only data collected at each of the levels can eliminate the possibility that there may be several causes of poor results: poor performance, weak skills and problems of commitment.

The positive

We tend initially to frame these discussions about the use of the chain of impact around its use for detecting problems and errors.

But it is, of course, equally powerful and important for identifying strengths and showing how they can be capitalised on.

Example 4 (Figure 10.9)

We have decided to bring our sales procedure up to date, with a new online tool and an updated sales process. This is being trialled with one of five sales teams in the organisation, with the intention that it will be rolled out as soon as possible. The purpose is to have a single tool and approach on which all team members are trained (which has not been the case up to now), to increase the efficiency and effectiveness with which enquiries are handled and progressed through the sales cycle, and to assure that the correct advice is given to customers on what they should order. If this happens it should result in improved sales, customers more satisfied with the customer experience and many fewer goods returned because they were not what the customer wanted.

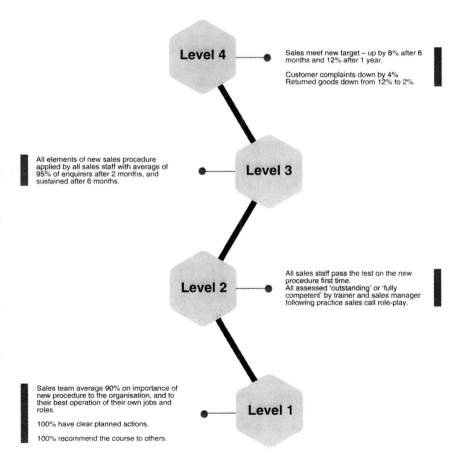

Level 4 — Sales meet new target – up by 8% after 6 months and 12% after 1 year.

Customer complaints down by 4% Returned goods down from 12% to 2%.

All elements of new sales procedure applied by all sales staff with average of 95% of enquirers after 2 months, and sustained after 6 months. — **Level 3**

Level 2 — All sales staff pass the test on the new procedure first time. All assessed 'outstanding' or 'fully competent' by trainer and sales manager following practice sales call role-play.

Sales team average 90% on importance of new procedure to the organisation, and to their best operation of their own jobs and roles.

100% have clear planned actions.

100% recommend the course to others. — **Level 1**

FIGURE 10.9

What does Figure 10.9 tell us?

1. The very strong level of buy-in at Level 1 told us that the sales procedure was acceptable to the sales team and that the course was going to get a positive report from them when other colleagues received it.
2. The Level 2 results – particularly because the sales manager was involved in assessing the role-play – provided strong confirmation that the course was fit for purpose and could be rolled out without further changes. This, and the Level 1 results, also built confidence in the outside organisation which had been contracted to do the training, and it was immediately invited to make proposals for new courses in stock control and project planning.
3. After two months the organisation could see from the Level 3 results that the planned changes in staff's behaviour as they applied the procedure had in fact taken place. On this basis it was able to give the go-ahead for the other four sales teams to be introduced to the procedure and given the course.
4. All the teams had been trained by the time that the Level 4 impacts began to be seen at six months. The sales manager was able to report to the board that the new procedure and the course had provided excellent value for money and that the early data collected had enabled the whole process of training the five teams to be accelerated with confidence.

Continuously monitoring the data in a world hotel chain

The chain operates a large number of properties in North America, Europe, the Middle East and Asia. As part of its mission to offer the highest-quality products and services, its Learning and Education department is offering the Certificate in Professional Bartending course to its bartenders. However, to be selected for the course, learners must have passed the initial interview and pre-examination, had a follow-up interview with the Hotels Executive Committee and attained above-average ratings on their most recent Performance Development Review.

Following training, the bartenders go back to their hotels and, with the support of their Director of Food and Beverage (DOFB) and the other bartenders, continuously create new beverage concoctions. Monitoring and evaluating the impact of this training course includes:

- Level 1: engaging the bartenders – the head bartenders are to agree to compiling two new recipes each month, keeping a record in their Menu Engineering Reports.
- Level 2: learning – bi-monthly training of bartenders, who will be measured on specific skills, e.g. timed preparation of cocktails, tests on product

knowledge and simulation exercises describing complete recipes. These will be recorded in the Bartender Training Reports.

- Level 3: implementing learning – the head bartenders must visit their local market to identify new ingredients, keep a record in their Market Visitation Logs, liaise with spirit suppliers to identify the top two current brands and introduce cocktails to 30 per cent of guests.
- Level 4: business impact – increase in the average revenue percentage ratio food : drink.

Check-list

Table 10.1 provides a check-list of some of the uses to which early data at each of the levels can be put, and some caveats to ensure that too much isn't read into these early reports.

TABLE 10.1

Level		Caveats
4	Improved efficiency Improved effectiveness	These measures may all, in some circumstances, be subject to seasonal and financial cycle variations, so short-term data can be misleading.
	Customer or client satisfaction Staff satisfaction	Even if no month-on-month variations are anticipated, remember that whenever we form a conclusion on the basis of limited and short-term data we are in effect suggesting a trend and projecting it in our own minds into the future. We know that the projection may be risky, but we may trust it so long as we believe that a trend has been established. None of this is safe unless we are satisfied that we have collected enough data to provide some evidence to support our confidence. This is made much easier if we have set short-term impact objectives on the basis of what we expect to have achieved by a certain time (after 3 months, after 6 months . . .). We have then thought out in advance how we expect the trend to have developed.
	Progress towards organisational compliance or improved status	This will normally be based on aggregation of data from Level 3, so it should be dependable – but needs to be monitored for sustainability.
3	Tasks performed Behaviour changed Individual compliance – operating to standard	Assuming that Level 3 objectives have been constructed to answer the questions, 'Who?', 'What?', 'When?' and 'To what standard?' the caveat regarding early Level 3 data is whether it reflects settled behaviour. Unless it can be shown that what has been reported is overwhelmingly likely to be repeated and sustained, it will be of limited value.

(continued)

TABLE 10.1 (Continued)

Level		Caveats
2	Improved knowledge Improved skills Improved confidence	In an operational context there is always a danger that a taught course or a briefing session or a piece of role-play may not be the true end of the learning (Level 2) activity. It may continue through some on-the-job learning. Therefore, if Level 2 results are reported too early, there is always a danger that the results of classroom or e-learning may be reported but not reflect improvements that come from practice and from improvements in confidence.
		Apparent changes in attitude can occur when someone knows they are being observed and follows 'good practice'. This does not necessarily mean that they will do the same when it is 'business as usual'. We need to be careful that we measure what is important to changes in performance and behaviour or to the information and process steps that we need someone to know so as to complete a task. Having a good result on an assessment of knowledge may not tell us that a person is actually able to do something to the standard. Knowing what and knowing how are different!
1	Importance to organisation Relevance to role/job Recommend to others	No caveats – these only provide early data. That is their importance.
	Clear planned actions	These are of significance only if they are clearly relevant both to what is learned at Level 2, and to what is expected to be done at Level 3. The capacity to name planned actions is itself of only general significance.

11

MEASURING IMPACT

Impact outcomes need to be sustainable in order to be worthwhile. Temporary peaks in achieve-ment are rarely of much significance. Impact outcome data will come from one of six broad groups of outcomes, and the information will generally be held centrally within organisations. This may often be harder to access than expected, or than should be the case. Access to it may well need to be signalled and negotiated in advance – at the planning stage of the project, programme or activity in question. Many organisations now use dashboards and scorecards for reporting – the Balanced Scorecard is popular and useful. Alerting those responsible for compiling these scorecards, and understanding the limited responsibilities of contractors and sub-contractors, are important aspects of planning impact measurement.

What are impact outcomes?

Impact outcomes are the eventual and sustainable changes resulting from the ini-tiative, project or activity that is being evaluated. Two words are important here: 'eventual' and 'sustainable'.

'Eventual' is not a scientific word, but it does describe changes that take place as a result of a process or a series of activities. In other words, it describes the final link in the chain through engagement, learning, performance and behaviour change to reach the level where we can answer the question, 'Did we achieve the impact that we set out at the start as being the reason why we were making the investment?'

Sustainability is very important. In any operational context, improvements in impact outcomes will give the greatest value if they can be maintained or even improved on. Of course, we may get our value for money from a short period when the impact outcomes far outweigh the costs. But for most organisations, impact outcomes are intended to deliver sustained and sustainable change.

Temporary peaks in achievement are rarely of much use. Here the link with the data gathered at Level 3 is crucial. True value is only likely to come from sustained and consistent changes in performance and behaviour.

So an impact outcome that is measured once and never again needs to be treated with suspicion. It may simply reflect a false peak. It may disguise a trend that is still going in the wrong direction. In fact, using trends to confirm impact is often very good practice. The point at which a series of good and sustained results ensures that an annual trend is now heading in the right direction is far more likely to signal significant achievement than any number of isolated small peaks in results. Of course, some trends will eventually come to an end. A reduction of customer complaints to zero cannot be improved on! But if our project delivers this result, that's what we want to sustain.

The lesson for us is that no single piece of data should be taken solely on its face value. The evaluator must always look for evidence of sustained results, and must always have an eye on trends.

The idea of legacy as impact

Our experience of many social and policy change projects is that, in many cases, the aim is to deliver a 'systems' change. For example, a new standard of quality in school meals, or perhaps a new directive by a ministry of education to implement equality of access to education, regardless of gender.

This idea of legacy has also, of course, to be sustained and sustainable. One policy maker saying that they support a change is weak evidence of sustained change. The change must be embedded into the 'systems'.

Measuring the impact of social change

Measuring the impact of social change is one of the most challenging evaluation activities. However, it can be done successfully. An international development project aimed to develop greater participation by citizens in a country that had been involved in conflict and political restructuring. Recognising that people had become more connected than ever before, through culture, politics and economics, the project's guiding principle was 'globally connected, locally engaged'. It aimed to make a positive contribution to social change by developing a global network of influencers who learned to address global and local issues together.

The evaluation objectives were:

- to establish the efficacy of the project design to deliver positive social change within six months of the end of the project
- over twelve months, to identify good practices of social and cultural influences that contributed to a 'tipping point' for increasing the number of community members developing and/or delivering fresh social actions as a direct result of their experience with the project.

Do we know what really caused our impact outcomes?

In addition to knowing how single items of impact data can deceive us as to their true significance, there is something further to consider before we can feel confident that our investment has achieved a result.

This is the possibility that some or all of our impact may have been caused by something other than the investment we are evaluating.

Dealing with other factors

These changes can be positive or negative, intended or unintended, and/or primary or secondary. These outcomes are ascertained in impact evaluations, which are focused on determining the ultimate impact results of an initiative on the organisation and/or community.

When we are assessing human capital initiatives, invariably other factors will also influence the results. Therefore, it is important that impact assessments include isolation of the factors that contribute to the results, and attribute to the initiative only those factors that can be linked to it. The chain of impact (also called the causal impact chain) is used to 'prove' the links between the inputs of the initiative and the ultimate outcomes. It is more challenging to prove impact outcomes, since the results are sometimes achieved long after the initiative is completed.

Sources: Herzberg (2008); OECD (2002).

Isolation and attribution are the subjects of Chapter 12. For the rest of this chapter, we will continue to consider the collection and analysis of impact data.

Finding impact outcome data

In Chapter 4, we discussed setting impact objectives, and divided them into six principal groups:

- achieved operational targets (including efficiency)
- improved financial performance
- successful and sustained innovation
- achieved organisational compliance
- enhanced reputation (internal and external)
- attributable legacy.

Using these convenient classifications we can look at common data sources and some of the practical and professional issues that project managers and evaluators face as they gather impact data and use it for measurement.

The main sources of data for each of these groups are likely to be found in the records of the organisations, companies and projects behind the activities that are being evaluated. For instance, in large companies and organisations the financial and performance data should be recorded by the relevant departments and stored by them or in the organisation's Management Information Systems (MIS). It should then should be recorded on whatever form of dashboard is used for regular reporting.

In smaller organisations – public and private or not-for-profit – the same should apply, and often does. But in many cases, where planning is more intuitive and systems are less developed, data is likely to be harder to locate. Cultures and systems differ widely in organisations, and this has a powerful effect on the way in which plans are laid and results are recorded and reported.

Financial data is often hard to find

Financial data should be the easiest to find. However, our experience is that this may be more difficult than is at first assumed. Someone working in the HR department of a company may not have access to data on overall income and expenditure, or to that of other departments.

This needs to be understood and discussed at the project-planning stage, especially when targets for increased sales, improved margins, operating efficiencies or reduced costs are amongst the objectives of the project. Furthermore, it is essential to understand that, for example, increased revenues may be due to multiple products, services and influences. The project in question may be measuring the effect of only one or two of these. It may not be a straightforward matter to get access to the full breakdown of the sales improvement and specific additional revenue earned. It may well have to be negotiated well in advance. The same may be true of full cost breakdowns.

Difficulties may also arise when it comes to slicing and dicing income and expenditure across departments, and even across regions and countries.

Although these sound like difficulties, they are really valuable to consider because any project owner, if she or he is to be held accountable for the achievement of planned impact objectives, must automatically 'own' the benefits as well as the costs. This means having full access to the numbers.

Increasingly, organisations are recognising that the more transparent and accessible the key data can be across the organisation, the easier it is to 'engage' everyone in making a contribution to the organisation's achievement. In publicly quoted companies there is an obligation to report income and expenditure, cash flow and balance-sheet data to shareholders, although this is limited to financial statements rather than other really valuable data such as customer satisfaction or repeat business.

We have experienced a surprising lack of knowledge across many managers and project owners with regard to 'whole organisation' performance data. Focusing only on their own department, many of these individuals are unaware of the main performance indicators that the chief executive reports to the board and to other governing or funding bodies. Yet they are responsible for large projects that are intended to contribute to improvements to these very performance indicators.

Project managers need to know

We strongly encourage those running projects and initiatives to ensure that they are fully familiar with organisational performance data, where it is sourced, when it is updated and what it means. When the time comes to measure their contribution to improvement, they will then know where to go and what to look for. Moreover, if the existing MIS does not include the data they are looking for, they will know whom to ask for it. They can specify the reports they need.

If data is not being shared, this needs to be recognised in the planning stage. It needs to be made clear that if the person responsible for the project or programme has no access to key data, she or he will be hampered in doing the job. If this is made clear and access to data is still not forthcoming, there is every likelihood that the project planning, most especially the setting of implementation objectives, will be inadequate.

The result is likely to be vague impact objectives which have been planned without baselines. Change will be hard or impossible to evidence and the whole measurement exercise will lack credibility.

Dashboards and scorecards

Many organisations use dashboards of one kind or another to report results. Some important tools are becoming increasingly widely used.

The Balanced Scorecard is one of these. Where it is being used, or being developed, it signals both an increased awareness of the need to capture and use impact data, and often a maturing culture of accountability. Because it covers a variety of performance data, and not just financial results, it offers a useful source of data for the project manager. However, it may not consistently, or in the current period, capture the specific data that the project manager will want to use to measure impact outcomes. Then it is always worth consulting those who have responsibility for annually refreshing the scorecard indicators to see if specific time-bound indicators can be added on a temporary basis so that the data in question can be collected through the scorecard.

The Balanced Scorecard

The Balanced Scorecard is a framework for a strategic measurement and management system. It translates the mission and strategy of the organisation into a set of performance measures from four perspectives:

1. Financial
2. Customers
3. Internal business processes
4. Learning and growth.

(Continued)

(Continued)

Financial measures track past information, while the other three measures drive performance and are indicators of future financial measures. Companies use the scorecard to:

- clarify, gain consensus, communicate, review and improve strategy
- align departmental and personal goals and targets to those of the organisation
- link long-term and annual budgets to the strategic objectives.

The Balanced Scorecard can be used as a systematic process for implementing and receiving feedback on the organisation's strategy.

Source: Kaplan and Norton (1996).

Where an organisation has business-critical regulatory compliance requirements, these may be included on the Balanced Scorecard. Even where organisations do not use the Balanced Scorecard, regulatory audit approval may indicate a stop/go, or may flag up potential significant risk to the organisation.

This kind of data is invariably compiled and held within organisations, though recognition or accreditation may often be provided by outside bodies. Recording and recognising compliance within the levels we use in our approach sometimes causes confusion if it is not done properly. The rule to remember is that individual compliance is an aspect of performance and behaviour, and is therefore tracked and reported at Level 3. But the result of all the individuals in an organisation meeting the compliance standards and formal internal and external audit is organisational compliance, and this is an impact outcome and is tracked and reported at Level 4.

Reputation

Reputation is very important to most organisations, but to some, it forms a major proportion of the impact outcome data they collect and monitor on a regular basis. It is most important where competition is strong. This can produce what may seem to be contradictory attitudes to reputation. If low cost airlines sometimes appear unconcerned about their reputation for service, this does not mean that they are unconcerned about reputation per se. They may be jealously determined to maintain a reputation for value for money and for punctuality and efficiency: less concerned to be liked than to be valued. So reputation involves both public approval and public respect. Among the most avid trackers of reputational improvement and change are:

- retail companies
- hospitality and food sector companies
- financial advice service organisations

- public sector, private and social enterprises that provide public services, especially those in health and social care as well as local government, transport and education services, which pay increasing attention to their public image.

In the rest of this chapter we will discuss sources for further impact outcome data, and also address some of the challenges that face evaluators when they come to measure impact data.

Below are various types of impact that connect with organisational targets and priorities.

First, some hypothetical examples (Table 11.1).

A glance at these examples is enough to confirm that the sources of this range of data will be quite extensive. A further moment's thought will confirm that the nature of the evaluator's relationships with them will also be diverse.

The way in which all data is accessed and interpreted requires thought, but the relationships involved with colleagues and data providers are particularly important factors in accessing and using impact outcome (Level 4) data and, of course, performance and behaviour data (Level 3). Here we are concerned with impact data, and the issue is that without the consent and collaboration of colleagues and stakeholders it can be impossible to make constructive use of the lessons gained from the data that is collected. The same people who own the data, in the sense of being its gatekeepers, are often the most important potential users of the results.

These 'data owners' fall broadly into three groups, as described in the next two sections.

Colleagues and other stakeholders

Most impact outcome data comes from these sources:

- internal to an organisation, where the achievement of a key operational target is being evaluated – in these cases, organisations generate their data regularly and as a matter of business as usual;
- as part of a wider partnership or stakeholder group, when a project or programme is devised to pool resources or capacity, share expertise or guarantee local delivery – in these cases the partnership agreements need to incorporate clear references to the data that needs to be provided, the responsibilities for providing it and the timing and standards involved.

Contractors and sub-contractors

In general Level 4 impact outcome data is not going to come from contractors and sub-contractors – unless, of course, the whole project has been commissioned from them. Then they may also be responsible for reporting its results.

TABLE 11.1

	Examples of impact			
Type of impact	Manufacturing	Retail and services	Health and social care	International development
Achieved operational targets (including efficiency)	Product quality targets exceeded and maintained	1,000 new customer orders processed daily	Reduction in numbers of hospital-acquired infections	Projects completed to time and at lower than average cost per person-hour
Improved financial performance	Cost per unit reduced without loss of quality	Profit margin of 30% maintained across all departments	Cost per nurse consultation reduced by 15% over the year	Travel and subsistence costs reduced by 5%
Successful and sustained innovation	One new product idea tested per month, and two new products into full production annually	Three new product lines introduced every 6 months, of which 60% justify retention	New theatre utilisation plan improves numbers of scheduled procedures completed by 20%	Online resource website attracts 10,000 resource downloads in the first year
Achieved organisational compliance	Factory safety record exceeding sectoral average and standard by 10%	Hazard Analysis and Critical Control Point audit passed first time without recommendations	Commissioning for Quality and Innovation scores improved from previous audit and maintained above national average	Donors sign off audit on achievement of project outcomes
Enhanced reputation	**Internal** Staff survey shows 90% rating for conditions of work Staff survey shows 85% rating as a quality employer **External** Company rated no. 1 for best product	Customer satisfaction with product returns policy rises from 70% to 90%	A&E facilities rated 'good' or 'excellent' by 80% of patients and carers.	Organisation ranks no. 1 on trust index
Attributable legacy	Reconfiguration of production process enabling return on capital employed (ROCE) to increase by 20%	Number of existing customers signing up to loyalty cards increases by 5%	Reduction in Type 2 diabetes as a result of well-being campaign	New teacher-training standards implemented nationally

But if the nature of their work is to provide training or another service, their responsibilities for providing data are likely to end at Level 2. They should always be expected to check and report engagement. They must provide evidence of successful learning. But they may not be in a position to check on performance and behaviour, and the impact outcomes will come from the organisation that has contracted them, or from independent sources.

In these situations, difficulties in obtaining data from sub-contractors stem pretty much entirely from faults and omissions at the contracting stage. If contractors have the achievement of specific Level 3 and Level 4 impact objectives built into their contracts, as well as a clear obligation to report them, there should be no problem with acquiring the data. If, on the other hand, contracts are imprecise, and if the evaluation is expected to report on unspecified outcomes, difficulties are inevitable. Contractors will complain, perhaps with justification, that they are being held to account for things that were not made plain to them at the outset. They will almost certainly protest that they are being asked to collect unplanned data.

Measurement

Most of this data about impact comes from organisational units concerned with finance, operations and HR. But the nature of the data can differ a great deal and the sources may not always be immediately obvious. The examples in Tables 11.2 to 11.8 are drawn from a wide variety of sectors and settings and refer to a number of generic groups of impact data.

TABLE 11.2 Achieved operational targets (including efficiency)

Major occupation group	How will it be measured?	Where will the data come from?
Product quality targets exceeded and maintained	Quality is often measured in the negative, by counting the number of incidents of inadequate quality, number of substandard items, processes that have to be repeated, items that need to be exchanged or repaired, fees or prices that have to be partially or wholly refunded	It is most likely to come from operations managers and to be verified by finance managers, or vice versa
1,000 new customer orders processed daily	Shipping and invoice data	Logistics, Finance
Reduction in number of hospital-acquired infections	Numbers of infections by category	Hospital records
Projects completed to time and at lower than average cost per person-hour	Comparison with average cost per hour on previous similar projects	This will come from project records and reports, and from Finance

TABLE 11.3 Improved financial performance

Type of data	How will it be measured?	Where will the data come from?
Improved profitability	Profit margin of 30% maintained across all products/services	Finance
Cost per nurse consultation reduced by 15% over year	The 'unit of measure' will be 'a consultation'. This will need to be defined. Cost may be reduced as a result of less time, fewer missed appointments, better scheduling	The time data will come from whoever administers the nurses' time and work. Missed appointment data will come from department records, as will scheduling changes
Travel and subsistence costs reduced by 5% per person	Comparison with average cost on previous similar projects	This will come from project records and reports, and from Finance

TABLE 11.4 Successful and sustained innovation

Type of data	How will it be measured?	Where will the data come from?
One new product idea tested per month, and two new products into full production annually	From records of team/section/department/organisation. There needs to be complete clarity about what constitutes a 'new product idea', what constitutes 'testing' and what is meant by 'full production'	It is likely to come from a production, lab or operations manager; or it may come from individuals and be verified (signed off) by a manager
Three new product lines introduced every 6 months, of which 60% justify retention	The definition of a 'product line' is essential and it is equally important to be clear as to what is meant by 'justify retention'. Does it imply a trial period? For how long?	Operations managers

| New theatre utilisation plan improves numbers of scheduled procedures completed by 20% | By comparing completed schedule procedures for a fixed period and comparing the result with that for a similar period before the plan was introduced | Operating theatre manager |
| Online learning resource website attracts 10,000 resource downloads in first year | Data generated by the website software | The website manager, who will analyse the data on an agreed periodic basis |

TABLE 11.5 Achieved organisational compliance

Type of data	How will it be measured?	Where will the data come from?
Factory safety record exceeds sectoral average and standard by 10%	Safety data; records of accidents, including records of accidents by type or by level of seriousness	In most organisations, from HR
Passes HACCP audit first time without recommendations	Audit report	Externally provided audit record
CQUIN scores improved from previous audit and maintained above national average	Audit report	Externally provided audit record
All projects in the last year monitored and evaluated to donors' standards and requirements	Donors' planned impact outcomes versus actual	Donors sign off audit on achievement of project impact outcomes

TABLE 11.6 Enhanced internal reputation

Type of data	How will it be measured?	Where will the data come from?
Staff survey shows 90% rating for conditions of work	Annual or periodic staff survey, from rated questions showing degrees of approval, not just a yes/no response	All staff, preferably with breakdowns showing data by gender, job and role and location

TABLE 11.7 Enhanced external reputation

Type of data	How will it be measured?	Where will the data come from?
Company rated no. 1 for best product in external ranking index	Ranking on index past compared to present	External index
Customer satisfaction with product returns policy rises from 70% to 90%	Customer survey; possibly questionnaires sent out after each incident of a return	Sales or Marketing
A&E facilities rated 'good' or 'excellent' by 80% of patients and carers	Percentage change on patient survey	Patient relations staff
Organisation ranks no. 1 on trust index	Ranking change	External index

TABLE 11.8 Attributable legacy

Type of data	How will it be measured?	Where will the data come from?
Reconfiguration of production process, enabling ROCE to increase by 20%	Change in ROCE	Finance
Number of existing customers signing up to loyalty cards increases by 5%	Percentage change in existing customers with loyalty cards	Marketing and Sales
Reduction in Type 2 diabetes as a result of well-being campaign	Data on Type 2 diabetes cases in target population subjected to a rigorous isolation/ attribution process using more than one formal method	Local and national sources for the data; local application of the isolation/attribution
New teacher training standards implemented nationally	New standards implemented in national policy	Education Ministry records

Measuring the impact of creating a Cardiology Centre of Excellence in a medical clinic

In response to reports that the country has the second-highest percentage of obese people, relative to the size of the region's population, a Middle Eastern medical clinic decided to set up a Cardiology Centre of Excellence. The clinic is a privately owned acute care hospital. Currently, it is licensed for only a Diagnostic Catheter Lab and not for an Interventional Catheter Lab, authorised to insert stents and pacemakers. Patients requiring these services have to be transferred to other facilities. To achieve its goal of creating a Cardiology Centre of Excellence, the clinic needs to prepare a theatre for open-heart surgery, acquire the licence for an Interventional Catheter Lab, and have its staff learn and apply the appropriate skills for these procedures.

The cost of the new equipment for the centre is high, and the clinic does not expect a positive ROI for the first three years. However, the clinic has set impact objectives for its new centre's first year:

- zero patient transfers to any other facility
- increase revenue for the Cardiology Department by 20 per cent
- grow the number of patients for the Interventional Catheter Lab from 0 to 500 in the first six months.

This information will provide the clinic's managers with initial simple performance data.

12

ISOLATION AND ATTRIBUTION

Credibility is the evaluator's first concern. It is not possible to show direct causality. This is why it is essential to build a robust chain of impact and why, also, attribution and isolation has to be carried out before any impact outcome is reported. This will be credible only if it is done systematically. There are five main tools that can be used for this. Control groups are widely regarded as reliable, but are hard to set up in most operational settings. They depend on a strong match between groups, no ethical or competitive issues and no risk of contamination between groups. However randomised control groups are widely used in some contexts. Forecasting is not often used, but can be powerful. It requires a mathematical relationship to be established between a particular investment and an effect. It can be seen in use in advertising. Regression analysis is a statistical technique for estimating the relationship between variables. It is valuable for analysing the effect of a number of influences. Trend line analysis can be used to show the likely continued influence of a trend that has been established over a significant period of time in the past, and can be seen to continue through the lifetime of whatever is being evaluated. Finally, estimation is the most commonly used. It is highly effective, but only when done systematically and with great rigour, often through focus groups. It can help to establish and drive accountability.

A credible view of impact

An evaluator's highest priority and greatest test is achieving credibility.

All impact (Level 4) data collected must be treated as raw data until it has been tested against the possibility that some or all of the improvement it represents may have been caused by influences other than the project, programme or investment.

It is not possible to show direct causality: no one can. Building credibility starts with the recognition that attributing improvement to one or more 'causes' is not and never will be an exact science. At best, the attribution of influence is a rigorously tested and transparent judgement based on the highest-quality evidence. Our purpose has to be that our stakeholders and readers will be sufficiently confident of the claims we report that they will be prepared to commit to further action based on them.

The good news is that there are attribution techniques we can use to achieve this. We say that one or more of them must always be applied. The process can be demanding, and it can be made less straightforward and more testing by the fact that stakeholders and other readers of evaluations may look at a situation from very different perspectives. These may do a lot to shape their judgement as to whether a report is credible or not. These differences may be driven by any one or several of the following:

- their expert knowledge of some aspect of what is being evaluated
- their prior knowledge of the stakeholders in the evaluation
- their prior knowledge of the evaluators, or of the approach to evaluation that is being used
- the demands or opinions of funders or policy stakeholders
- their desire to see certain results reported.

All responsible project commissioners and managers make some attempt to take these factors into account as they decide whether anything other than the project inputs and activities should be given some, or even all, of the credit for any observed improvement.

We are complex beings. We function in complex social environments, not in controlled laboratories. Many internal and external forces and factors can affect our performance and achievements. The existence of some of these factors, let alone the extent of their effect, may not always be obvious until we go looking for them. Our starting point should always be that it is unlikely that an improvement in one of our key objectives or indicators is the result of one influence, and one only.

Evaluators may consider:

- getting participants or experts to help them attribute improvements to different influences
- analysing and re-analysing data to see how it relates to previous experiences, or to statistical models, if they exist.

They may do this by investigating whether the project or programme has been based on a plausible Theory of Change (see pages 32–5). If it is, they may map the results against it. This may also involve:

- checking data to see if it is consistent with what might be expected, and looking at the circumstances in which change occurred
- checking data against estimates of what might have been the case if nothing had been done
- looking for possible alternative explanations.

If this seems a bit haphazard . . . well, in a way it is. Which is why we want to demonstrate that there are better and more organised ways of tackling attribution.

The fact that an organised approach has been developed, that these reliable techniques have been developed and tested, has to be attributed to Jack Phillips, the chairman of the ROI Institute, based in the USA. We learned these principles of rigour and good practice from him, and are working hard to develop them further and to ensure that all of our students and colleagues have appropriate techniques available to apply in the enormous range of projects and settings in which they operate.

Jack Phillips' key principle is that impact outcomes should not be reported until they have been tested against the possibility that some other factor or influence may have caused some or all of the benefit that has been recorded. This can be tested, and credible attribution done, only after a piece of formal process has been applied.

This needs to be done with the same rigour that goes into the planning and collection of high-quality data.

The systematic approach

It is not necessary to claim that the tools we do have available will produce a scientific, absolute measure of attribution. They will not. But if they are used responsibly and with rigour they will provide cautious, evidence-based conclusions about the proportional influence on impact outcomes of each of the main contributory factors. They will enable us to be credibly conservative about the claims we make for the impact of the projects, programmes and approaches we are evaluating.

This is the one time in the whole planning, monitoring and evaluation cycle that we specifically advise clients, and suggest to you as a reader, that unless you have a background in research techniques or in statistical analysis or both you may wish to bring in an external person to assist you in your project evaluation.

At present, we use five techniques, often in combination:

1. control groups
2. forecasting
3. regression analysis
4. trend line analysis
5. estimation.

Each is briefly described below.

Control groups

If asked which they would regard as the most reliable route to take to attribution, many people would select control groups. Their reputation is built on the frequency of their use in scientific trials.

The problem is that they prove extremely difficult to use in many working or organisational settings. Two examples illustrate this.

Control groups

1. A large, low-price retail chain sells mainly identical products at set prices in stores that conform to the same specification in almost every respect. Its customer base is firmly established and very settled. Could it use control groups to perform isolation/attribution of the impact of its training spend on sales or customer satisfaction? In principle, yes. It might be possible to match staff groups from any store or group of stores, their managers and their customers. The organisation would be largely confident of avoiding contamination by selecting groups quite distant or separate from one another. But what if the product distributor learns about sales point or customer interaction improvements from one store and decides to pass this information on to another store? In that case, the control group may become 'contaminated' (in other words, adopt some of the good practice from our trained group), and will no longer function as a control group.

2. A chain of care homes develops a new job aid to ensure that elderly, dependent residents are kept hydrated throughout each day and regularly checked to go to the toilet whenever they need. A control group could easily test the effectiveness of the approach, but it would clearly be unethical to risk any residents being insufficiently hydrated, and therefore at risk, during the attribution exercise.

Research theories: control groups

There are a number of techniques that can be used to isolate and attribute the outcomes of an initiative. These can be classified as experimental (e.g. randomised control groups), quasi-experimental (including non-randomised control groups and regression analysis), and non- experimental (such as participatory approaches). We use a number of these techniques based on the situations of the initiatives being implemented.

We use control groups selected via randomised and non-randomised methods.

Randomised control groups

Randomised control groups follow the same guidelines as RCTs. That is, before the initiative begins a randomly selected sample is drawn from the population of interest. Two groups are randomly created from this sample: the group

(Continued)

(Continued)

where an intervention will take place (for example training) and the control group. Randomisation in this way avoids the effects which can arise from selection choices, including bias. The participants in both groups will share similar characteristics and therefore the only difference is the initiative being implemented. However, since this method only 'controls' for differences within the particular setting, concluding that the same would apply to others in different contexts would not be valid. To address this, a large enough sample drawn from the same eligible population, with implementation in different settings, would be required.

Then, at the end, the outcomes of both groups are compared to estimate the impact of the initiative. Statistical analysis could also be carried out to test the 'significance' of this impact, with larger samples yielding more precise statistical inferences.

However, this method needs to be planned and managed carefully to avoid risks of (1) different rates of attrition (e.g. caused by dropouts), (2) contamination (spill-over effects) and (3) unintended behavioural responses.

As noted above, there are many benefits in using this method, but there may be ethical reasons why initiatives cannot be withheld from a group of persons.

Most importantly of all, the key is to be quite sure that you can randomly select a population within the same context with the same characteristics and, within the population, randomly select the intervention group and the control group.

Non-randomised control groups

In some circumstances it is impossible to carry out randomisation, for various reasons, such as the evaluation being requested after the initiative has already begun, voluntary participation in the initiative, as well as the initiative requiring a phased implementation. In these cases, other methods are used to create comparison groups.

Judgement matching

The intervention and comparison groups (e.g. teams, staff groups, education areas, local population areas, households or individuals with the best match of characteristics) are created by using descriptive information about relevant matching characteristics, combined with other information (e.g. geographic information, survey results, interviews etc.) and in consultation with key informants (clients and other 'experts'). However, this method is less precise and is prone to subjectivity biases; therefore more qualitative work is necessary to identify unobserved differences, so the report should always attach appropriate caveats to the results.

Pipeline approach

Where there is a plan to implement an initiative gradually, especially in large projects, this approach compares the group that participates (treatment/ intervention) with the group that is yet to participate (comparison). However, selection bias may be introduced and therefore it is important, again, to check that the relevant characteristics of both groups are similar.

Propensity score matching

Here the aim is to undertake statistical matching to create a comparison group with a similar set of observed and relevant characteristics to those in the intervention group. Propensity score matching uses all available information to create a comparison group after the intervention by statistically matching each participant in the intervention group with a non-participant. The pairs are formed based on the observable characteristics and on the basis of the non-participant group having similar probabilities of being included in the sample to the intervention group at the start of the initiative. However, it should be noted that there are no guarantees that all relevant characteristics will be included. To ensure that the best matching variables are identified, a larger sample will often be required. This method is also prone to the potential risk of bias caused by failing to take into account unobserved differences between groups. This can be addressed by combining this method with the double difference technique.

Double difference (or difference-in-difference)

As long as the unobserved differences between the treatment/intervention and comparison groups remain constant with time, so that the response to intervention does not depend on the time when it is applied (this is called 'time invariant'), the double difference (or difference-in-difference) technique can be used to deal with this bias. The differences between the two groups are measured before and after the initiative has been implemented. Since this method eliminates the initial differences between the two groups, it gives an unbiased estimate of the effects of the initiative, provided that they are time invariant. When combined with propensity score matching (see above), the effects of unobserved selection biases can be eliminated. However, this works better when the differences between both groups are eliminated as much as possible. This method can also be combined with regression analysis to deal with unobserved selection effects. It should be noted that this method is more prone to the presence of measurement error in the data and therefore the quality of the data has to be carefully managed.

Sources: Bamberger (2006); Haynes et al. (2012); Leeuw and Vaessen (2009); Scriven (2008).

Control groups are hard to use in many contexts

It should come as no surprise that many of those who start out believing they will be able to use a control group to isolate the degree of benefit they can ascribe to the investment or activity they are evaluating end up having to change their plans. Control groups are more readily applied to clinical or scientific pilots, and are much harder to apply in business and social settings, where issues of matching characteristics, context and contamination make them impractical. Their conditions require that:

- two groups share the same characteristics and are exposed to the same influences and circumstances/context
- the control group is not exposed to any risks not experienced by the group that has benefitted from the improvement
- there are no competitive issues between the two groups
- there is no risk of contamination between the groups.

Isolating the impact of a strategic skills training project

A leading operator of restaurants and pubs in the UK encourages 'promotion through the ranks' among its more than 40,000 employees. Over the years, many of its area managers had taken advantage of this opportunity. However, some of these managers lacked the strategic skills necessary to successfully lead their teams to maximise sales and profits, particularly during the global recession.

To improve performance, the organisation embarked on a training project that would enable its area managers to develop the required strategic skills. Working in partnership with a major university, the Masters in Multi-Unit Hospitality Leadership learning programme was designed. The learning outcomes covered four modules – Strategy and Finance, Finance and Business Models, Service and Quality Leadership, and Operational Excellence.

A project of this importance required evaluation to determine its ROI. Based on sales growth, customer satisfaction and team turnover, this was determined to be 539 per cent. It was thought that the sites that had significant investments would be excluded from the evaluation, since this investment might influence business levels. To calculate the ROI, three techniques for isolating the impact of the training were used. These included:

1. *control groups*: a comparison between the group of area managers who were participating in the project and a group who were not participating
2. *time series*: pre- and post-programme performance comparisons
3. *estimation*: participants, supervisors and the HR Process and the Evaluation manager gave their estimates of the amount of impact the project had on the outcomes, alongside their percentage level of confidence in their estimates.

Forecasting

Forecasting can be defined as estimations made about future events, generally by making calculations using historical data.

The Lancaster Centre for Forecasting has identified three classes of methods used in forecasting:

1. *Judgemental.* These methods are based on subjective opinions. They include judgements based on individual opinions, without reference to other forecasts, surveys on intentions (e.g. intentions to buy), committee consensus, experts' opinions (e.g. sales force), and Delphi.
2. *Extrapolative.* These methods make forecasts for a particular variable based on patterns identified in that variable's history. The patterns are assumed to hold into the future. Methods include trend curves, decomposition, exponential smoothing, Box-Jenkins or ARIMA and Neural Nets.
3. *Causal or structural.* These methods try to identify relationships between variables which have held in the past and which are assumed to hold in the future. Methods include single equation regression, simultaneous system, VAR models, simulation and cross-impact analysis.

Source: Fildes (2010)

We use forecasting for isolation in the few cases where we have another factor of influence for which there is a good deal of reliable historical data that links it to a particular effect. The historical data will have been significant to build a mathematical (econometric) model to use to forecast the influence of other factors. For instance, it may be known for a particular product that a given amount of TV advertising will always generate a minimum number of additional sales. In that case it should be possible to encapsulate this in a simple econometric formula. Then, if a performance incentive were introduced to encourage sales growth, it would be possible to use the formula to account for any proportion of extra sales growth that should be attributed to advertising, as opposed to the incentive.

Regression analysis

This is a statistical technique for estimating the relationship among a number of variables. For example, in a case where we are interested in studying the factors that influence the production of a specific crop (our dependant variable), the factors or independent variables might include the amount of sunlight, temperature, water, soil quality etc.

Regression analysis is concerned with the analysis of the relationship between a dependent variable, on the one hand (our crop), and one or more independent variables (all those other factors), on the other. The dependent variable is called 'dependent' because its value is influenced by the value of other variables that are called 'independent variables'. In particular, the purpose is to measure the change in the dependent variable that follows the change in each of the independent variables while holding the others fixed.

In this case, for the most simple and basic technique, we need certain conditions to be in place in order to deploy this method of isolation.

- Condition 1: The relation between the dependent variable and the independent variables is linear.
- Condition 2: In the studied population, the unobserved influencing factors are present independently of the observed factors.
- Condition 3: The sample is large enough and its observations are identically and independently distributed.
- Condition 4: The explanatory factors (or the factors included in the analysis) are not perfectly correlated.
- Condition 5: Large outliers are excluded.

Regression analysis

Human capital initiatives come in all types and sizes, being both discrete and continuous, and can be affected by other factors external to the initiative. As long as the treatment/intervention and the characteristics of the subjects in the sample can be measured, regression analysis is a popular, flexible approach for dealing with the heterogeneity of the treatment/intervention, the heterogeneity of the characteristics of participants, multiple initiatives/interventions, interactions between initiatives, as well as interactions between initiatives and specific characteristics.

Regression analysis uses modelling techniques to analyse the relationship between the dependent and independent variables of interest. It does this by examining how the dependent variable changes as one of the independent variables changes, with the others held constant.

Using this method, it may be possible to estimate the contribution of a specific initiative to the total outcome or to estimate the effect of the interaction between two initiatives. Control groups can be used in the analysis.

Unobserved selection effects and endogeneity biases can be dealt with by combining this method with the double difference technique. In doing this, analysis is carried out on the changes within groups over time instead of between groups.

Regression discontinuity analysis

In this popular method, a cut-off point for eligibility is assigned to the initiative using, for example, the participants' income. The treatment/intervention group is compared to a comparison group that is made up of participants at the cut-off point who have not participated in the initiative. Therefore, it is less likely that the results will be biased by unobserved variables.

Sources: Bamberger (2006); Leeuw and Vaessen (2009).

Trend line analysis

This approach can be highly effective in isolating the influence on the planned impact outcome of a single known factor that may be responsible for a medium- or long-term trend – either positive or negative.

In the example in Figure 12.1, unique visitors had been gradually but slowly growing. A new marketing campaign aimed to give a lift to the visitor numbers. Nothing else was introduced either at the same time or after the marketing campaign.

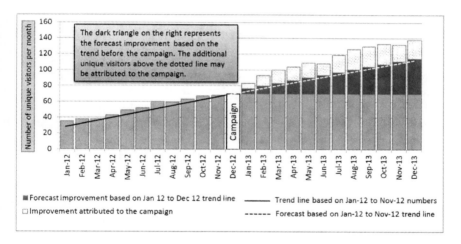

FIGURE 12.1

You can use trend line analysis only under the following conditions:

- *There must be a trend.* This sounds obvious, but needs careful thought. What is a trend? Could it become clear through three months' data? Will it need six months'? Is it safe to work with trends only if you have at least twelve months' data? The only safe way to proceed is to begin from the assumption that a trend needs to be visible over a full twelve months. This is the least required to deal with issues of seasonality, which can be strongly influential inside organisations, as well as in the wider world. Inside organisations the impacts of summer holidays and winter infections are obvious. Outside of them, influences like seasonal buying patterns (December, for instance, is the dominant month in sales of men's clothing) and major winter weather incidents are vital considerations. This is not to say that it is impossible to discern and persuade people of trends evident over periods shorter than a year, just that they should be approached with great caution.

- *There must be consistent data.* There must be as much data establishing the trend as there is relating to the activity or improvement alongside which it is being set. The data must be collected in relation to the same intervals (weekly, monthly, quarterly).

- There must be every reason to suppose that *the trend will have persisted over the whole period of the evaluation*, and no reason to suppose that it may have been halted.

Monetising video conferencing

A remote and rural healthcare educational alliance is to develop the educational needs of NHS practitioners living in remote and rural communities. It links educational providers with remote and rural health services, advises on the uses of appropriate methods for educational delivery to remote and rural staff, supports learner access to education by working with technology experts and evaluates remote and rural education.

One of the methods of educational delivery is by videoconferencing. However, a barrier experienced in adopting this technique is human error, due to the lack of technical expertise, leading to unused expensive equipment. To resolve this, an educational package was commissioned to increase skills, knowledge, competence and confidence in using the videoconferencing equipment. Following course completion, each participant was given the educational package, which included data-collection tools for the evaluation, to carry out cascaded training within his or her organisation.

This project attracted high interest from among the management team, as well as political and local interest. It was evaluated to Level 5, ROI. To isolate the impact of the educational package, estimates from managers, leads from HR and L&D, as well as participants were collected. Their percentage level of confidence was used to adjust the estimates given. Trend line analysis of data on videoconferencing activity was also collected from the IT department. Of the isolation techniques available, these were seen as the most appropriate. Control groups were not used because contamination could not have been avoided and it was deemed unethical to prevent other groups from participating in the communication skills opportunity. Forecasting and regression analysis were also not appropriate.

Estimation

Estimation is likely to be the least-trusted form of isolation – at least until people have seen it done well.

The suspicion around it comes as no surprise. The word 'estimation' suggests guesswork, making things up. We have all been treated to estimates that have borne little relation to what has subsequently happened. Interestingly, when considered within a qualitative approach to data collection and analysis, and especially when built into a participatory evaluation approach, it is treated with less suspicion. As if by magic, it becomes 'qualitative research' in which careful adjustments are made through careful referencing and iterative reviews to arrive at an agreed interpretation of results. This, of course, is exactly what happens in a robustly managed estimation approach.

One of the most frequent estimation exercises of which we are all conscious is the quarterly reporting of UK national Gross Domestic Product (GDP). It is interesting that only relatively recently have the press reports of this, quite rightly, taken to emphasising that these reports are estimates. They have to be. We hear them in the following quarter, and they tell us, in effect, what the country has earned in the preceding quarter. But we can't really know that soon. VAT returns are made three months in arrears, so it is too soon to gather data from them. Individual tax returns come at the end of the year. Too early for them.

In fact, this GDP estimate is made on the basis of not much more than 40 per cent of the data on which a final account of what we earned will be made a year or eighteen months down the line. No great surprise, then, that these particular estimates have a reputation for having to be revised later to such a substantial degree that it is clear that they should be treated with caution by policy makers.

This example highlights two of the main problems that we need to overcome if we are to use estimation effectively as a means of isolating and then attributing benefit within our own projects and programmes:

1. clarity about the basis on which estimations are being made
2. confidence in the realism of the estimates themselves.

Estimates will achieve a satisfactory degree of credibility so long as we undertake them rigorously and arrive at them through strong process (Figure 12.2).

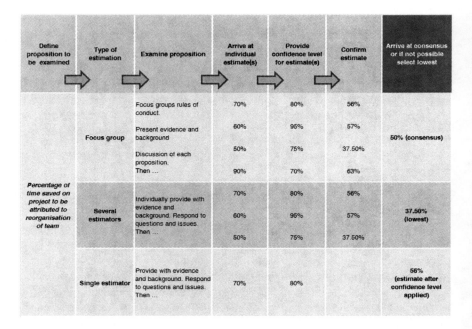

FIGURE 12.2

Whose estimation?

The opinion or judgement of experts can be used to estimate programme outcomes. This is a data-gathering technique that utilises the perception, knowledge and experience of experts in given functional areas. Since it is subjective, it is best used to supplement other objective measures, or to replace them where objective measures are not available. The process includes the systematic collection and summarisation of experts' opinions. It can be done at one time (e.g. via a survey or panel/focus group) or iteratively (e.g. using the Delphi method).

There are many advantages to using expert opinions, which include flexibility, ease of use, being quick and being inexpensive. However, there are many criticisms as well. It is subjective, i.e. based on the experts' perceptions, and therefore not deemed credible because of perception bias. Subjectivity also refers to the experts having different bases, e.g. for using numbers such as on a rating scale. Other difficulties include identifying suitably qualified experts and a sufficient number of experts.

Source: Minister of Public Works and Government Services (2010).

Margin of error

The margin of error is an 'analytical technique that accounts for the number of acceptable errors in an experiment'. It is given so that reviewers of experimental (or survey) results can determine their levels of accuracy. The larger the values of the margin of error, the less trustworthy are the results. The value of the margin of error is usually followed by the confidence interval.

Source: www.businessdictionary.com.

References: American Statistical Association: www.amstat.org; National University of Singapore Department of Statistics and Applied Probability: www.statistics.nus.edu. sg; Economic and Social Research Council (ESRC) Quantitative Methods Initiative: www.quantitativemethods.ac.uk.

Managing an isolation/attribution process

The principle that no account of impact and benefit is valid until it has been tested is often hard to maintain in practice. In addition, the isolation and attribution tools we have discussed need to be used well, and the process itself must be carefully and well managed. They must also be used in ways that respond to three sets of challenges that all those reporting on results must meet and resolve whenever they use data to report.

Challenge: establishing relationships and avoiding bias

The first challenge is establishing the relationship between an investment of time, effort and resources and the impact or impacts caused by it. Or are they? That is the point. This relationship needs to be demonstrated, and can never be taken for granted.

Validity, errors and biases

There are four types of validity that need to be considered when carrying out impact evaluation. However, there is no one impact evaluation method that addresses all four types; therefore a mix of methods is usually recommended.

1. Internal: establish the causal relationship between the outputs of the initiative and the processes of change that leads to the outcomes and impacts.
2. Construct: ensure that the variables that are measured adequately represent the underlying realities of the initiatives that are linked to the processes of change.
3. External: establish whether the results can be generalised to other settings.
4. Statistical conclusion: make sure the degree of confidence about the existence of a relationship between the initiative and the impact variable, as well as the magnitude of change, is accurate.

Source: Leeuw and Vaessen (2009).

Causality

The Oxford Dictionary defines causality as 'the relationship between cause and effect' and 'the principle that everything has a cause'. This suggests that every effect has factor(s) that caused it to occur. Causality has been discussed and studied for many centuries in both the physical sciences (e.g. biology, physics and engineering) and social sciences (e.g. psychology, economics, statistics, law and management).

The *Stanford Encyclopaedia of Philosophy* provides a useful summary of the many theories of causality that are discussed in these fields. Two that are relevant to impact evaluation are:

1. Probabilistic causal theories: how 'causes change the probability of their effects', noting that 'an effect may still occur in the absence of a cause or fail to occur in its presence'. Two different kinds of causal claims that have been identified in this theory are singular and general. Singular causal claims refer to particular individuals, places and times, while general causal claims refer to event-types or properties.
2. Theory of causal processes: the focus is on identifying and understanding the possible cause(s) of an observed effect.

Sources: Dowe (2008); Hitchcock (2012); Morris (2005).

Challenge: Accounting for the elapse of time, and the way in which time is managed

The more time passes between, say, a training course and its impact, the more likely it is that other influences or circumstances may have influenced the result. And the greater the possible cumulative influence.

An obvious example is a sales training programme. Say that one is held in January. It is then reasonable to track its impact over the next twelve months to see how much improvement there has been in sales and revenue (and, importantly, in the profit from that revenue). The task of attribution after one year may well have to take account of a number of other influences (price fluctuation, position of competitors, management attention), but these things will be quite fresh and the task is manageable. If it is being done, at least in part, by estimation, the estimators should be able to get a fairly clear view of the circumstances.

But move on another year. How easy is it at that distance to be clear and credible about the degree to which sales improvements in that year should still be attributed to the training that the salespeople experienced that first January? Much less straightforward.

However, for many projects, especially for those intended to influence social or economic change, the impact outcomes may take many years to be realised.

We may need to collect data over a long time period and we need to build up our results taking into account what can happen over time.

Time series

The STatistical Education through Problem Solving (STEPS) website defines the term 'time series' as 'a sequence of observations which are ordered in time (or space)'. Data for an observed phenomenon is captured over time and plotted on a graph, a scatter plot. Usually, X is the data of the phenomenon being observed and Y is the independent variable, time. Two kinds of time series data have been identified, continuous ('an observation at every instant of time') and discrete ('an observation at [usually regularly] spaced intervals').

There are four components of time series:

1. trend: 'a long term movement in a time series'. this can be depicted using a straight line on a scatter plot to identify the underlying direction of the data observed
2. cyclical: a description of any regular fluctuations
3. seasonal: a description of regular fluctuations that are dependent on the time of year
4. irregular: the residual remains after all other components are accounted for.

Source: Easton and McColl (1997).

Challenge: comparing competing influences

Even once some relationship has been established in respect of the project, programme or initiative that is the focus of measurement, it is often extremely important to conduct a more extensive attribution exercise that apportions causality between a number of competing initiatives or influences. This can be of crucial importance in a partnership, or in an organisation where a number of teams or departments are contributing to a series of broad aims.

This often occurs in respect of customer, client or patient sentiment. An organisational priority to improve the results of regular surveys is likely to be supported by one or more specific initiatives, by a general managerial push to improve the client or customer interface and perhaps by some improved communication technology. It is important to the organisation that customer sentiment ratings are improved. But it is also vital that the sponsors of these initiatives continue to work together. It will be pointless and damaging if they descend into argument over who should take the credit for improvements.

Attribution

The Organisation for Economic Co-operation and Development (OECD) defines attribution as 'the ascription of a causal link between observed (or expected to be observed) changes and a specific intervention'. It refers to isolating and ascertaining the contribution of an initiative/intervention to the outcome so as to determine how much credit can be ascribed to the initiative or to the performance of other partners/organisations. It takes account of anticipated or unanticipated confounding factors and external shocks.

Howard White, Executive Director of the International Initiative for Impact Evaluation (3ie), identifies two applications of impact evaluation, based on interpretations of the definition for impact. In the first, when impact is interpreted as 'long term effects', impact evaluation examines the long-term outcomes of an initiative. The second is more of an 'attribution analysis', where impact evaluation studies the indicator of interest to see what happens with the initiative and what would have happened without the initiative (the counterfactual). White emphasises that neither is right or wrong and that they may overlap, but they are completely different.

The former types of impact evaluation draw on work carried out in the fields of management (e.g. Root Cause Analysis) and psychology (where people attribute reasons for behaviour and events). The latter types of impact evaluation usually draw on work carried out in statistics and economics (used in experimental and quasi-experimental approaches such as RCTs and regression analysis). However, it is important to note that as long as there is quality impact data, you should always consider the benefits of using statistical methods, even if you wish to also use more qualitative approaches as well.

Sources: Leeuw and Vaessen (2009); OECD (2002); White (2009).

The attribution activity and results will, in some ways, be different every time. But the process should always be the same. It is important that this is done systematically, and, from the point of view both of the person undertaking the evaluation and of stakeholders and colleagues, that it is done to a consistent pattern. For this reason we recommend a step-by-step approach, and the use of a prompt tool like the one shown below.

In this example the results of a leadership programme are being isolated.

Step 1: orientation (Table 12.1)

At the early planning stage, the project team should be thinking hard about the other factors that might also be driving the very improvement they are tracking. We encourage them strongly to think both about the external factors and forces that might account for improvement. We also focus them on the internal forces. Often, doing this in the planning stage helps project teams to recognise the likely scale of their contribution as well as the factors that may negatively influence any results. This is really helpful in managing project risk!

TABLE 12.1

	Step 1: Orientation (Record the raw data related to each impact – understand the possible or probable influences – select for isolation – select isolation approach)		
	Impact 1	*Impact 2*	*Impact 3*
Level 4 outcomes	Audit achieved	10% improvement in staff satisfaction after 1 year	Reduction in number of client complaints from an average of 10 per month to an average of 2 per month after 1 year
Possible/probable external factors/ influences that may have caused/ contributed to each impact	Changes in the compliance requirements	None	None
Possible/probable internal factors/ influences that may have caused/ contributed to each impact	New managers	Staff have received an above-inflation pay rise	Additional customer service staff
Influences selected for isolation	Changes in the compliance requirements	Staff have received an above-inflation pay rise	Additional customer service staff

Step 2: isolating individual impact (Table 12.2)

It is vital that all impact data is subjected to one of the available isolation/attribution tests. Some may even need to be subjected to more than one if it is considered essential to build trust in the results. Different results may require different methods. In the above example, regression analysis might be applied as well as estimations.

In such a case, the trend line would be used to make an initial adjustment to the attributed benefit, and the estimation would then take into account further influences, and adjust it further. Example: raw Level 4 impact data shows time taken to complete a process to a set degree of accuracy improved from fifteen hours to nine hours over a one-year period after a management training initiative. Trend line information going back eighteen months before the initiative shows that there was already an established trend of improvement which, without the management training, would have brought the time down from fifteen to thirteen hours. An estimation exercise involving a range of key stakeholders decided that improvements in working conditions during the year would have accounted for a further two hours of improvement. This left two hours of the improvement attributed to the training.

TABLE 12.2

	Step 2: Isolation of individual impacts (Use one method for each impact to establish a conservative individual view of how much of the improvement should be credited to the investment in question)		
	Impact 1	*Impact 2*	*Impact 3*
By trend line	None	None	None
By comparison/ control group	None	None	None
By forecasting	None	Staff have received an above-inflation pay rise	None
By regression analysis	None	None	None
By estimation	Changes in the compliance requirements		Competing organisations have received some adverse publicity
Value of impact after isolation	All customer-facing teams assessed as fully compliant with the organisation's standard after 1 year. *Expert estimation attributed 80% of this improvement to the leadership programme.*	10% improvement in staff satisfaction after 1 year. *An established mathematical relationship between above-inflation pay settlements and the staff satisfaction index resulted in 5% of the improvement in satisfaction being attributed to the leadership programme.*	Reduction in number of client complaints from an average of 10 per month to an average of 2 per month after 1 year. *Managers' estimates attributed 80% of the reduction in complaints (8 per month) to the improved practice resulting from the leadership programme.*
Focus group estimates of attribution	100%	90%	90%
Confidence levels	90%	90%	80%
Consensus attributions	90% = (90% × 80%) 72% of improvement finally attributed to the leadership programme	84% of improvement finally attributed to the leadership programme	72% = 6 per month finally attributed to the leadership programme

13

MONETISING

It is often difficult to calculate the money values of impact outcomes. If it is possible, there is a straightforward formula for calculating value, based on the conventional business benefit cost ratio. There is growing pressure to show value for money for human capital investments. To do this we must know the value of one unit of the impact in question. Arriving at this is likely to need the cooperation of others – often the finance department. It will already have some known and standard values. But external research may be necessary. Colleagues may need to be asked to provide fresh internal data. Values must always be validated. We never get over difficulties in monetising by using proxies.

Getting rid of infectious and dangerous waste

A health centre needed to improve the efficiency and effectiveness of managing infectious and dangerous waste. Every hour of every day, staff would dispose of waste which comprised infectious and non-infectious waste. For several years, staff had been trained to separate waste and ensure that the appropriate disposal units were used. The waste was collected daily by specialists who removed it from the site.

The cost of removal was calculated by the disposal company based on categories of waste and how much time was required for sorting, as well as the weight and volume of waste.

Local residents and businesses often complained about the waste disposal collection and many expressed concerns about the way waste was stored outside the health centre and the potential danger to them and their families.

(Continued)

(Continued)

The health centre decided to change its practice and introduced new waste management technology which meant that the waste was partly processed on site and the volume and cost of disposal was significantly reduced. But the new equipment required that the sorting of waste had to be 100 per cent accurate at the point of patient treatment.

The management introduced a range of activities to manage the change: not only the introduction of new units in treatment rooms for different types of waste, but new notices, labelling, training and inspection systems. Moreover, new security was introduced to ensure no tampering or potential leakage of waste from the new equipment, so as to assure local residents that it was safe to store the waste on site.

Calculating the money value of the initiative was extremely difficult. It was not a simple question of reduction in the cost of disposal, as several costs were on-going and these needed to be factored in. And even then, when the day-to-day cost reduction was calculated, initial capital, training and other costs had to be calculated to identify whether the whole initiative had in fact achieved value for money.

The residents were happier with the new arrangement and there were fewer complaints, less concern expressed at local residents' meetings and fewer negative reports in the local media.

Going to money

The above example demonstrates several issues when calculating value for money.

The first is that it is often difficult to calculate the money value of any impact outcome. The main impact outcome was the reduction in the volume and frequency of waste collection, which saved the health centre significant operational cost. However, some on-going new costs were incurred, so the net reduction in operational costs needed to be calculated.

And then, of course, before the question 'Did we get value for money?' can be answered, the costs of the equipment, of training, notices, signs and everything else involved, including the time of those implementing the change, needed to be calculated. Some of this might be spread over a period of time, but some would have been expenditure that needed to be accounted for at the time it was incurred.

Then there is the question of the reduction in numbers of complaints from local residents, and arguments in residents' meetings and bad publicity in the local media. Could this be monetised? After all, fewer negative notices and a reduction in complaints might improve the health centre's image and save hospital staff time in dealing with these.

Why do we need to put money value on our impact outcomes?

We monetise the impact outcomes or, in other words, the improvements we achieve, in order to see if it was worth spending the money to get there. Many call this evidence of value for money.

If we know the monetary value of some or all of these impact outcome improvements, we can compare them to what they cost us and report the results either in the form of an ROI percentage or in the form of a benefit cost ratio (BCR), one of the most commonly used business ratios, well understood in both the public and private sectors.

So what money value should we use if we are going to calculate a BCR or ROI?

The formula is simple. We divide benefits by costs. Consider the example below and ask yourself what is wrong with it.

$$\frac{Sales\ income\ of\ \pounds2,000}{Cost\ of\ \pounds500} = 4.0$$

This ratio suggests that we got £4 of benefit for every £1 we invested.

But did we really get that much benefit?

Actually, no, because in the example above we have taken our gross revenue (sales income) and assumed that it is all profit. It's like saying that the value we get from selling a tube of toothpaste is the price the customer pays. It is not, of course. The value we get is the profit on the tube. Now the question is, what profit: gross profit or net profit? And when we say net profit, do we mean before or after interest, dividends and tax?

Our advice is always use net profit, and before any interest, dividend or tax.

We acknowledge this when we report value for money in responsible and credible evaluations. We adjust the calculation so that, instead of comparing gross revenue with cost, it compares profit or margin with cost. That means that we subtract the costs from the benefit before we create the ratio. So our example becomes:

$$\frac{Benefit\ (profit)\ of\ \pounds1,000}{Cost\ of\ \pounds500} = 2.0$$

This tells us a different and more accurate story about what we have achieved. Now we can say that for every £1 invested, we have a benefit of £2. We can also, if we wish, express this as an ROI percentage:

$$\frac{Benefit\ of\ \pounds1,000 - Cost\ of\ \pounds500}{Cost\ of\ \pounds500} = 1.0 \times 100 = 100\%\ ROI$$

This helps us understand what we get back after we have taken away the cost of achieving the benefit.

That is the easy part. More demanding is establishing credible monetary values in the first place.

Dr Jack Phillips was the first to highlight the need to ask the question 'Was it worth doing?' His work was sober, cautious and conservative. He was right to ask the question and he led the way in showing that calculating ROI on human capital investments can be done. He also sensibly advised that if you are going to calculate ROI, you really need to have a deep insight into why one investment achieved a certain ROI while another similar one didn't.

However, not everyone has followed his sensible path, and many others have come along and decided that you can monetise just about anything and, without any recourse to econometric modelling of any kind, have made huge assumptions about the money values of outcomes that are simply too weak and ill-founded to take seriously.

To monetise or not to monetise

'Did we get value for money?'

This must be one of the most frequently asked questions in organisations of all kinds. It must also be one of the questions most often asked without any realistic chance of getting an accurate answer.

There is serious pressure, quite rightly, in both the private and the public sectors to show value for money. However, in many cases the political pressure (we use the word political here to refer to internal as well as external political expectations), has led to many cases of attempts to put a money value on something that is simply not credible. Fewer young offenders re-offending, more out-of-work individuals taking up jobs, an increase in the number of individuals eating more healthy food are examples of the types of outcomes that result from perfectly effective interventions which are then undermined by fantasy money values being placed on these improvements. The private sector often falls into the same trap: better customer satisfaction, improved ranking as a place to work, increased staff engagement are just a few of the impact outcomes that we have also seen monetised without any credible basis for the calculation.

How do we monetise?

The issue is essentially simple: we can monetise a benefit only if we know the value of one unit of it. And if you don't, you shouldn't try making it up!

A typical example: 'We reduced the numbers of customer complaints for poor service from thirty to ten over the previous year.'

This example poses a number of issues:

1. Do we have a definition for 'a complaint'? Is it a complaint that has gone beyond a certain point and has not been able to be resolved by an automatic process? Are there several categories of complaints?

2.   If that is the case, do we have some data about the cost of handling complaints in the past? Does the cost of managing each category differ?
3.   What information do we need to find so as to establish the cost of a complaint? Time spent, refunds, replacements? How do these differ by category of complaint?

These are all good questions, and need to be asked in order to come up with a standard value for 'a complaint' that can be accepted by the organisation as a whole. That means that it will certainly have to be endorsed by the finance department as well as, perhaps, by others.

Another example: we have changed our order and dispatch processes and we can now process an order to the point of collection for delivery using three hours of one person's time and equipment to pack and stamp the goods; and, because of the shorter time, we can reduce warehousing because we can move the goods through faster. This means that we need to calculate the increased value in the reduction of time, space and machine usage. This additional value will add to our profit margin. We need to compare the cost of all inputs before and after. Once we have done this we can ascertain our savings. The most likely source of expertise to help us do this is our colleagues in finance. They may already have a known (standard) value which they apply to calculate the increased value from the changed process. They may have used a TDABC model to make these calculations.

Known values are those that finance, HR or some other colleague is able to produce without further research. They are exactly that: 'known' in the organisation already. An example might be the margin used in sales or, in financial services, the known contribution from each customer account.

Standard values are those which have been used before and are the latest approved and adjusted version that has been signed off by the responsible person or department. These may have been used for budgeting, or developed for tendering.

External research may often involve published data from other similar organisations or projects. For instance, the UK-based Chartered Institute for Personnel and Development publishes an annual survey of recruitment and retention. This can be accessed online and may provide useful values for average recruitment costs in a wide range of sectors and occupations. Research through Google Scholar may also be useful, though any research should always be scrutinised carefully to determine its scope and context (and therefore transferability), and its age (and therefore relevance and credibility).

Internal data may well involve colleagues being asked to undertake some specific collection and analysis of past data. Often this data will be available elsewhere in the organisation. Organisations are likely to have multiple uses for data on employees' full costs, costs of grievances, costs of absences, standard costs of meetings, but even so, a proportion at least of the cost of the research, including the cost of researchers' time, should be included in the costs of the evaluation as a whole.

Validation is crucial. If you are presenting a monetised benefit based on a newly researched value to either an internal or an external group, it is vital to have taken the time to have it validated beforehand. For an internal group, the validation should be done by the original owner of the data (maybe finance), or by the person or department most likely to raise an objection or a doubt (often finance again). If you are using an external source, it is more likely that the process will be questioned. If there is a solid methodology that is clear and logical, and the result has been signed off by someone with appropriate expertise, this may be sufficient to quell any doubts.

Monetising leadership development

An agricultural organisation was established many decades ago as a cooperative to serve its customers, members and community. After a major merger and expansion drive, it embarked on a leadership development programme aimed at transforming its managers into a new group of pioneers that would reposition its offer to the retail food market. These pioneers would focus on prioritising local customers and communities and the organisation's values so as to achieve a competitive advantage.

The leadership development programme was designed to improve the managers' leadership skills and thereby improve their behaviour. It was developed as a course over several months that combined classroom and on-the-job training. With a substantial investment of this kind, it was vital that the effectiveness of the leadership development programme was evaluated.

It was hoped that the programme would demonstrate value for money quickly, not least to demonstrate to its members that this substantial investment had been worth it. In order to calculate the ROI, the full costs needed to be captured. In addition, the benefits of the programme had to be identified and monetised, where possible.

Increases in sales could be monetised. So too could reductions in waste/losses from damage to product. Better buying patterns also reduced waste. Improved loyalty from local customers and members was also measured, but not monetised. It was recognised that while this might be possible to monetise in future, if and when a large set of data might be available to build evidence of a clear relationship between sales increases and customer loyalty, this would take several years to build. No attempts were made to put money values on staff engagement or embodiment of values, for two reasons. The first was that the unit of measure 'staff engagement' was neither stable nor standardised, the second that embodiment of values was not possible to measure in any rigorous way.

This degree of rigour is important because it helps to ensure that any presentation or discussion can be freed to focus on key conclusions and recommendations, and any danger of its becoming mired in disputes about the credibility of money values is avoided.

Bad driving behaviour

A local police authority was faced with budget cuts which were likely to have a potentially significant impact on its ability to serve its community. It sought ways to reduce costs without reducing police presence on the ground. One problem identified was the fact that when an officer was found to be driving in a dangerous manner, they had to be immediately removed from active duty in the community until they had undertaken a refresher course and demonstrated the correct behaviours. While there were costs incurred in damage to cars and handling complaints from the public (and luckily, no injury to the public), these costs were incidental by comparison with the loss of police officers available to drive patrol vehicles. In this case, therefore, the benefits of reducing poor behaviour were focused on the value of the capacity (measured in hours) that could be available to deploy officers in the community. One way of monetising this was to use the cost of overtime although this would have given a limited picture. Rather than monetise, our advice was to concentrate on measuring the capacity of the force to deploy the resources in patrol cars that were needed to attend to public needs in the fastest possible time, at any time.

Reporting costs and benefits

We can also report value for money by comparing the cost of our project with our outcomes, including reporting all of those that we cannot monetise. In this case, we are presenting the results in tabular form rather than as a monetary calculation. Remember that BCR or benefit cost ratio is exactly that, a ratio. But here we are not setting up a ratio, we are stating our impact outcomes (after attribution) and analysing them against the cost of achieving them.

For example, in a community project, one kilometre of river bank was cleaned of rubbish and maintained consistently over two years and the accountability for its maintenance was adopted by the local school as part of its third-year science class.

The cost of cleaning, removing the rubbish, training the team leads, regular clearing of the banks, planting new riverbank plants and the development of materials for the school curriculum was matched against the outcomes.

One kilometre of riverbank cost £10 per metre. Cost of maintenance is £0.02 per citizen within a one-kilometre radius. Cost of learning about maintaining the natural river environment is £0.10 per child.

We spend a lot of time and effort trying to build the confidence of clients and participants who feel that if you cannot put a money value on an impact outcome that somehow it means the impact outcome is less important or beneficial. This is simply not the case. Of course, you must be comparing *impact* outcomes *after* attribution, and not any other type of outcomes and not before isolation.

Interestingly, our experience is that those with a longer-term, more strategic perspective are usually less interested in the outcomes that can be monetised than in other outcomes. We call these non-monetised outcomes, the signals of a healthy organisation: one with high trust, brand recognition, loyal customers, engaged and committed staff etc. Improvements in these impact outcomes tell the senior team that it is leading a ship in fair waters and in the right direction, with a good team.

Ironically, the impact outcomes that can be monetised are, more often than not, those that are reporting historical results: in other words, what happened in the past. More goods sold, fewer errors, better margins achieved, higher productivity levels. All very good, and hopefully sustainable. And one could not deny that these too may be indicators of a healthy organisation. But when we monetise the results we have achieved, we are monetising the past achievement. This may be great for justifying expenditure in the short term, but does not necessarily tell us much about our positioning for the future.

Proxy values

How far should we allow ourselves to be pushed or persuaded into finding a money value for some achievement? Policy makers are often keen that we should go a considerable distance. As a result, there will always be those who are prepared to attempt to indulge them. Hence the work that has been done recently on developing the means to attach proxy values to otherwise non-monetisable achievements and benefits.

Proxy values/variables

The term 'proxy' may refer to having the authority to act on behalf of someone, or to a computer server that acts as an interface for a service. The online Oxford English Dictionary provides another definition for proxy, 'a figure that can be used to represent the value of something in a calculation'.

Within social science research, a proxy variable is used as an alternative when a quantity of interest cannot be observed. That is, when it is difficult or impossible to quantify or obtain a figure for the variable being observed, a substitute is used. Since a proxy variable is not a direct measure, care should be taken that it is strongly related to the variable being observed.

Sources: Oxford Dictionaries (2012); Clinton (2004).

The caution in the definition above is well-framed.

We reject the idea of using them because we regard it as more or less impossible to articulate proxies that are strongly enough related to the measures they represent to be credible, unless there is a sound mathematical model built from a well-established time series set of data for the two variables.

That might be the end of the discussion. But proxies are attractive in some circumstances, and to some funders and stakeholders, and as a result they have been quite actively promoted, especially to the public and the voluntary and third sectors. It is easy to see why: many of the impacts sought in those sectors are inherently both hard to measure and even more difficult to value directly. But they do have considerable policy importance, and those who achieve them are constantly being pressed to tell policy makers what they are worth to the donor or the taxpayer.

To illustrate some of the problems with proxies, it is useful to look at four examples of values arrived at in an evaluation done in a higher education context. They relate to an evaluation of a number of university local outreach programmes. The data relates to volunteers in schools and is attributing value to a series of outcomes that have been measured but are impossible to monetise by other means.

TABLE 13.1 Example 1

Outcome	Indicator	Financial proxies	Total
Increased learning	Number of hours of one-to-one tuition over a school year	Average cost of a private 1-hour tuition session	£223,668.00

The first problem with the example is the measurement of 'increased learning' by the number of hours of tuition. Increased learning is not an impact outcome. It isn't a learning outcome. The implication is that more knowledge has been measured, but that is not the case. Only time spent in class has been measured, which is not the same thing. The financial proxy is the 'average cost of a private one-hour tuition session'. Why? Were these not state schools? Is the average cost of a classroom teacher in a state school greater or smaller than that of a private tutor?

TABLE 13.2 Example 2

Outcome	Indicator	Financial proxies	Total
Higher aspirations	We used the average across three studies to estimate an increase in the aspirations of 14% of the pupils involved	The difference in earnings between those who do and do not go to university and the gain in tax	£680,552.40

In the example in Table 13.2 we are presumably being asked to assume that having higher aspirations inevitably includes attending university. Again, we have the problem that 'aspiration' is not an impact outcome. It is a hope, maybe an intention at best. The calculation behind the estimated gain of £680,552.40 is a result of multiplying the average extra earnings of university graduates as compared to those who have not been to university, plus the extra tax these earnings would have yielded to the Treasury by the forty-seven (the actual number behind the 14 per cent of those involved) who noted higher aspirations. This calculation has conflated the returns to two beneficiaries, the ex-pupils and the state, thereby increasing the actual sum of the supposed benefit. It has also used an average of extra income and applied it to a notional earning year of these pupils' lives. Even were this to work in itself, which it does not, it would be valid only as a net benefit once the notional costs of the university education had been deducted.

TABLE 13.3 Example 3

Outcome	Indicator	Financial proxies	Total
Greater enjoyment of reading	Based on a similar programme, we estimate that 15 pupils will see an improvement in their reading fluency and hence enjoyment of reading	Average number of books read by an 8-year-old multiplied by the average cost of a children's book	£1,544.52

In Table 13.3 the supposed outcome of 'greater enjoyment of reading' is based on a correlation with improved fluency that has been supported by research. Again, the question is 'What is the impact outcome?' It is a hard stretch of the imagination to propose increased enjoyment of reading as an impact outcome. And the proxy, which assumes that this will have raised the pupils' consumption of books to that of the average eight-year-old, and which then attaches the average price of a children's book, has lost the link with the idea of enjoyment. And what does the proxy mean? The financial benefit goes to the publishers and the authors. And what is the benefit? Is it the average price of the book, or the average margin of profit on the book? If the pupils who now enjoy reading more do not have the price of these books, presumably they will not be in a position to buy and read them, or will they purchase them second-hand or borrow them? If we are to assume that they purchase the books, do we assume Amazon prices or the non-discounted full cover prices?

TABLE 13.4 Example 4

Outcome	Indicator	Financial proxies	Total
Greater cultural awareness	We assume that all children involved will gain some cultural awareness through working with international students	Cost of a 1-hour assembly on different countries and local council budget for community cohesion projects	£47,692.95

The final example, in Table 13.4, is not based on any data at all, but on an assumption that 'some cultural awareness' would have been gained by pupils as a result of working with international students. We do not know what 'cultural awareness' is meant to convey. What is the unit of measure? If we assume an impact outcome is a long-term legacy where a real change in 'systems' can be said to have been realised, it might be possible to consider this an impact outcome. Moreover, a financial proxy and a figure of benefit both seem to have been pulled from the air.

These examples show the difficulties and dangers of trying to provide artificial measures of financial benefit. The more deeply you scrutinise them, the less they seem to tell you.

In each case the impact outcome presents problems of definition of a standardised unit of measure. In each case, the stated indicator is not an impact outcome and requires us to make large assumptions, but offers us little assistance in understanding why we should regard them as credible. The financial proxies are confusing. They do not represent savings in any real sense, it is not clear to whom the savings might apply, and on occasion they would need to be offset by other costs, which are not mentioned.

Ultimately, the danger is that the financial proxies appear to provide data on which policy can be developed when all they do is conjure an illusion of achievement based on compounded assumptions.

Value for money in the chain of impact

Finally, it is important to see the discipline of monetising impact outcomes where possible as only one link in the chain of impact. The value of the chain is in the data provided at each level, and the use to which that can be put. Remember Rule 4: 'Report results at each level when they are available to all those that can influence outcomes. There should be no surprises.'

In Chapter 10, we looked at a hotel where the training school ran a course for managing bar beverage service and how it was being monitored and evaluated. In this case, reporting the results at each level allowed the project team to learn what was working and where improvements could be made to how outcomes were achieved, without changing the actual outcome objectives. Reports would be generated at each level as follows:

- Level 1: Reports of the number and percentage of bartenders who rated the training course as relevant to their daily job responsibilities (scoring at least 4 out of 5).
- Level 2: Results of the training of bartenders, which included tests on product knowledge, simulation exercises to describe complete recipes, as well as skills test, e.g. 5 minutes to prepare a cocktail; collating these from the Training Reports.
- Level 3: Reports on the head bartenders' Market Visitation Logs, which are records of the head bartenders' visits to their local markets to identify new ingredients. Also monitored are reports of the head bartenders' meetings with

spirit suppliers to identify the top two current brands and their introduction of cocktails to guests.

- Level 4: At the scheduled time, reports on the average bill and revenues.
- Isolation is necessary to identify the influences of other factors, such as increased traffic to the hotel from other drivers (new visitor attractions, conference centre) and adjust the results after attribution.
- When calculating value for money, increased bill values and overall revenues can be monetised using margins.

As can be seen in this example, the chain of impact can be built up all the way through, right up to and including calculating value for money. But the chain should always remain as strong, even if it is not possible to monetise the final outcomes.

14
PROOF AND RULES

A vital element in any evaluation is the framework of rules that underpins its approach and its conduct. Rules can be defined as 'red tape' (bureaucratic, complex and rigid), or 'green tape' (clear, with valid means–ends relationships, employing optimal control, consistently applied and well understood by stakeholders). These rules are identified with the green tape concept. To be effective, they need to assert credibility, ensure consistency and guarantee fairness and equity.

The eight rules of the 'green tape' approach to planning, measuring and evaluating are:

1. *Always use full costs.*
2. *Never extrapolate from a small set of data or assume that the result from one group or project applies to another group or project.*
3. *Always carry out attribution/isolation for impact outcome data (and only impact outcome data), whether or not you intend to calculate ROI.*
4. *Report results at each level when they are available to all those that can influence outcomes – there should be no surprises.*
5. *Avoid averages except as benchmarks.*
6. *Never ever use proxy data for money values – it can destroy the credibility of the whole evaluation.*
7. *Never confuse correlation with causality – there must be a chain of impact.*
8. *Stories illustrate outcomes but the data must come first.*

Proof

Research rigour

Research rigour can be defined as examining the research methods used to ensure that they are scrupulously and meticulously applied in carrying out the research under study. This examination is constantly repeated throughout the research to ensure that any resulting claims of the research can be supported and justified.

When considering research rigour, researchers try to answer questions such as:

- Can the results be trusted?
- Were the measures used valid?
- Were the most appropriate methods used to answer the research question?

Sources: Members of the Research Methods Seminar (E600) taught by Mike Palmquist in the 1990s and 2000s (1994–2012). Glossary of Key Terms. Writing@CSU. Colorado State University. Available at http://writing.colostate.edu/guides/guide.cfm?guideid=90; Mentzer (2008).

We would all love to be in a position to state that evaluations of projects, programmes and activities had 'proved' that a particular investment of money and effort had resulted in a specific impact.

However, there is no way *ever* to demonstrate direct cause and effect. As you will have realised, reading thus far, there are too many variables; in other words, other influences which are likely to have played a supporting or contributory role in the achievement of impact.

We are not, therefore, very often in the zone of proof. We are normally in the zone of credible conclusion.

This means that there are always going to be questions raised about the credibility of what we and you report. There may always be challenges to the conclusions. Colleagues and stakeholders will watch very carefully to ensure that they are fairly dealt with as we attribute benefits to one cause or another.

One of the most important resources that we have with which to address these issues is a clear set of rules, governing our conduct as evaluators and communicating our values and standards of practice to others.

Dr Jack Phillips led the way in developing a set of rules for evaluations of learning and development. He called these 'Guiding Principles'. In setting out these rules, he pioneered the important realisation that in any organisation all results need to be treated fairly and consistently. This will allow fairness of treatment between one investment and another. Moreover, comparisons of investments across organisations, if the same 'Guiding Principles' are adopted, will enable a measure of reasonable comparison.

What Phillips set out in his 'Guiding Principles' are a set of rules similar to those that are applied in financial reporting. In the financial world, a set of rules or accounting standards are applied in order to provide confidence that a standard has been applied to the treatment of financial data. And, of course, it enables investors as well as the tax authorities to make decisions about the financial performance and status of the organisation.

Rules

An evaluation is an exercise in consent. As such, it can work only if it has behind it the force of an implicit or explicit contract.

The nature of the contract is that some people will furnish information and data to others who will examine it through an agreed process and, as a result, produce a report that respects both the information and the process itself.

Any announcement in an organisation that an evaluation is to be executed is greeted at the very least with some nervousness, and at worst with outright suspicion and hostility. Sometimes this hostility is bred of a concern that behind the evaluation is an agenda that will result in a biased presentation of data and conclusions. Sometimes it results from sensitivity to the process being used. Sometimes, of course, it is driven by a mistrust of the competence of the evaluators.

There are, of course, occasions on which some people are determined not to cooperate with any form of evaluation. They may feel that the timing is inappropriate. They may believe that their status, or that of their work, renders evaluation by others irrelevant or inappropriate. If that occurs, the problem may be resolvable only by the intervention of a higher authority.

But mostly this is not the case, and the path of an evaluation needs to be smoothed by more conventional means: agreement on the rules that will govern and condition the conduct of the evaluation.

The Oxford Dictionary defines 'rules' as 'one of a set of explicit or understood regulations or principles governing conduct or procedure within a particular area of activity'. Rules are usually set by the governing body of an organisation to regulate its activities. Research has shown that rules can deter flexibility and creativity. Even so, other research has shown that rules can have 'positive social psychological effects for employees'. This leads to rules being classified as 'red tape' and 'green tape'.

- Red tape: rules that are complex, rigid and formulistic, that tend to be used in bureaucratic environments. Reducing red tape releases the entrepreneurial spirit and improves performance.
- Green tape: also known as effective organisational rules, described by five attributes: '(1) Written requirements, (2) with valid means–ends relationships, which (3) employ optimal control, (4) are consistently applied, and have (5) purposes understood by stakeholders.' These attributes are expected to increase technical capacity, as well as improve rule acceptability with stakeholders, who explain, enforce or comply with the rules.

Source: Oxford Dictionaries (2012) 'Rules' [online], available: http://oxforddictionaries.com/definition/english/rule?q=rules [accessed 10 November 2012].

We identify our rules clearly with the green tape concept.

Green tape rules in practice

The point of having a set of rules is to understand how the highest principles and practice will affect each evaluation. This means that consideration of the application of the rules must be an important feature of the planning of each evaluation.

When this is done it will become apparent that all of the eight rules play a part in ensuring the credibility of the evaluation, and it is important to think this through and to draw it to the attention of other stakeholders at the planning stage and, of course, in reports. Credibility is the first prism through which any reader will view any evaluation.

Stakeholders and colleagues are then likely to turn their attention to practical and personal implications. What does the evaluation mean for the way in which such things are done in the context of these two groups, or in the organisation? Have they, or those with whom they may have relationships, have been treated fairly in the evaluation?

Source: DeHart-Davis, L. (2009) 'Green Tape: A Theory of Effective Organizational Rules', *Journal of Public Administration Research and Theory: J-PART*, (2), 361.

---

abdi Green Tape Rules for impact evaluation

This concept of green tape exactly describes both the spirit and the structure of the rules required to lie behind formative (improvement focused) evaluation. They need to underpin three crucial concepts:

1. credibility: by including rules that assure rigour and conservatism
2. consistency: by ensuring that each evaluation will be conducted to the same standards and within the same limitations
3. fairness and equity: by ensuring that all stakeholders are fairly represented, that the data provided by them and about them is handled with transparent regard for their rights and interests, and that conclusions and recommendations are clearly linked to data.

As well as acknowledging these concepts, rules are needed to guard against prevalent bad habits, and occasionally to defend evaluators against the desire of stakeholders to see conclusions reached, whether or not there is evidence to support them.

The eight rules in Tables 14.1 to 14.8 – the green tape of responsible impact evaluation – address these requirements.

Rule 1: Always use full costs

In Chapter 9 we looked at a programme working to eradicate avoidable blindness in Africa, and saw how the project team discovered that the true cost was almost double what was initially calculated. Initially, only the direct costs were considered. However, by applying the rule 'Always use full costs', the project team captured the direct costs (spectacles, travel, accommodation, evaluation cost etc.), as well as the indirect costs (salary of participating teams such as specialists and trainees, costs of running eye departments in the developing country, use of hospital facilities for training for both parties etc.). These were categorised under Needs Assessment and Analysis, Design and Development, Acquisition, Delivery/Implementation, Evaluation and Overheads (relating to the training and development team).

The project team realised that although it was not calculating the ROI of the programme, it was still beneficial to capture the full costs. Capturing full costs was especially helpful for future budgeting. It was also helpful for future projects to identify the categories and costs associated with a programme of this kind. In addition, calculating the fully loaded costs gave weight to the need for a rigorous evaluation approach when the project team communicated with stakeholders (Table 14.1).

TABLE 14.1

Rule 1: Always use full costs.

Rationale: It is impossible to calculate a benefit unless you first know how much you have had to spend to achieve it – including items like people's time.

Credibility	Consistency	Fairness and equity
Only full costs provide a realistic basis for reporting value for money. Even if the impact outcome data cannot be monetised, full-cost information is vital to provide a realistic perspective on what has been achieved.	Wherever regular evaluations are being conducted it is important to establish conventions about full-cost reporting, and to ensure that costs are calculated and recorded in the same way, and following the same structure, every time.	Reporting indirect as well as direct costs, and ensuring that full costs are always reported, guarantees a fair view of the relative value for effort and money of activities that may be very differently structured and financed.

Rule 2: Never extrapolate from a small set of data

In a reassessment of the information in an evaluation carried out in Nigeria, a second set of evaluators issued questionnaires to test the conclusions of the first evaluation. The first evaluation was based on around a third of Nigeria's thirty-six states, and data had been scarce in some of them because of the security and logistical challenges of collecting it. The second evaluation (the evaluation of the evaluation, if you like) questioned the conclusions reached on the basis of the data gathered in the first one. But a closer look at the second evaluation showed that the data it had collected had come from only two states, and the vast majority of it from only one. Nigeria is such a large and diverse country that it is extremely dangerous to assume that data collected in one state will be relevant in any others (Table 14.2).

TABLE 14.2

Rule 2: Never extrapolate from a small set of data or assume that the result from one group or project applies to another group or project.

Rationale: In impact evaluations we frequently find ourselves taking decisions about how much data we need to collect, and we are often in a position where we cannot collect all that we'd like to have. We then look for data that will provide reliable indications of outcomes. We may collect data from only a proportion of a group or cohort, but we must be satisfied that this proportion at least matches the principal characteristics of the group (gender, geography, age, location, for example). But there must be some data. In the case of small populations, we usually aim to collect the outcome data from the whole population. In larger populations, only if we deploy randomised representative sampling can we be confident that the results represent a close approximation to the results we might find for the whole population (see Chapter 12 for guidance on sampling and likely margin for error).

Credibility	Consistency	Fairness and equity
We can never assume that just because another group shares some or all of these characteristics any results will be replicated.	It is important to establish conventions and guidelines on sampling so that the approach taken in each case can be seen to be consistent with prior guidelines or agreements on the collection and treatment of data.	Assuming, without direct evidence, that similar behaviour and results will be observable in different contexts will always be unreliable and is likely to be unfair. It may provide evidence that leads to underestimates or overestimates of outcomes.

Rule 3: Always carry out attribution/isolation for impact outcome data

In the example of the restaurant and pub group in Chapter 12, the evaluator was able to report an ROI of 539 per cent as a result of a strategic leadership training investment. But this was acceptable only after three forms of isolation had been used: control groups, time series (comparisons between pre- and post-performance, which is not a formal isolation process, but was certainly a useful check in this case) and estimation by a number of internal stakeholders (Table 14.3).

TABLE 14.3

Rule 3: Always carry out attribution/isolation for impact outcome data (and only impact outcome data), whether or not you intend to calculate ROI.

Rationale: It is always essential to analyse any report of impact by asking 'Is there anything else that could have caused all or part of this, and if so, how much of the impact should we attribute to what we have done?'

Credibility	*Consistency*	*Fairness and equity*
Taking a claim of benefit at its face value without examination by a formal attribution process is the equivalent of attributing climate change to human activity without taking account of other influences on the weather.	Applying, reviewing and refining the attribution process ensures that all claims of impact outcomes are expressed conservatively and respect the reality that rarely, if ever, is a result due to only one action or a single investment.	Wherever in an organisation, or amongst stakeholders, there are competing initiatives or influences capable of having contributed to an impact, a systematic process of isolation will enable agreement, sharing of the credit and building on the results.

Rule 4: Report results at each level when they are available to all those that can influence outcomes

In Chapter 10, the example of an initiative to track the implementation of a Funding, Monitoring and Evaluation Framework shows how the data collected at Levels 1, 2, 3 and 4 is being communicated quarterly to project leads to enable them to make changes and improvements in the way they use a specific fund to shift the balance of care for older people to care in the community (Table 14.4).

TABLE 14.4

Rule 4: Report results at each level when they are available to all those that can influence outcomes. There should be no surprises.

Rationale: We use this approach and the data we generate to improve projects and programmes while they are in progress. This has the benefit that key stakeholders are prepared for the results produced by evaluations well before they are finally reported.

Credibility	*Consistency*	*Fairness and equity*
Early and prompt reporting reinforces positive engagement with evaluation and its results. More importantly, it affords an opportunity to use the data to address where improvement can be made and increase the potential for achieving value for money.	If engagement, learning and application of learning data are consistently reported promptly and in the same way, colleagues and stakeholders are likely to understand their usefulness for improvement not only of the activities or programmes that are being evaluated, but also for other related activities and programmes.	It is important to show how each link in the chain of impact plays its part in the whole achievement of the impact of an activity or programme, and in doing this to emphasise the contributions of involved participants, colleagues and stakeholders.

Rule 5: Avoid using averages, except as benchmarks

A reading of Chapters 10 and 11 should make it clear that averages are of limited use in reporting outcomes. It is important to look at range as well as average. Averages can provide some direction when establishing future targets for achievement. In Chapter 4, we use the common issue of complaints in an organisation to illustrate the value of averages or trends, and the danger of focusing on single data points, which may easily represent blips, or exceptions simply occurring by chance (Table 14.5).

TABLE 14.5

Rule 5: Avoid using averages, except as benchmarks.

Rationale: Once we have compiled a set of results, we need to make sense of the data. There are lots of ways to view the data in order to reflect on what it might tell us. If we are looking at improvement, say, in error rates across teams, an average of the data may be useful to help set a minimum benchmark for error rates. However, looking at only the average may mean that we fail to spot the range of performance: the average may mask very great differences between different teams.

Credibility	*Consistency*	*Fairness and equity*
We must show that we have fully understood what is going on behind any piece of data. Averages can conceal that full picture. A well-informed and experienced manager will see that, and attach less weight to conclusions as a result. If averages are used to arrive at a compromise between two conflicting views of impact, the result will always dissatisfy at least half of those involved. This means that there will be insufficient credible consensus for action to be taken as a result.	Averages pose problems for consistency. There will always be arguments that medians should be used instead, and if there are instances where consistent data has been gathered over time it may be possible to report trends. For consistency, it is always better to report hard data, even if it is conflicted, or trends. Either of these can provide sufficient common ground for subsequent actions.	Averages disguise the distinct contributions that make them up, and therefore make it more difficult to recognise and work with the results achieved by different stakeholders.

Rule 6: Never, ever, use proxy data for money values

The four examples of proxy values in Chapter 13 underline the dangers of using them. Each one is readily seen to be plausible, but the more closely it is examined, the less robust it seems to become. The intention in evaluation has to be that the opposite is the case: the closer the scrutiny, the greater the confidence (Table 14.6).

TABLE 14.6

Rule 6: Never, ever, use proxy data for money values: it can destroy the credibility of the whole evaluation.

Rationale: Any report of value for money needs to be based on hard, real financial benefit. It is better to say openly that it is impossible to attach a money value to benefits than to fabricate a value based on estimation or association.

Credibility	Consistency	Fairness and equity
Proxy values are, by definition, not real. Therefore, they can be and are challenged very frequently and, while they may seem to offer a magic result, will quickly be recognised for what they are – 'made up'. Project leaders and evaluators can find themselves being pushed into 'making up' economic value and, no matter how much in their report they may caution about the validity of the calculation, it is the number, not the caution, that will be noted and given the headline. The result of this is that the credibility of the evaluation becomes the focus of all discussion around it, at the expense of the conclusions and recommendations that can be drawn from the collected data. It also undermines confidence in any future attempts to report results.	It is deeply undermining to the concept of evaluation to apply stringent rules and etiquettes to the collection of data on engagement, learning and application of learning, and then to suspend them in favour of hypothesising data related to monetary value.	One of the most common motivations for developing proxy data is to provide the basis for making comparisons between different projects, programmes and their suppliers. If the basis for proxy data is insecure, these comparisons will, by their very nature, be weak. The comparisons risk being invidious and unfair. Of course, on these terms, the process of comparison itself becomes self-defeating because the basis for making a choice between one approach and another lacks substance.

Rule 7: Never confuse correlation with causality

In Chapter 10 we looked at a programme to reshape care for older people by shifting the balance of care from acute/care home settings into the community. The case outlined the chain of impact for the implementation of the change team's integrated Funding, Monitoring and Evaluation Framework, repeated here:

• Level 1: the Framework is considered user friendly by at least 80 per cent of project leads.
• Level 2: project leads and stakeholders wishing to apply for project funding are able to use the Framework to apply for funding and to provide monitoring data that meet the objectives of the Change Plan.

- Level 3: two months after implementation, 100 per cent of project leads are completing their Applications and Monitoring returns that reflect the Framework.
- Level 4: 100 per cent of project leads adhere to the quarterly, six monthly and annual monitoring as outlined in the Framework.

In this case, the chain of impact clearly shows the performance that is required at Levels 1 to 3 to achieve the impact outcomes (Level 4). Therefore, although it cannot be said that implementing the Framework *caused* 100 per cent of projects to adhere to the scheduled monitoring as outlined in the Framework, the data collected at each level can demonstrate a credible chain of impact (Table 14.7).

TABLE 14.7

Rule 7: Never confuse correlation with causality – there must be a chain of impact.

Rationale: The fact that a targeted impact has been achieved at a time and in a context that is consistent with an investment that was designed to drive it does not mean that the investment was responsible for the achievement. To show that, we need to collect enough data through the chain of impact to demonstrate that the people in whom the investment has been made have actually performed the tasks and functions assigned to them.

Credibility	*Consistency*	*Fairness and equity*
Evaluations are often undermined either because no attempt has been made to show what has caused changes, or because unsubstantiated claims based on weak assumptions have been made about causality.	This is one of the most basic and most important issues on which clear consistency is essential for evaluators. If it is understood that we never take the short-cut of trying to suggest that the impact is caused by one intervention simply because no one else is claiming the credit, we may on occasions have to admit that we can offer no conclusions, but when we do offer them it will be clear that they have some foundation.	The bottom-up discipline of collecting sufficient data to establish a chain of impact is one that offers a much clearer view of individual and shared accountability. It establishes fairness of treatment both to immediate stakeholders, and, through isolation and attribution, to others outside the immediate stakeholder groups.

Rule 8: Stories illustrate outcomes, but the data must come first

At the end of Chapter 3 we cite a case of setting objectives for reduction in the incidence of pressure ulcers. The treatment of these is estimated to account for as much as 4 per cent of total NHS expenditure.

The specific objectives set were percentage reductions in the prevalence of pressure ulcers, the rate of infections from them and the amount of nurse time spent caring for patients suffering from them. Obviously, any reports of improvements in these metrics would be enhanced by some anecdotal evidence, from patients who had previously suffered from pressure ulcers, of the improvement in the quality of their lives as a result of better practice. But if those observations from patients were to be offered on their own, without the data, they would be unlikely to stimulate the same level of interest from managers. They would certainly not supply the basis for future decisions (Table 14.8).

TABLE 14.8

Rule 8: Stories illustrate outcomes, but the data must come first.

Rationale: Case studies and interviews are interesting and revealing, but it is not safe to generalise from them; they should be used to supply context to reports of quantified outcomes.

Credibility	*Consistency*	*Fairness and equity*
A success story is just what it says it is: a story of a single success. It does not tell us that anything else has been a success. Its value is as an illustration of what has been explained through data.	Good practice is to use success stories (how often do we see failure stories?) as illustrations only where data has been supplied to provide a proper context for them.	If success stories are used in a way that encourages a distorted view of results, this fails to recognise that it is the whole investment that is being measured. One good story may be the exception.

Communicating credibility, consistency and fairness

The above descriptions and explanations of the rules establish a general case for the green tape discipline. Organisations should publish, communicate and promote these rules as evidence of their commitment to fairness, consistency and transparency. In doing so, it helps to build credibility and engagement in the process. It is an equally essential aspect of good practice to review and note any issues, challenges, qualifications or lessons learned during the evaluation or as a result of the publication and presentation of the evaluation and its conclusions and recommendations. There should always be some reference to the underpinning rules in final evaluation reports.

Green tape tool

The simple template in Table 14.9 is all that evaluators will require to make their thinking, and their experience, transparent.

TABLE 14.9

abdi Green Tape Rules (evaluation application of rules template)

Rule	Contribution to the credibility of the evaluation process and its results	Practical and personal implications		Issues noted during the evaluation (any challenges, changes, qualifications, lessons for future good practice)
		Consistency	Fairness and equity	
1. Always use full costs.				
2. Never extrapolate from a small set of data or assume that the result from one group or project applies to another group or project.				
3. Always carry out attribution/isolation for impact outcome data (and only impact outcome data), whether or not you intend to calculate ROI.				
4. Report results at each level when they are available to all those that can influence outcomes. There should be no surprises.				
5. Avoid using averages, except as benchmarks.				
6. Never, ever, use proxy data for money values: it can destroy the credibility of the whole evaluation.				
7. Never confuse correlation with causality – there must be a chain of impact.				
8. Stories illustrate outcomes, but the data must come first.				

15

STRATEGIC REMINDER

This book has been written primarily for those with a responsibility for evaluation. Some will regard themselves as professional evaluators. Many others will be project and programme commissioners, managers, organisational development and HR managers and directors, consultants and education and training providers. Indeed, professional evaluators are likely to be in a minority. This reflects the definite trend towards managers at all levels in organisations being charged with providing some evidence of the outcomes, impacts and benefits of the investments for which they are responsible. There is a greater understanding of the importance of setting SMART objectives, but not necessarily always a concomitant ability to frame them to an acceptable standard. There is much less appreciation of the challenges of collecting and analysing data generated by these objectives. These tasks – indeed the responsibility for improving the way we plan, measure and report what we spend our money on – clearly cannot be left to evaluators. They are central to the tasks of managers.

This final chapter has two functions, which we have rolled into one message: A Memo to Chief Officers.

It sets out first to encapsulate some of the key ideas and messages that have punctuated the preceding chapters.

Its second function is fulfilled by addressing it to chief officers and senior executives. They need to understand that achieving higher levels of professional planning, measurement and reporting is demanding, but essential in any well-run organisation.

The ideas behind what we do and help others to do are not hard to grasp, but they are always challenging to apply. Within organisations this means that there must be willing and pro-active cooperation from immediate colleagues and from others in key positions and functions.

Our experience, shared with many others, is that change of this kind will be very hard to embed successfully unless it has the endorsement and support of those at the top. The most senior managers are unlikely to be directly involved in monitoring and evaluation or to be directly involved in measurement activities. But we have seen very senior people react rapidly and positively to brief, focused explanations of what can be done, and how.

We hope that they react with enthusiasm. Whenever they do, the chances of driving through real change will have increased dramatically because, whereas planning, monitoring and evaluating is generally conducted in the middle ranks of an organisation, the culture and key standards are set from the top. If the most senior executives are not positive supporters of these disciplines, it becomes very hard for others to promote and sustain them.

A memo to chief officers and senior executives

Three relevant questions to ask yourself and share with your senior team

1. Do you plan, track and report the impact achieved by at least 25 per cent of your significant investments in human capital?

The *majority* of projects and programmes we have seen and heard of have been planned with insufficient – often zero – needs analysis. It is rare to come across an investment with really SMART outcome objectives that can be monitored and evaluated.

This suggests a failure to question whether human capital-intensive investments are delivering impact. It suggests that the data is lacking with which to make sound investment decisions, and indicates that the analysis on which future improvements can be based cannot be done.

2. Are your investments in human capital driven by demand, or are they essentially supply sided?

All human-capital spending plans need to be interrogated as a matter of course, until each one can be aligned directly with key organisational objectives.

'Because we have a budget for this', or 'Because this supplier has a particularly good course', or 'Because we generally do one of these at this time of year' are not valid reasons for launching a project or a programme.

Justifications for training such as 'We need to strengthen leadership amongst middle management' need to be questioned until the answers become specific in terms of saving money, saving time, improving customer satisfaction or staff relations, improving quality or driving some form of innovation.

Human-capital spending plans need to be treated with the same rigour as that applied to decisions on purchasing expensive equipment.

3. Do you know, and do you report, the true cost of these investments?

When costs are reported for human capital projects and activities, they generally leave out the most important element: the cost of the people's time. For every human capital investment, ask to see the full cost of the time that staff spend away from their work, including the cost of any backfill required. Ask also to see the share (pro-rated) of any unallocated overhead costs for any project or HR activity. Make it clear to others that these indirect costs of the people attending activities are very real to the organisations, and that they can multiply the overall costs of these activities and projects by between three and ten times.

Three constructive answers

1. Good planning depends on sound principles and good habits

- Demand that every investment is linked to a key organisational priority.
- Start each plan by stating the impact it is intended to achieve.
- Require each investment plan to show that baselines have been researched, and all the stakeholders have been identified and their potential contributions and expectations analysed.
- Ensure that all plans include SMART objectives for performance and behaviour, knowledge, skills and confidence and the buy-in of all key people.
- Require a full cost forecast (not the same as a budget).

2. Achieving professional measurement

- No one can show absolute proof that an investment in any human capital project delivered a specific result – the best that can be done is to establish a chain of impact that demonstrates the relationship between each set of outcome data that you have 'tested' firmly in terms of the links in the chain.
- You can never accept that a piece of outcome data is the result of a specific investment until it has been subjected to a specific isolation/attribution process to acknowledge and account for the efforts and influences of others.
- The smartest organisations collect data to drive improvement, and collect enough of it to provide credible evidence.
- Avoid falling into the trap of confusing correlations with causality. Over the years, we have read and reviewed many reports that state categorically that the investment in A correlates with improvement in B and therefore A caused B. You cannot make that leap.

(Continued)

(Continued)

- By building a strong body of evidence you will have the means to make better decisions for planning future investment.

*3. Responsible reporting is about communicating
what has really happened*

- Even if it is a disappointment, good data helps you move on and improve; this happens only as a result of open minds and hard work.
- Do not embark on improving measurement practice if all you want to do is prove what a great investment you have made – you will almost certainly miss most of the key learning, and may find that it has not been quite as successful as you hoped.
- Dummy tools (mainly now online) claim that if you put in your numbers they will tell you what value you've achieved. Even though they are based on models that were tried elsewhere, this does not mean that they will give you the same results. They provide a short-cut to unreliable answers, fail to provide any measure of accountability and are a poor basis for decision making.

Three immediate steps to take

1. *Review your human capital spend and your projects* to make sure that you know the extent to which your spending is aligned with the priorities and objectives you have identified as most important to your organisation, and check that costs you have been told about are indeed the true, *full* costs.
2. *Require all future spend to be justified* in terms of the impact outcomes it is expected to achieve, or at least to which it is expected to contribute.
3. *Ensure that your organisation has the capacity to do sufficient measurement*, which means having people with the right skills, baseline data for all your key organisational priorities and indicators and a presumption that all your biggest spend and all your pilot activities will be measured, and their impact reported.

Now . . .

Make sure that your organisation reaps the benefit of doing this well. Only those at the top of the organisation can demand the discipline, seek the engagement and commitment, and take the lead by showing a respect for evidence and a determination to use quality data for analysis and decision making. Be open about the results of investments, share them and be prepared to learn from them.

The prize is future improvement.

A final word to practitioners

We all need to learn with and from each other. We need support.

If you have read this book and, like us, want to continue to learn and develop your planning, measurement and improvement techniques, join our Moodle Group immediately.

Go to www.abdi.eu.com.

As well as the Moodle discussion group, you'll find the following further resources on the website:

- case studies
- further reading list
- further learning.

LIBRARY. UNIVERSITY OF CHESTER

GLOSSARY

Some definitions taken from *The Monitoring and Evaluation Handbook for Business Environment Reform* (Herzberg 2008), *Glossary of Key Terms in Evaluation and Results Based Management* (OECD 2002), and the Oxford Online Dictionary; other sources referenced when used.

Action plan   A documented plan that breaks down goals/objectives into smaller, manageable activities. Action plans should include:

- proposed actions: 'will do' → 'so that' → 'by start date'
- resources: 'required resources' → 'source of resources'
- problems: 'barriers' → 'solutions to barriers'
- evidence of completion: 'date completed' → 'evidence'

Activities   Actions taken to mobilise inputs to produce specific outputs. Also called 'actions' or 'tasks'.

Aggregating data   The act of collecting data from a combination of measurements and summarising the collected data.

Application   The on-the-job practice of knowledge or skills that were learned as part of a human-capital learning initiative, such as a training programme (Level 3 in abdi's approach).

Attitude   An evaluative reaction to someone, or something, exhibited in one's feelings, beliefs or intended behaviour.

Attribution   Isolating and proportioning part of the total benefits to a specific area, in order to compare the benefits with the cost.

Baseline data   Data collected prior to the start of an initiative that can be used to compare new data and thus serve as a reference point in terms of relative success or failure.

Benchmarks   The assimilation of best practices within a particular sector to form a standard for other practices to be compared or assessed.

Benefit cost ratio (BCR)   This equation compares the cost of an initiative with the monetary value of the benefits obtained from carrying out the initiative: total benefits/ total costs.

Benefits   Positive outcomes generated from an initiative, which can be monetary on non-monetary.

Bottom line   The last line of a financial statement or balance sheet, used to show net profit or loss.

Case study   An intensive study of an initiative; provides a detailed record and narrative of the process and outcome.

Chain of impact   The steps taken to demonstrate the links between an initiative/activity and the long-term outcome (impact). These steps include: activity → reaction → learning → application → outcome and impact. All the links in the chain need to be clearly articulated.

Comparative data   An examination of two or more sets of data to identify similarities and/or differences.

Competence   The ability to do something successfully or efficiently.

Compliance   Adherence to rules, regulations, orders.

Conservation   Purposely and cautiously reporting the lowest figures (percentage of attribution, etc.) relating to benefits derived as a result of the initiative.

Consistency   The quality of being uniform or constant in the performance or treatment of measurement techniques.

Credibility   The quality of being trusted, convincing or believable.

Data frameworks   The basic structure that outlines planned action with regard to key performance indicators, data collection and monitoring.

Data set   A collection of a related set of variables or information, which is composed of different elements.

Direct costs   Costs for activities, resources, material or services that can be directly traced to the initiative.

Dosage   The amount of investment (whether that be costs, time, human capital or level of training) that an initiative requires.

Engagement   The commitment of key stakeholders to learn, execute and/or support the activities of the initiative. For abdi's approach, this is at Level 1. It is important to evaluate the stakeholders' views on the relevance of the initiative to their roles and the organisation, the amount of new knowledge gained as a result of the initiative, whether they would recommend it to others and any specific planned actions that are directed towards changed behaviour.

Evaluation   A systematic and objective assessment of an on-going or completed initiative, including its design, implementation and results. An evaluation should provide information that is credible and useful, enabling the incorporation of lessons learned into the decision-making process.

Evidence base   A body of facts or information that indicates whether a belief or proposition is true.

Forecasting   Used to isolate the effects of an initiative. The actual performance of a measure related to the initiative is compared to the forecasted value of that measure. It is useful in organisations that have created mathematical formulas for output variables as a function of one or more inputs. (From: Phillips, J. J. (2003) *Return on Investment in Training and Performance Improvement Programs, Improving Human Performance*, 2nd edn, USA: Butterworth-Heinemann.)

Formative evaluation   An evaluation conducted while the initiative is being implemented to improve performance.

Fully loaded costs   All monetary input that can be identified and linked to a particular initiative. It is the denominator in the BCR and ROI equations. In the ROI equation, it is also part of the numerator, where it is subtracted from the total benefits.

Impact   Long-term and sustainable change as a direct/indirect result of the initiative. This can be positive/negative, primary/secondary or intended/unintended. Also called 'impact outcome'.

Impact measurement   Assessment of the long-term outcomes of a particular investment.

Indicator   A variable that provides a means to measure achievement. 'To indicate' means 'to point out' or 'to show'. When used in monitoring and evaluation, indicators point towards the fulfilment of objectives.

Indirect costs   Costs which cannot be applied to a specific task or method but which are relevant in calculating the total cost of the project.

Initiative   Programmes, projects, policies and interventions that are implemented to improve a situation or resolve a problem.

Input   That which goes into the initiative, such as financial, human and material resources.

Isolation   Identification and separation of the factor(s) influencing an initiative for further examination.

Iteration   The act of repeating a process or set of procedures for a specified number of times or until a desired outcome is achieved.

Know-how   The required level of existing skills, knowledge, competences and practical abilities.

Know-what   The information needed to do what is required to the standard expected, or pure knowledge.

Meta-analysis   Used for combining studies across different projects that use measures that can be compared or converted to a common metric.

Monetising   Converting impact data to monetary value.

Monitoring   A continuous process involving the systematic collection of data on specified indicators, which is used to indicate the progress and potential achievement of an initiative's objectives.

Non-monetised impact   An impact that has not had a monetary value attached, either because it was not possible to do so in a credible manner, or it was not planned to do so.

Objectives   An individual's, group's or organisation's desired aims or goals for an initiative.

Outcomes   The likely or achieved short-term and medium-term effects of an initiative's outputs.

Output   The products, capital goods and services that result from an initiative; may also include changes resulting from the initiative that are relevant to the achievement of outcomes.

Proxy   A figure used to represent the value of something in a calculation.

Qualitative data   Data that describes the attributes or features of something, sometimes called 'soft' data. Can be hard to standardise or convert to money.

Quantitative data   Data that is represented by numerical values, sometimes called 'hard' data. Can be standardised and is often easier to collect than soft/qualitative data; may also be relatively easy to convert into monetary values.

Randomised controlled trial (RCT)   Random selection of participants for testing from at least two groups (intervention and control) from the same eligible population and a comparison of the testing outcomes. Considered the 'gold standard' by many evaluators but very difficult and costly to implement.

Relevance   The extent of alignment or connection between an initiative and the organisation's objectives.

Reliability   The closeness or consistency of an initial estimated value to subsequent estimated values.

Return on investment (ROI)   An indicator of the value-for-money of investments in human capital initiatives. It uses the formula:

$$ROI = (Benefits - Fully\ Loaded\ Costs)/Fully\ Loaded\ Costs \times 100$$

ROI forecasting   ROI forecasting is when the future ROI is predicted either before an initiative has been implemented or using reaction, learning or application data.

Root Cause Analysis   A type of problem-solving approach that aims to identify the source(s) of a problem or incident.

Scorecard   Tracks key elements of an initiative's strategy through a clear set of performance indicators.

Selection bias   Errors that occur in the selection process when a research study is being undertaken, i.e. when choosing the persons or groups that are to take part in the study.

Settled behaviour   Changes in a person's typical actions as a result of an initiative (observed at Level 3 in abdi's approach).

Skills   Proficiency in performing a specific act.

Stakeholder   Any person or group who has an interest or concern in, or can influence, the objective(s) or outcome(s) of an initiative.

Standard values   Primary business measures that already have monetary values developed for each unit of measure. E.g. cost of individual absence and staff turnover.

Summative evaluation   An assessment of the extent to which an initiative has achieved its intended outcomes. It is carried out at the end of implementation or at a particular stage in the implementation.

Systems Analysis   Dissection of a system to investigate its component parts in order to identify problems or areas for improvement.

Systems and process maps   Flow diagrams that clearly outline the sequence of activities that convert inputs into outputs.

Theory of Change   An initial planning tool that describes an initiative to show all the assumptions, intentions and links within it that are often not explicit. It describes the causal logic (sometimes called the 'program logic') that shows that the initiative is expected to lead to a particular goal.

Unit of measure   The standard of measure used to assess the amount or quantity of something.

Validity   In terms of an evaluation and measurement instrument, the extent to which it measures what it intended to measure.

Variable   A feature of a unit being observed that may assume more than one of a set of values to which a numerical measure or a category from a classification can be assigned (e.g. income, age, weight, etc., and 'occupation', 'industry', 'disease', etc.).

BIBLIOGRAPHY

ActKnowledge Inc. (2012) 'Theory of Change', [online], available: www.theoryofchange. org [accessed 15 August 2012].

Bamberger, M. (2006) *Conducting Quality Impact Evaluations under Budget, Time and Data Constraints*, World Bank [online], available: http://lnweb90.worldbank.org/oed/ oeddoclib.nsf/DocUNIDViewForJavaSearch/757A5CC0BAE22558852571770059D8 9C/$file/conduct_qual_impact.pdf [accessed 10 April 2013].

Bassi, L. (2011) 'Decision-Science: Measuring and Valuing Training Investments' (podcast) *Human Resources IQ.*, www.humanresourcesiq.com/corporate-learning-measurement/ podcasts/decision-science-measuring-valuing-training-invest.

Blanchard, K., Zigarmi, P. and Zigarmi, D. (1985) *Leadership and the One Minute Manager*, USA: William Morrow and Company, Inc.

Bloom, B. S., Engelhart, M. D., Furst, E. J., Hill, W. H. and Krathwohl, D. R. (1956) *Taxonomy of Educational Objectives: The Classification of Educational Goals. Handbook 1, Cognitive Domain*, London: Longman.

BRC Global Standards (2012) 'Understanding Root Cause Analysis', *BRC Global Standards*, www.brcglobalstandards.com/Portals/0/Books/Rootcause/rootcause/assets/basic-html/ page1.htm [last viewed 8 January 2014].

Clinton, J. (2004) 'Proxy Variable', in Lewis-Beck, M. S., Bryman, A. and Liao, T. F., eds, *Encyclopaedia of Social Science Research Methods*, Thousand Oaks, CA: Sage Publications, Inc.

Cooper, R. and Kaplan, R. S. (1988) 'Measure Costs Right: Make the Right Decision', *Harvard Business Review*, 66(5), 96–103.

DeHart-Davis, L. (2009) 'Green Tape: A Theory of Effective Organizational Rules', *Journal of Public Administration Research and Theory: J-PART*, 19(2), 361.

DePoe, J. M. (2013) 'Knowledge by Acquaintance and Knowledge by Description' [online], available: www.iep.utm.edu/knowacq [accessed 24 September 2013].

Doran, G. T. (1981) 'There's a S.M.A.R.T. Way to Write Managements's Goals and Objectives', *Management Review*, 70(11), 35.

Dowe, P. (2008) 'Causal Processes', *The Stanford Encyclopedia of Philosophy* [online], available: http://plato.stanford.edu/archives/fall2008/entries/causation-process [accessed 8 April 2013].

Dreyfus, S. E. (2004) 'The Five-Stage Model of Adult Skill Acquisition', *Bulletin of Science, Technology & Society*, 24(3), 177–81.

Dreyfus, S. E. and Dreyfus, H. L. (1980) *A Five-Stage Model of the Mental Activities Involved in Directed Skill Acquisition*, Washington, DC: California University Berkeley Operations Research Center.

Easton, V. J. and McColl, J. H. (1997) 'Time Series Data', *Statistics Glossary v1.1* [online], available: www.stats.gla.ac.uk/steps/glossary/time_series.html [accessed 8 April 2013].

Fildes, R. (2010) 'Forecasting: The Issues (Revised Version)' [online], available: www.lums.lancs.ac.uk/research/centres/Forecasting/Material/ [accessed 21 December 2012].

Haynes, L., Service, O., Goldacre, B. and Torgerson, D. (2012) *Test, Learn, Adapt: Developing Public Policy with Randomised Controlled Trials*, London, UK: Cabinet Office Behavioural Insights Team.

Hernandez, P. R., Schultz, P. W., Estrada, M., Woodcock, A. and Chance, R. C. (2013) 'Sustaining Optimal Motivation: A Longitudinal Analysis of Interventions to Broaden Participation of Underrepresented Students in STEM', *Journal of Educational Psychology*, 105(1), 89–107.

Herzberg, B. E. (2008) *The Monitoring and Evaluation Handbook for Business Environment Reform*, USA: Investment Climate Department, The World Bank Group.

Herzlinger, R. E., Kaplan, R. S. and Porter, M. E. (2011) 'How to Solve the Cost Crisis in Health Care: Interaction', *Harvard Business Review*, 89, 22–3.

Hitchcock, C. (2012) 'Probabilistic Causation', *The Stanford Encyclopedia of Philosophy* [online], available: http://plato.stanford.edu/archives/win2012/entries/causation-probabilistic/ [accessed 20 October 2013].

Hordijk, L. (2007) 'The Art and Craft of Systems and Analysis', *Options* (winter), www.iiasa.ac.at/web/home/about/achievments/scientificachievementsandpolicyimpact/young scientistssummerprogram/Systems%20analysis_1.pdf.

International Finance Corporation (2007) *Stakeholder Engagement: A Good Practice Handbook for Companies Doing Business in Emerging Markets*, Pennsylvania, USA: International Finance Corporation, World Bank Group.

Kaplan, R. S. and Anderson, S. R. (2004) 'Time-Driven Activity-Based Costing', *Harvard Business Review*, 82(11), 131–8.

Kaplan, R. S. and Norton, D. P. (1996) *The Balanced Scorecard: Translating Strategy into Action*, Boston, MA: Harvard Business School Press.

Kaplan, R. S. and Porter, M. E. (2011) 'How to Solve the Cost Crisis in Health Care', *Harvard Business Review*, 89(9), 46–64.

Koedinger, K. R. and Corbett, A. (2006) 'Technology: Bringing Learning Sciences to the Classroom', in Sawyer, R. K., ed. *The Cambridge Handbook of the Learning Sciences*, New York: Cambridge University Press, 61–75.

Kotter, J. P. (1995) 'Leading Change: Why Transformation Efforts Fail', *Harvard Business Review*, March–April.

Kotter, J. and Whitehead, L. A. (2010) *Buy-In: Saving Your Good Idea from Getting Shot Down*, Boston, MA: Harvard Business Review Press; London: McGraw-Hill.

Krathwohl, D. R. (2002) 'A Revision of Bloom's Taxonomy: An Overview', *Theory into Practice*, 41(4), 212.

Krathwohl, D. R., Bloom, B. S. and Masia, B. B. (1964) *Taxonomy of Educational Objectives: The Classification of Educational Goals. Handbook 2, Affective Domain*, London: Longman.

Leeuw, F. and Vaessen, J. (2009) *Impact Evaluations and Development: NONIE Guidance on Impact Evaluation*, Washington, DC: Network of Networks on Impact Evaluation.

Locke, E. A. and Latham, G. P. (2006) 'New Directions in Goal-Setting Theory', *Current Directions in Psychological Science*, 15(5), 265.

MacLeod, D. and Clarke, N. (2009) *Engaging for Success: Enhancing Performance through Employee Engagement*, UK: Department of Business, Innovation and Skills.

Melia, S. (2011) 'Do Randomised Control Trials Offer a Solution to "Low Quality" Transport Research?' [online], available: http://eprints.uwe.ac.uk/16117/ [accessed 30 July 2012].

Mentzer, J. T. (2008) 'Rigor Versus Relevance: Why Would We Choose Only One?', *Journal of Supply Chain Management*, 44(2), 72–7.

Meyer, P. J. (2003) *Attitude Is Everything: If You Want to Succeed Above and Beyond*, USA: Meyer Resource Group, Incorporated.

Minister of Public Works and Government Services (2010) 'Program Evaluation Methods: Measurement and Attribution of Program Results' [online], available: www.tbs-sct.gc.ca/cee/pubs/meth/pem-mep04-eng.asp [accessed 8 April 2013].

Morris, D. R. (2005) 'Causal Inference in the Social Sciences: Variance Theory, Process Theory, and System Dynamics', in *23rd International Conference of the System Dynamics Society*, Boston, USA.

OECD (2002) *Glossary of Key Terms in Evaluation and Results Based Management*, Paris: OECD Publications.

Oxford Dictionaries (2012) 'Rules' [online], available: http://oxforddictionaries.com/definition/english/rule?q=rules [accessed 10 November 2012].

Patton, M. Q. (2011) *Developmental Evaluation: Applying Complexity Concepts to Enhance Innovation and Use*, New York: Guilford Press.

Phillips, J. J. (2003) *Return on Investment in Training and Performance Improvement Programs, Improving Human Performance*, 2nd edn, USA: Butterworth-Heinemann.

RAND Corporation (2009) *Performance Audit Handbook: Routes to Effective Evaluation*, Cambridge, UK: RAND Corporation.

Scardamalia, M. and Bereiter, C. (2006) 'Knowledge Building: Theory, Pedagogy, and Technology', in Sawyer, R. K., ed., *The Cambridge Handbook of the Learning Sciences*, New York: Cambridge University Press, 97–115.

Scriven, M. (2008) 'A Summative Evaluation of RCT Methodology: And an Alternative Approach to Causal Research', *Journal of MultiDisciplinary Evaluation*, 5(9), 11–24.

Shields, R. W. (2001) '1965 Benjamin Bloom publishes *Taxonomy of Educational Objectives: The Classification of Educational Goals*', *History of Education: Selected Moments of the 20th Century* [online], available: http://fcis.oise.utoronto.ca/~daniel_sch/assignment1/1965bloom.html [accessed 15 August 2012].

Simpson, E. J. (1966) *The Classification of Educational Objectives, Psychomotor Domain*, Urbana, IL: Illinois University.

Townsend, C. and Liu, W. (2012) 'Is Planning Good for You? The Differential Impact of Planning on Self-Regulation', *Journal of Consumer Research*, 39(4), 688–703.

Weiner, B. (2000) 'Motivation: An Overview', in Kazdin, A. E., ed. *Encyclopedia of Psychology, Vol. 5.*, Washington, DC and New York: American Psychological Association and Oxford University Press, 314–17.

White, H. (2009) *Some Reflections on Current Debates in Impact Evaluation, 3ie Working Paper 1*, New Delhi: The International Initiative for Impact Evaluation (3ie).

White, H. and Phillips, D. (2012) *Addressing Attribution of Cause and Effect in Small Impact Evaluations: Towards an Integrated Framework, 3ie Working Paper 15*, New Delhi, India: The International Initiative for Impact Evaluation (3ie).

INDEX